T0267567

A Canadian Chaplain in the Great War

Revisiting B. J. Murdoch's
The Red Vineyard

Edited by ROSS HEBB

NIMBUS
PUBLISHING
— NIMBUS.CA —

Nimbus Publishing Limited
3660 Strawberry Hill Street, Halifax, NS, B3K 5A9
(902) 455-4286 nimbus.ca

Printed and bound in Canada

NB1684
Editor: Marianne Ward
Editor for the press: Angela Mombourquette
Design: Jenn Embree

Nimbus Publishing is based in Kjipuktuk, Mi'kma'ki, the traditional territory of the Mi'kmaq People.

Library and Archives Canada Cataloguing in Publication

Title: A Canadian chaplain in the Great War : revisiting B.J. Murdoch's The red vineyard / edited by Ross Hebb.
Other titles: Revisiting B.J. Murdoch's The red vineyard
Names: Murdoch, B. J. (Benedict Joseph), 1886-1973, author. | Hebb, Ross N., 1960- writer of added commentary, editor.
Identifiers: Canadiana (print) 20240392620 | Canadiana (ebook) 20240392647 | ISBN 9781774713259 (softcover) | ISBN 9781774713266 (EPUB)
Subjects: LCSH: Murdoch, B. J. (Benedict Joseph), 1886-1973. | LCSH: World War, 1914-1918—Personal narratives, Canadian. | LCSH: World War, 1914-1918—Chaplains—Canada—Biography. | LCSH: Chaplains—Canada—Biography. | LCGFT: Personal narratives. | LCGFT: Autobiographies.
Classification: LCC D622 .M8 2024 | DDC 940.4/78092—dc23

Nimbus Publishing acknowledges the financial support for its publishing activities from the Government of Canada, the Canada Council for the Arts, and from the Province of Nova Scotia. We are pleased to work in partnership with the Province of Nova Scotia to develop and promote our creative industries for the benefit of all Nova Scotians.

CONTENTS

INTRODUCTION

❧

THE RED VINEYARD, A UNIQUE VOLUME AMONG CANADIAN Great War writings, is a little-known and vastly unappreciated treasure. While Canadians know something of our nation's contributions in the First World War, they seldom, if ever, think of the presence and role of army chaplains during the conflict. This work addresses that deficiency. Canada was a much more overtly religious nation a hundred years ago, and over 500 chaplains served in the Canadian Expeditionary Force (CEF) during the war. Of this group, almost 450 served overseas.[1] Out of all these chaplains, only two wrote lengthy first-hand accounts of their experiences, and they did so quite soon after the November 1918 Armistice.

The first account was penned by the well-known Quebec City Anglican, Canon Frederick George Scott. His *The Great War As I Saw It* was published in 1922. Known before the war as a poet and churchman, Scott had become an iconic national figure well before his Toronto publisher, F. D. Goodchild Company, released his volume. Although overage at fifty-four in 1914, Scott had sailed with the First Contingent and eventually sneaked out of England to France to minister to the "boys" at the front. Through his unconventional behaviour of chatting not only with generals at headquarters, but also with privates in the trenches, he became a beloved fixture in the Canadian Corps. Although frustrated by his unorthodox wanderings, the authorities dared not sack him and send him home. He rose to become the senior chaplain of the First Division.

Whereas Scott was famous for his wartime exploits before he published, Father Benedict Joseph Murdoch was not. Murdoch was a young, recently ordained Roman Catholic cleric from the small town of Chatham, New Brunswick. He went overseas to England in 1916. There, his locally raised, predominantly Catholic 132nd Battalion was unceremoniously broken up and its soldiers scattered. He was not sent to France until June of 1917. He served in the coastal military hospitals until finally, in December 1917, he was reassigned as Roman Catholic chaplain to the four infantry battalions of the 3rd Brigade. Father Murdoch was but one of many chaplains in a highly structured Canadian Corps, but his account reveals that he saw everything imaginable at the front, including combat. At war's end, he returned home a changed man. He, like Canon Scott, felt compelled to write of his experiences, not for glory or profit, but to honour the "great hearted Catholic lads"[2] of the Canadian Expeditionary Force. As Murdoch relates in a later publication, the first one thousand copies of *The Red Vineyard* were published in July of 1923.[3] Unlike Canon Scott, Murdoch had had to finance the publication by an American publisher out of his own pocket. Thankfully, it was successful and by 1958 *The Red Vineyard* had gone through ten printings totalling over ten thousand copies. Unfortunately, it has not been republished since 1959.

HUMBLE BEGINNINGS

Benedict Joseph Murdoch was born on March 21, 1886, the first son among Robert Murdoch and Mary Allen's six children. His maternal grandfather, Captain James Uniacke Allen, was born in Passage, Ireland, in 1821. After the Crimean War, Captain Allen moved to Chatham, married his sweetheart, and settled down to amidst the strong Irish Catholic heritage of the Miramichi region of New Brunswick. His grandson, Benedict Joseph, was raised in a staunchly Roman Catholic family. Not only did Benedict become a priest, but two of his sisters proudly entered the religious life.[4] Benedict Joseph studied at St. Dunstan's College in Charlottetown before going to the Grand Seminary in Quebec City for his priestly education and training. After four years in Quebec, he was ordained a priest on June 29, 1911, by Bishop Barry of Chatham. Over the next three years he served in several French-speaking Acadian parishes as assistant and then pastor.[5] In May of 1914, his bishop granted him leave from parish ministry. The cause was Murdoch's desire to travel to Baltimore in order to explore the possibility of a vocation to a religious order that specialized in teaching. After considerable inner turmoil, he realized his error and returned to Canada, a nation visibly transformed by the call to arms.

Upon returning to Chatham, Murdoch's bishop placed him as assistant to Fr. Dixon of St. Mary's, Newcastle, across the river from Murdoch's hometown.[6] In early 1916, the recruitment drive for the 132nd Infantry Battalion stirred the entire Miramichi region. Attending many of the rallies, Fr. Murdoch one night volunteered his services as the unit's chaplain—before he had episcopal permission to do so. Thankfully for Murdoch, the battalion's leadership also approached his bishop. Permission was granted and Fr. Murdoch donned the khaki and became Padre Murdoch, chaplain to the 80 percent Catholic 132nd Battalion of the CEF.

THE CANADIAN CHAPLAINCY SERVICE (CCS)

Although some effort was made to secure the part-time services of two rabbis,[7] the Canadian Chaplaincy Service (CCS) of the CEF was an overtly Christian enterprise. Not only was it Christian, but its ethos was markedly Protestant. The CCS was administered by Anglicans and comprised almost every conceivable Protestant denomination—including the Salvation Army. As a result, Roman Catholics were treated somewhat differently from everyone else.[8] When a battalion was raised in Canada, the chaplain chosen was usually the same denomination as the majority of the recruits within its ranks. In practice, this meant that few battalions sailed with a Roman Catholic chaplain. This created a problem, for while most units had some form of Protestant chaplain, many had a sizeable minority of Roman Catholic recruits. These men were effectively left without any functioning minister. A Protestant chaplain, no matter how well meaning, could not hear confessions or celebrate Mass let alone give last rites to the dying. These functions required a Catholic priest.

The solution eventually seized upon was to assign a priest not to each battalion of the CEF but to each brigade. Brigades comprised four separate infantry battalions. When he reached the front in December of 1917, Murdoch was responsible for all Roman Catholics in the 3rd Canadian Infantry Brigade, which amounted to all the Catholics spread across four battalions of almost one thousand men each. For the practical purposes of transportation, billeting (shelter), and messing (eating), he was attached to the 16th Infantry Battalion—the Canadian Scottish.

While it is perhaps difficult to grasp from a secular, twenty-first-century perspective, chaplains were not only an accepted, but an expected part of the Canadian military in the Great War. Canadians expected their soldiers to have access to religious and spiritual services and resources as a matter of course. Chaplains provided the obvious weekly public worship, but also counselled, advised, encouraged, admonished, exhorted, and consoled those who sought their ministrations. Their most appreciated function was often the most passive—their physical presence. Being present, not only on the parade ground and behind the lines, but in the forward areas, up to and including the actual trenches, was often their most appreciated ministry. By so doing, chaplains shared the mud, the lice, the fear, and the danger. They too might be, and were, wounded and killed by enemy action.[9] Canon Scott was one of the twenty-one Canadian chaplains wounded during the conflict. Fr. Murdoch's friend and fellow Roman Catholic priest Fr. Crochetière, who is mentioned several times in *The Red Vineyard*, was killed by enemy artillery fire in April 1918.[10] When Fr. Murdoch assumed his duties with the 16th Battalion, it was clear that military chaplaincy at the front was a dangerous vocation.

As well as the generic ministrations of all chaplains, the role of Roman Catholic chaplains included work that was significantly more focused and precise. Their task was to be the bearers of the Church's sacramental life. Confession, daily celebration of the Mass, and administering Holy Communion and, if necessary, the last rites was why they were in the army. As individual confession was the prerequisite to receiving the Sacrament,[11] *The Red Vineyard* contains constant references to hearing confessions at all times, day or night, and under every imaginable circumstance. If at all practicable, immediately after the hearing of confessions came the celebration of Mass and congregants' reception of the Sacrament. Whether in little French churches, out of doors, or while down in a shallow trench under German artillery bombardment, if at all possible, Mass was celebrated. Often the influx of soldiers and the constraints of time, especially before battle, meant that this work had to be done in pairs with one priest breaking off hearing confessions to celebrate Mass and to administer the Sacrament. Murdoch records one such busy day in late September 1918 and notes "feeling that my men were now ready, spiritually, for battle."[12] Over one hundred years later, it must be noted that the emphasis here was not on the aggression and violence of battle but on being prepared for the very real and immediate threat of death and what came next. In fact, Murdoch concludes the entire work with his reflection upon those who "knelt to ask pardon of God, and to become fortified with the Bread of the strong…[and then] answered so quickly the final roll call."[13] Whether the reader shares this outlook on preparing for death or not, it was essential to Murdoch's world view and key to comprehending his Great War experience.

NOTABLE FEATURES

The Red Vineyard is the record of Benedict Joseph Murdoch's Great War chaplaincy. It starts when he signs up at Newcastle, NB, in May of 1916 and ends as soon as he leaves occupied Germany on Christmas Day, 1918. He does not even bother to record his return to England, his trip home, or his demobilization. Once he ceases ministering to the Catholic lads on active service, his tale is concluded.

For an exclusively wartime story it lacks certain elements many readers might expect. Chief among these are expressions of jingoism and hatred of the enemy. Murdoch neither welcomes nor relishes the war but accepts it as a fact of the world in which he lives. Indeed, being the introspective man that he was, at the outset he examines his motives for becoming actively involved. Furthermore, he expresses no hatred of the enemy. His account includes an incident when a crowd on the ground watched a German airplane under intense ground fire. The pilot appeared to succumb to the barrage directed his way only to fake a spiralling descent (so the firing would cease) and then pull up at the last moment and so safely escape beyond danger. "What did we do, gentle reader? For a few seconds, overcome with amazement, we stood there gazing skywards, then from all over the area there were sounds of clapping hands as we good-humouredly applauded 'Old Fritz.'"[14] It is difficult to conceive of sentiments further removed from bloodthirstiness than these. But Murdoch goes further and provides an even more revealing story.

Perhaps no incident is more telling and better encapsulates Murdoch's attitude than his account of ministering to wounded and dying German soldiers. Once he determined that the dying German was a Catholic, he would kneel beside him with the Sacrament, wait until he had prepared himself, and then, "I would give him Holy Communion." Finally, he would anoint the man. Murdoch relates, "it was a beautiful sight to see the tears of gratitude come into the eyes of those dying Germans…invariably they reached out and gripped my hand before passing out." Of those German soldiers, Murdoch concluded, "Many lads were ushered up to the gates of heaven that day"[15]—the same words he used to describe his dying Canadian soldiers under the same circumstances. In essence, the needs of the faithful and the duties of the priest transcended the distinctions of friend and foe, of warring sides, and of nationality. All were Catholic lads in need of priestly ministrations.

The Red Vineyard is, however, much more than a tale of battles and suffering. Murdoch repeatedly relates the beauty of the French countryside, the rustic charm of the peasants as they worked their fields, and the simplicity of traditional rural French living. He even devotes an entire chapter to what was to him their unusual bread-making technique. While recording the natural beauty of the land and the resilience of its people, he cannot help but reflect how the war has marred it all. All the countryside within the battle zone is shell-pitted, desolate, and unkempt. Murdoch notes that no men were seen working the fields; all, including all military-age French priests, had been called to arms to defend the nation. Moreover, typical of numerous Canadian soldiers' documented reactions, he notes two sights that particularly affected him—civilian refugees and civilian malnourishment and starvation. Murdoch notes his dismay at the sight of refugees fleeing the German spring advance of 1918. In the later autumn of 1918, what he found especially difficult was seeing French children in the regions formerly occupied by the Germans. Murdoch relates, "It was pitiful to see the little boys and girls playing in the streets. At first it seemed to me that they were all too tall for their years; then I knew it was that they were undernourished."[16] Tellingly, it was the suffering of the civilian population, not of the combatants, that made such an impression on Murdoch.

The Red Vineyard has its lighter moments as well. Murdoch relates the reaction of English soldiers while watching a baseball game between Canadians and Americans. The English are bewildered by the banter directed at the pitcher, and they muse about what appeared to them to be the absence of fair play. As Murdoch relates, "to them it seems quite abusive, and judging by their talk they are disgusted." They walk away shaking their heads. By contrast, the little French boys follow the strange game and mimic its manoeuvres. They are seen "sliding to some imaginary home plate, [and] one can hear such expressions as 'Safe!' and 'Hat a-boy.'"[17]

In a very different vein, Murdoch also relates the disinterment of a buried casket in recently liberated French territory in the autumn of 1918. Initially he declined the priest's invitation to witness more gruesome scenes, but the smile on the French priest's face piqued his interest. The casket to be disinterred had been buried as the Germans entered the town four years earlier. The occupying forces observed due decorum, even saluting the deceased. Once opened, Murdoch noted that the casket had been filled with the "beautiful vestments and precious altar vessels, together with municipal books and documents."[18] The French priest had ingeniously duped the invading Germans.

Murdoch relates another humorous incident, but this one requires a degree of historical context. He states that during his early months in France, while serving as a priest in the large Canadian tent hospital complexes, he happened upon a mysterious ward. Upon entry, a nurse expressed surprise at his appearance and commented that, despite being full, no one ever died on that ward. Murdoch was perplexed. He was soon to learn that the ward was filled with P.U.O.s, cases labelled "Praxis of Unknown Origin," otherwise known as "put one over" on the doctors. These unhappy men were also known as malingerers. The ward was run by a French-Canadian doctor nicknamed Boots, who, when Murdoch met him at mess, was complaining that he had been sent a soldier who was actually sick with a skin ailment. Boots was most offended. Realizing Murdoch's curiosity, Boots invited Murdoch to visit his ward in order to observe treatment. But Murdoch had to make a promise—he could not laugh. Murdoch agreed. The next day he walked down the aisle of the ward and observed the men undergoing treatment. He states, "some held the handles of a galvanic battery in their hands while their bodies squirmed and twisted...; others had their feet on steel discs in tubs of water, while others underwent electric treatment in different ways. The doctor moved from bed to bed, inquiring with simulated solicitude as to the state of each patient." Not surprisingly,

Murdoch heard two men tell the doctor that they felt well enough to return to their battalions. Upon exiting the ward, Murdoch relates that he "laughed and laughed. The fat doctor had been so funny and also the poor fellows, squirming and twisting under treatment that was not at all necessary for them."[19] In retrospect, and with our fuller appreciation of the psychological strains of warfare, our amusement might well be more muted. However, given the level of knowledge at the time, the institutional approach that Murdoch describes was certainly better than jail, hard labour, or a firing squad.

One of the most novel and refreshing aspects of *The Red Vineyard* is Murdoch's broadening of the reader's perspective well beyond the front-line trench and no man's land. By so doing he reveals the extensive war-related infrastructure that sustained the front. He shows us the rear areas of war—the hospitals, the troop trains, the rest areas of baths, baseball games, and original amateur plays and entertainments. Of the nurses, he relates they "were most attentive to the wounded, without the slightest display of maudlin sympathy; but they worked hard and long and one never heard the least complaint from their lips." Tellingly, he concludes, "it was a common occurrence…to see a nurse being ordered away for a complete rest, made necessary by the terrific strain of her work."[20]

Murdoch's excellence as a storyteller is well displayed as he relates his tale of the troop trains. The military tent hospitals were always located next to rail lines for ease of transportation. While serving at No. 7 Canadian General Hospital, Murdoch often saw trains on their way forward "with their hundreds of khaki-clad lads leaning out from car windows, cheering, singing, and waving." The French children would gaze "wide-eyed at the soldiers who had come from across the seas. They wondered too what those words meant that someone on the troop trains always called out and which brought such a thundering response." The children soon learned the words and at every stop they too would ask, "'Har we doon-hearted?' Then, mingled with the laughter…would come thundering the answer, 'No!'"[21] But Murdoch's story does not end with this touching interaction between French children and Canadian troops. His tale has a sobering punch. He relates that other trains would make the return journey. The French children noticed the differences with these trains. "Everything seemed very silent.… [O]n the side of every car was painted, in the middle of a large white circle, a red cross. No groups of laughing faces appeared at the open car windows, though now and again the white, drawn face of someone lying in a berth peered out through the glass. On these trains, no one called out, 'Are we downhearted?'"[22] These were the returning hospital trains filled with wounded. The conflict generated a steady stream of such silence and suffering. Murdoch has made his point and made it most powerfully.

Murdoch's function as a chaplain afforded him a perspective that was very seldom expressed in the literature of the period—the link with the home front, especially with the women left behind. One of his tasks was to write to wives and mothers and tell them of the death of their loved one "and how they had been prepared to meet God."[23] These women often wrote back to Murdoch, expressing their thanks for both his ministrations and his communication. Murdoch devotes an entire chapter to this return correspondence. He reflects, "I thought of how many women there must be over the world bearing great sorrows, but the eyes of the world are not focused on these." The world focuses on marching men, on flags and bands. But after the marching, these women "would go back into silent rooms where so many little things would remind them of their men. Then as the days would pass, to many would come the words to chill the heart and makes homes desolate: 'Killed in action.'" For Murdoch, the only solace at this point was to link their sorrow with that of another mother, Mary, and her son, Jesus. From Murdoch's perspective, there was no human experience, especially human suffering and sorrow, beyond the comprehension and theological embrace of his faith.

Finally, a word of caution. For Murdoch, as for us, it is impossible not to be a creature of the age in which we live. In his case, this meant that he shared certain attitudes and outlooks that now strike us as prejudiced, biased, and unacceptable. One instance of this would be Murdoch's reference to the Maori among the New Zealand troops. He notes that they "were treated by the white men with the same courtesy that they showed one another,"[24] but goes on to add, "the Maoris were the most intelligent-looking men of the yellow race I had ever met." Though his words are meant as a compliment, linking intelligence to race in any manner is, of course, unacceptable today. Murdoch does add approvingly that "those of the Maoris who were Catholics were excellent ones."

This leads into the other area that stands out one hundred years later, namely relations between the various Christian denominations. While it is true that the Great War saw a significant lessening of denominational barriers among the chaplains and an increased appreciation of one another's strengths, stark differences of perspective persisted. Murdoch was completely immersed in the perspective of Catholic exceptionalism, namely that the only complete, historic, and assured expression of Christianity was to be found in the Roman Catholic Church. It was the only proper "home" for Christians. All other expressions were incomplete, deficient, and insecure. He relates several instances of men returning to the Catholic Church from other denominations or of being baptised into its ranks as the cause of great joy and thanksgiving. He even relates an incident involving Canon Scott. Scott had addressed a group of men, encouraging the Anglicans among them to attend Holy Communion, but secured only a few takers. When Murdoch then had the opportunity to address the Catholics present, all thirteen of them responded to his invitation to confession and Communion. Murdoch went on to expound upon this instance of one-upmanship, concluding with the sentiment that the Catholic men truly loved their priest. Regrettably, this leaves the reader with the clear implication that such was not so much the case with Canon Scott and his Anglican soldiers.[25]

THE CURIOUS THING ABOUT GEORGE

An odd feature of Murdoch's *The Red Vineyard* is his handling of the individual named George. Although George is mentioned in the text fifty-three times, Murdoch never gives George's full name. We first encounter George as a nameless helper in chapter 39 (XXXIX) when Murdoch arrives at the front in December of 1917. The man remains nameless until chapter 44 (XLIV) when Murdoch simply calls him George. George is constantly preparing Murdoch's sleeping quarters, moving Murdoch's kit from place to place, and presenting him with food. Murdoch does not highlight the fact that as an officer, he was, as a matter of course, assigned a personal assistant, termed in true British Army parlance, a "batman." When the two are forced to part ways in mid-September 1918, when Murdoch is transferred to the 14th Battalion, Murdoch calls him "ever-faithful George." Immediately afterwards, Murdoch endures what he calls the "most terrible day of my life," and immediately exclaims, "How I missed George."[26] By way of contrast, all we ever hear of Murdoch's new batman at the 14th Battalion is that he is an Englishman—his name is never mentioned!

This curious absence of a full name for Murdoch's batman created the mystery of who is George? How to go about discovering George's identity? The first problem was whether or not "George" is a first or a last name. Although likely the man's first name, in the army, such could not be assumed. Men were often known by their surnames. To cite only one notable example, Anglican chaplain Canon Scott called his batman "Ross," short for George Oliver Ross (29381). There are approximately three hundred men listed on the Library and Archives website who served in the Canadian Expeditionary Force with the last name George. Nonetheless, the odds are that George was the man's first name, thus rendering his discovery even more challenging. There are obviously thousands of Georges who served in the CEF.

In searching for George, my quest had to be circumscribed within reasonable parameters. As Murdoch was attached to the 16th Infantry Battalion, perhaps George was a member of that unit. The nominal roll for the unit, generated at the time of its recruitment in 1915, does exist. Fifty-seven men with "George" as part of their name are found on that list, but none of them was Murdoch's batman. The reason George was not to be found on the nominal roll lies with the turnover rate of a Canadian Great War infantry battalion. The 16th Battalion was raised in 1915, but Murdoch was attached to the unit in December 1917. By that date, death, wounds, sickness, and transfers would have witnessed approximately two thousand additional men move through the battalion. If a member of the 16th Battalion, George was obviously not one of the unit's original members.

How best to continue the search? A colleague suggested I investigate Murdoch's personal correspondence file. There, buried among its one hundred pages of mainly mundane chaplaincy matters, is a letter Murdoch wrote from France to his Chaplaincy superior in England. In this letter from May 1918, Murdoch asks if a transfer could be obtained for his batman, George Edward Martin (152853). Eureka—George's identity is finally unveiled. Murdoch explains that George is an optometrist by trade, and while he was a machine gunner in the battalion, he had been wounded and subsequently suffered from shell shock. Although Murdoch "would hate to lose him" and George was a "very fine fellow," he was "very anxious to get back to his own work."

George Martin's service record reveals that he joined the 79th Battalion at Brandon, Manitoba, in March 1916. Once in England, his unit was broken up and he was sent as part of a reinforcement draft to France where he joined the 16th Battalion in the field. In April 1917, he was appointed lance corporal. Soon after, he was wounded. While in the hospital system, George was diagnosed with shell shock. In December 1917, of his own volition, George Martin gave up his promotion, reverting to the rank of private. He was then transferred to the Canadian Chaplaincy Service to function as Murdoch's batman. Although George did not obtain the transfer that Murdoch attempted to facilitate, he did survive the war. George Martin returned to Canada and was demobilized in late April 1919.

A UNIQUE CONTRIBUTION

What might surprise some readers of *The Red Vineyard* is Murdoch's presence during actual combat. Although armed only with the Sacrament and holy oil, he served in the danger zone. This was especially true during the One Hundred Days Offensive at the end of the war. Although it constitutes only 10 percent of his time in the CEF, Murdoch devotes fully 20 percent of *The Red Vineyard* to recording the events of that intense period. He was attached to the field ambulance units as they followed immediately behind the advancing infantry battalions of the 3rd Brigade. Murdoch assisted the stretcher-bearers and Medical Officers (MO's) and ministered to the dying. On one occasion in September 1918, Murdoch records going forward with the stretcher-bearers while they sought out the wounded. Rushing out upon an open field, the bearers came under intense enemy fire, three "went down, two mortally wounded. I ran quickly to them and began to anoint them. The other bearers ran to points of safety and I was alone on the field. Those were the most terrible moments of my life. I knew the enemy could see me and was firing at me…. Terrified, I crouched flat on my stomach until I finished anointing the lad, who passed away before I had done my work. Then I rolled over and lay still, as if I were dead."[27] During the same period, Murdoch records being strafed by airplane machine-gun fire as he anointed the wounded, of being bombed nightly while sleeping in the open without trenches, and of repeatedly being under intense German artillery fire. "Sometimes the shells would come so near us that I would sit on my box, or kneel before the Blessed Sacrament, trembling, expecting each moment to be my last."[28] Not surprisingly, the accumulation of these experiences left their mark.

The Red Vineyard is remarkable not only because Murdoch records these events, but most unusual for the time, he also records the lasting effects they had upon him. In the summer of 1918, while on leave in England, he went on retreat to the same monastery as he had the previous summer. This time things were different, for he was different. "I did not settle down to the deep quiet of the monastery.… A strange restlessness possessed me, and I felt a distinct relief when my time was up."[29] He also realized why this was so: "The year at the front had done its work too well." His mental health was at issue. He knew, however, that he was not unique. "I now experienced the effects of that tension which all who have taken part in the World War know so well." He also describes instances of panic and indecision. After walking through an especially intense bombardment, he relates thinking that "that hurt, dazed look, which I had seen so often in the eyes of the men, was in my own eyes,"[30] describing what later in history became known as "the thousand-yard stare." He also describes waking from a deep sleep while in a bunker "trembling violently, I am not sure whether through cold or fear."[31] Murdoch gives a telling indication of his fragile emotional state in the autumn of 1918 when he relates his reaction to the gift of a pear. "These little acts of kindness of the old curé's sister used to affect me almost to tears. I think the awful strain of battle was beginning to affect us all."[32]

With these revealing examples, recorded so soon after they happened, combined with his thoughts at the time and their cumulative effect upon him, Murdoch breaks new ground in Canadian Great War literature. Using himself as the example of how the conflict affected his mental health, he becomes a spokesperson for the returned Canadian soldier. Long before even shell shock, let alone PTSD, were recognized as actual conditions—and with the legacy of the "Boots" ward as a backdrop—Murdoch was highlighting the ongoing mental health legacy of Great War service. Perhaps this self-effacing frankness concerning his own fragility is the greatest legacy of Fr. Murdoch's The Red Vineyard.

A NOTE ON THE TEXT

The Red Vineyard was first published in the summer of 1923 by The Torch Press, a small Catholic publishing house in Iowa. The most commonly available edition appears to be that of 1928, the first Canadian printing by Hunter-Rose of Toronto. This is the version available online at archive.org. The last known printing was the tenth, done by The University Press, Glasgow, in 1959. What all these printings have in common is that they were privately done, that is, Murdoch financed them all out of his own pocket. Murdoch was always his own publisher and distributor. Indeed, his last instructions to his executor concerned the debt remaining to the printer for his last book.

Over the course of all ten printings of *The Red Vineyard* there are few deletions, additions, or alterations of any sort. Layout and the text remain unaltered from the initial 1923 printing. This new edition continues that tradition, with only a minimum of changes to capitalization and spelling (including some proper names) so as to conform to contemporary usage and to correct errors. Furthermore, this volume is neither abridged nor condensed, although it is expanded. What is new, in addition to the introduction and afterword, is a running commentary. Although initially intending to let Murdoch's excellent writing stand alone, I became convinced of the need for explanatory text. These Editor's Notes are designed to provide contextualization, crucial historical background, and useful assistance to the reader. My goal has been to allow this great writer, patriotic Canadian, and faithful Maritimer to tell his story in his own words.

THE RED VINEYARD: A TIMELINE

MAY 1916: Murdoch joins the 132nd Battalion at Newcastle, NB

SUMMER 1916: Initial training at Valcartier Camp, QC

OCTOBER 1, 1916: Entrain for embarkation from Saint John, NB

OCTOBER 26, 1916: Depart Halifax, NS, on board the *Corsican*

NOVEMBER 5, 1916: Arrive in England

WINTER 1916–17: Bramshott Camp

SPRING 1917: Witley Camp

JUNE 17, 1917: Transferred to No. 2 Canadian Infantry Base Depot, Étaples, France

AUTUMN 1917: Chaplain at No. 7 Canadian General Hospital

DECEMBER 1917: Posted to 3rd Canadian Infantry Brigade as Roman Catholic (RC) Chaplain attached to 16th Battalion

MARCH 21, 1918: German Offensive Commences; B. J. Murdoch's thirty-second birthday

APRIL 1918: Ronville Caves

MAY 1918: Bedridden with influenza for a week

JUNE 22, 1918: Granted two weeks' leave to England

JULY 6, 1918: Rejoined 16th Battalion at Écoivres

AUGUST 8, 1918: One Hundred Days Offensive begins with the Battle of Amiens

AUGUST 26, 1918: Battle of Arras

SEPTEMBER 1, 1918: Battle of the Drocourt-Quéant Line

WEEK OF SEPTEMBER 15, 1918: Transferred to 14th Battalion but remains RC Chaplain to 3rd Canadian Infantry Brigade

SEPTEMBER 26, 1918: Battle of the Canal du Nord

OCTOBER 5, 1918: Brigade out of line to rest

OCTOBER 17, 1918: Brigade rests at Somaine; Germans retreating

NOVEMBER 11, 1918: The Armistice

DECEMBER 6, 1918: Crossed the Rhine into Germany with the Army of Occupation

DECEMBER 12, 1918: Encamped in the vicinity of Cologne with the Army of Occupation

DECEMBER 24, 1918: Christmas Mass in parish church in Germany

DECEMBER 25, 1918: Departs for leave in England and eventual demobilization in Canada

THE RED VINEYARD

REV. B. J. MURDOCH

Late Chaplain to Canadian
Expeditionary Forces

The cover of the 1923 Torch Press (Iowa) edition. (Library of Congress)

To the memory of all those men with whom I walked up and down the ways of the red vineyard, but especially to the memory of those who stopped in the journey and now rest softly in their little green bivouacs in the shadow of the small white crosses, this book is affectionately dedicated by their friend and comrade, the author.

Contents

I ❧ A Little Speculation

The year was 1916. All New Brunswick was astir with recruitment fever. Determined and competitive recruitment drives were sweeping and scouring every community in search of young men. Chatham was no exception. Besides the local 132nd Battalion, four other New Brunswick–based infantry battalions were attempting to raise their one-thousand-man quotas. The 140th and 145th Battalions were focused on Kent and Westmorland counties, while the 165th Battalion was targeting the province's Acadians. Finally, in the capital of Fredericton, the 236th (kilted) Battalion belatedly began its recruitment efforts in July. This is the context in which The Red Vineyard begins.

Padre B. J. Murdoch's story opens with a peek into a world that no longer exists—a fireside gathering of Catholic priests. As the topic of Murdoch's desire to become a chaplain arises, those assembled proffer their opinions. The first priest thinks Murdoch's hair will quickly turn grey in the trenches, and the second suggests that chaplaincy is contrary to his priestly vocation. The third priest admits to being a little envious of the opportunity; he suggests Murdoch will do much good, ushering many souls up to heaven. We will learn that Murdoch shares this perspective. But Murdoch is not yet in the army.

Not to be outdone by the local Protestant ministers, he spoke up at a recruiting rally for the 132nd Battalion and volunteered his services. Reading of this in the next morning's paper, his bishop was not amused—no permission to enlist had been granted. Murdoch had gotten himself in hot water. Fortunately for him, the Miramichi region that the battalion was drawing from was predominately Roman Catholic—80 percent of the recruits were of that faith. The battalion needed a Roman Catholic chaplain. As a result, the officer commanding the battalion, Col. G. W. Mersereau, paid a visit to Murdoch's bishop in Chatham. Murdoch was in. His attestation papers give his date of signing up as May 15, 1916. – RH

❝ I'll give you just three nights in the front-line trench before your hair will turn grey," said a brown-haired priest, looking at me with a slightly aggressive air. I remained quiet. "You'll not be very long in the army till you'll wish yourself out of it again," was the not very encouraging assertion of a tall, thin priest who suffered intermittently from dyspeptic troubles.

Still, I did not speak. Another priest, whose work was oftener among old tomes than among men, said slowly and, as was his wont, somewhat seriously, that it surprised him very much to note my eagerness to go to war. He did not consider it in keeping with the dignity of the priest to be so belligerently inclined. Did I not recall that I was an ambassador of the meek and lowly Christ, the Prince of Peace?

Had I obeyed the first impulse, I think my reply would have been coloured with a little asperity, but as I was weighing my words, a gentle, white-haired old priest, stout and with red cheeks, said to me as he smiled kindly, "Ah, Father, you are to be envied. Think of all the good you will be able to do for our poor boys! Think of the souls you will usher up to the gates of heaven!" He shook his head slowly from side to side two or three times, and the smile on his kind old face gave place to a look of longing as he continued, somewhat regretfully, "Ah, if I were a younger man I'd be with you, Father. All we older men can do now is to pray, and you may rest assured I shall remember you often—you and your men." I looked at the old priest gratefully. "Thank you, Father," I said, and I thought of Moses of old, with arms outstretched.

None of the other priests spoke for awhile, and I gazed into the fire of dry hardwood that murmured and purred so comfortably in the large open fireplace, built of small fieldstones. I was thinking earnestly and when the conversation was again resumed I took no part in it. In fact, I did not follow it at all, for I was wondering, among other things, if my hair would really turn grey after a few nights in the front-line trenches. However, I did not worry, for I concluded it would be wiser to wait until I should arrive at the trenches, where I might have the evidence of my senses.

I gave but passing thought to the words of the good priest who was a little dyspeptic. He had never been in the army, and where was his reason for assuming that I would not like the life? Of course, I did not mind what the old priest, whose work was so often amongst old books, had said about my being an ambassador of the Prince of Peace. I felt that this priest had got his ideas a little mixed. Not very long before, I had heard him vent his outraged feelings when the

French government had called the priests of France to fight for the Colours.[33] He had been horrified. So I surmised that he imagined I had voluntarily offered my services as a combatant. I had not.

The conversation continued, but I heeded it not. I was just meditating on the words of the saintly old priest with the red cheeks. How well he understood, I thought. And the flames of the fire shot in and out among the wood, purring pleasantly the while.

II ∾ The Bishop Writes

Up to this time I did not have the bishop's consent. In fact, I cannot remember having mentioned in his presence my desire to go to the front with the soldiers as chaplain, but I had talked it over frequently with priests, and it never occurred to me that the bishop had not heard of my wish, nor that he would not be in accord with it. But one morning I received a letter from the bishop telling me plainly and firmly that he wished me to keep quiet and not to talk so much about going to the front until I should know whether or not I would be permitted to go. He mentioned a recruiting meeting of a few nights previous, at which I had offered my services as chaplain to the battalion that was then being recruited in the diocese.

Perhaps I had been a little too outspoken at the meeting, but I had considered myself quite justified in breaking silence, since it had already come to pass that three ministers of different Protestant denominations had offered themselves as chaplains to the battalion, which, though still in rather an embryonic state, gave promise of being complete in a few months. I foresaw that it would be more than half Catholic, as the population of the district from which it was being recruited was three-fourths Catholic. So I offered myself generously, not wishing to be outdone by the ministers, and then had sat down feeling that I had done well.

The following morning, however, I was not altogether sure, for when I read my words printed in the daily paper, I felt just a little perturbed. What would the bishop think? I wondered. I had not long to wait before I knew exactly what His Lordship thought. His letter told me quite plainly.

I kept quiet. Keeping quiet, however, did not prevent me from following with interest the activities of others. Almost every evening recruiting meetings were held in different places throughout the diocese, at which old men spoke and orchestras played, and sometimes a young boy would step-dance. But most important of all, many young men enlisted. They came in great numbers, the Catholics far in the majority. Then, one morning early in the spring, the paper announced that the battalion had been recruited to full strength. The different companies would stay in the town till the following June, when the battalion would go into camp to train as a unit.

That evening a letter came from the officer in command, saying that as 80 percent of his men were Catholics, he had decided to take a Roman Catholic chaplain and that he intended going to see the bishop that evening. A few days later another letter came from the bishop saying that he had been asked for a Catholic chaplain, and as he remembered that I had seemed very eager to go with the men, he was glad to say that he was giving me permission to go. He had decided this, he added, on the Feast of the Seven Dolors of our Lady.

"The Seven Dolors," I said to myself quietly, two or three times. Then I fell to wishing that the bishop had made his decision on some other Feast of our Lady. I remember now, as I stood in the quiet little room with the letter in my hand, recalling the words of the priest—that he would not give me three nights in the front-line trenches before my hair would turn grey. But this thought did not bother me very long, for I began to think of something else; as I did the letter trembled a little with the hand that held it. "Perhaps I am not coming back," I said to myself. Then I repeated, "The Feast of the Seven Dolors! The Feast of the Seven Dolors!"

III ❧ A Little Adjusting

During the next seven or eight days, from all sides I heard one question asked by young and old: "When are you going to put on the uniform, Father?" Little children to whom I had taught catechism rushed around corners or panted up narrow streets of the little town where I was stationed and smilingly asked me. Their fathers and mothers, after saying good morning, remarked pleasantly, as an afterthought: "I suppose we'll soon be seeing you in the khaki, Father?" They seemed to anticipate real pleasure in seeing me decked in full regimentals. But the more I had evidence of this seemingly pleasant anticipation, the less inclined I felt to appear publicly in my chaplain's uniform. When the time came for a last fitting at the tailor's, I found other duties to claim my attention, until a polite little note from the proprietor of the establishment informed me that my presence was requested for a last fitting of my uniform.

Then one morning, when the spring birds that had returned were singing merrily among the trees with not the slightest thought as to their raiment, and when bursting buds were making the trees beautiful in their eagerness to drape them with bright green robes, I appeared on the public streets of the quiet little town clad in full regimentals. I had chosen an early hour for my public appearance, thinking that my ordeal would not be so trying. Since that morning I have had many exciting experiences, up and down the ways of war; I have witnessed many impressive scenes, beautiful, terrible, and horrible, but these events have by no means obliterated from the tablets of my memory the events of that morning.

Nothing particular happened until I had descended the hill and turned the first corner to the right in the direction of the town post office. A horse was coming at a leisurely gait down the quiet street, driven by a young fellow of about sixteen, who sat on the seat of a high express wagon with a friend. Both lads seemed to see me at once and started perceptibly. In his excitement, the driver pulled on the lines and the startled horse jerked his head quickly, is if he too was struck by my unwonted appearance. On the opposite side of the road a barber, who was operating on an early customer, stopped suddenly and came to the window, the razor still in his hand, while his patient, almost enveloped in the great white apron that was tucked about his neck, sat up quickly in the chair and turned a face half-covered with thick, creamy lather toward the window.

All along the way people stopped, looked, smiled pleasantly, and then passed on. I had almost entered the post office when the rattling of an express wagon that must have passed the winter uncovered, as every spoke in the wheels seemed loose, came nosily to my ears. The horse was reined up opposite me, and as I turned my head sidewise I was greeted by the two young fellows who had passed me but a few minutes before, only this time, three other lads with smiling faces were standing behind them in the wagon holding to the seat. After I got my mail from the box, I decided not to return by the same route along which I had come. There was a more secluded way. It was with a feeling of great relief that I found no one coming in my direction. I took out my new khaki handkerchief, unfolded it, and wiped my brow.

But, alas for my relief! I had not gone very far till I crossed a street running at right angles to my course. A number of schoolchildren were coming along this. I quickened my pace. They saw me and immediately a great bubbling of excited talk was borne to my ears. Then, as I disappeared from their view, I heard the sound of many eager feet pattering up the sidewalk. It ceased suddenly and I knew that again they were regarding me intently. There was a complete silence for a second or two, then I heard quite clearly the voice of a little girl, who in the last year's confirmation class had given me more trouble than any other of the candidates, call almost louder than was necessary for her companions to hear: "Oh, doesn't he look lovely?" A man just coming from his house on his way to his office smiled pleasantly and interestedly as he heard the small voice. Then he raised his hat. I saluted. As I walked up under the trees clothed in their beautiful spring garments and listened to the birds that sang so blithely this bright cool spring morning, with never a thought as to their raiment, I wiped my brow again. "These military clothes are warm," I said to myself—yet I knew that this was not the reason.

IV ◌ The Portable Altar

The subject matter of this little chapter is critical. No other item is as essential a clue to understanding what chaplaincy meant to Murdoch than this early mention of his portable altar. Not only were Catholic priests required to say Mass daily as part of their vocation, but it was the essential element of their employment. The priest interceded with God by offering up the Mass as worship and thereby recalling and invoking the sacrifice of Jesus on the cross. This is what Murdoch would do for the next two and a half years in the specific context of war. While foreign to most Canadians now, it is important to note that this daily activity of the Catholic priest entails a constant reminder of suffering and death. In sum, the suffering and death Murdoch was to encounter in war were not foreign elements in need of incorporation into his religion but central aspects of his faith that were already present.

Murdoch succeeded in bringing the portable altar back from the war and continued to use it for several decades. Regrettably, this tangible relic of his Great War service is now lost to us. In the 1950s, his residence was broken into and the portable altar stolen. It has not been seen since. – RH

After a few days a box about one foot and a half long, one foot high, and nine inches wide arrived. It was made of wood covered with a kind of grey cloth, with strips of black leather about the edges and small pieces of brass at every corner. There were leather grips on it so that it could be carried as a satchel. It was my little portable altar, containing everything necessary for saying Mass. One half opened and stood upright from the part containing the table of the altar, which when opened out was three feet long. Fitted into the oak table was the little marble altar-stone, without which one may not say Mass. In the top of the upright part was a square hole in which the crucifix fitted to stand above the altar; on either side were holders to attach the candlesticks. From the wall that formed a compartment in the upright portion, where the vestments were kept, the altar cards unfolded; these were kept in place by small brass clips attached to the upright. Chalice, ciborium, missal and stand, cruets, wine, altar breads, bell, linens, etc., were in compartments beneath the altar table. The whole was wonderfully compact and could be carried with one hand. As I write these words it stands nearby, sadly war-worn after its voyage across the ocean and its travels through England, France, Belgium, and the Rhineland of Germany. I have said Mass on it on this side of the ocean; on the high seas; in camp in England; in trenches; on battlefields; in tents, camps, and billets through the war-scarred areas of France. I offered the Holy Sacrifice on it placed on a low, wide windowsill in a German billet on our way through the Rhineland. It was carried across the Rhine December 13, 1918, in the great triumphal march. Now it is home again. In many places the cloth covering is scraped and torn; one of the brass corners is missing. It is very soiled from the mud of France and rifle oil stains, etc.; the leather edging is chipped and peeled. The table has been broken and repaired again, so has the little bookstand. The silver chalice and paten are slightly dented in many places. The little bell has lost part of its handle, but its tone is still sweet. One alb has been burned, but I have another. The cincture has been broken and knotted. I gaze at it now and think of the thousands of great-hearted lads who knelt before it, often on rain-soaked fields, or stood among piles of ruins and heard the sweet notes of the little bell warning them of the Master's approach, so that they might bow reverently when He came; of the thousands on field, on hillside, in caves and huts who knelt to eat of the Bread of Life, many of them going almost immediately with this pledge of eternal life before God to be judged; as I think of all this, there comes into my eyes a mist, and the little portable altar grows dim.

V ∽ In Training Camp

In early September 1916 the battalion left New Brunswick for Valcartier Camp. Located along the banks of the St. Lawrence River not far from Quebec City, Valcartier Camp had been hastily created in August of 1914. By September 1916, it was a well arranged and strictly run military training camp; however, as Murdoch's reference to shoeless military band members suggests, even at this advanced date there were insufficient quantities of such basic items as boots. His description of camp life communicates a sense of fresh air and the great outdoors. This is, of course, offset by his reference to the smoke-filled moving picture huts. As he explains, smoking was permitted because there were no ladies present.

Not surprisingly, Murdoch fondly recalls his open-air Masses on Sunday mornings. He also mentions as many as three thousand Catholic soldiers drawn up for service on the grassy plain before him. Finally, with a touch of Catholic indignation, he relates an incident in which Catholic soldiers missed his Mass for they had been ordered to attend a Protestant service! Murdoch immediately investigated. Citing the army's rule book, "K.R.&O." (King's Regulations and Orders), he convinced the Protestant clergy of their error and immediately received apologies. As he points out, "there was no such thing known in the army as a universal church service." – RH

In a few weeks we left for training camp, travelling all night and arriving at our destination early in the morning. We detrained and the whole battalion fell in, the band marching at the head of the column. Our camp was in a wide green valley, as level as a floor, flecked with hundreds of white bell tents; and in the distance on every side sloped gently upwards high solemn mountains that kept silent guard over the plain below. Through the whole length of the valley ran a long grey asphalt road over which passed all the traffic of the camp. All summer long, battalions of new soldiers came up this road and took over lines that had been assigned them. All summer long, and well on into the autumn, battalions of trained soldiers marched down the road to entrain for the port of embarkation for overseas. We marched up the smooth road, the band playing the regimental march, passed line after line of the different battalions quartered on either side. Soldiers from different units lined the way and voiced friendly criticism as to our appearance, etc. Many wagons from the farmlands beyond the hills were drawn up on each side of the road; grouped about them were many khaki-clad lads buying milk, little pats of butter, buns, and a number of other articles. We marched about two miles till we came to a great square of unoccupied bell tents. Here we halted and took over our lines.

In a few days we were in the ordinary routine of camp life, and I think most of the men liked the new order. Living in a tent seemed to give one a continual feeling of freshness and buoyancy. Every morning, very early, far away at general headquarters, a flag would run up the tall flagpole; then from all parts of the camp would sound the reveille, breaking in on the peaceful repose of honest sleepers, and when the last sound of the bugles had died away there would be heard a quick rattle of snare drums and a few great booms from the bass drum, then the exhilarating strains of a military march would break on the morning air. I had listened to the pleasant martial strains for perhaps a week or two, and naturally associated with them the idea of orderly marching bandsmen, fully equipped, polished and shining from head to foot, till one morning I untied the flap of my tent and looked out. More than half the bandsmen were in their shirt sleeves; five or six were in their bare feet, and now and again they jumped spasmodically, as they walked on a pebble or struck a hidden tentpeg; some who wore boots did not wear socks or puttees, and the trousers from the knee down were tight and much wrinkled, yet there was no lack of harmony in the stately, marching music.

All day long till four o'clock the men drilled or took different exercises, while the sun slowly shifted scenery on the great silent hills. Up and down the long grey road, huge-hooded khaki motor lorries rumbled with their loads of supplies for field and tent. In the evening toward sunset, after the men had washed and rested a little, the flag that had been flying at headquarters all through the day would drop slowly down the pole. Then two buglers would sound retreat, after which the guard would be inspected while the band played some slow waltz or minuet. To me this seemed the happiest hour of the daily military routine. The day was done and from all parts of the camp could be heard low, pleasant talk, as the band played soft music, the men standing about in little groups or moving from tent to tent, visiting neighbours. It always brought to my mind the idea of restfulness and peace.

After retreat the long grey road would become alive with the continuous movement of soldiers going and coming. The officers did not care to walk along this road, as it meant for them one continual return of salutes. Sometimes an open-air moving picture show would be in progress. There were also two halls where moving pictures were shown on rainy nights. In the early days it was a treat to the lads to visit these places. As there were never any ladies present, smoking was permitted. Sometimes the smoke rose in such density that it obscured the pictures on the screen. At ten o'clock last post would sound and weary men would roll themselves in their blankets on the hard ground and dispose themselves to sleep.

VI ⁓ Mass Out of Doors

On Sundays I would set up the portable altar on two rifle boxes placed one above the other, on a great green plain near the end of the camp. Nearly always an awning would be erected above the altar, and whenever the wind blew, canvas was draped about posts as a wind-shield so that the candles might not be extinguished. It was a wonderful sight to see the men draw up on the grass, every one of them reverent and quiet before the little altar as I vested for Mass. Often three thousand were drawn up on the green plain as level as a floor. Sometimes a number would wait till this late Mass—which was always said at ten o'clock—to go to Holy Communion, though I always said an early Mass for those who wished to receive.

Since the war, different men who were present at those open-air Masses have told me that never before had they assisted at the Holy Sacrifice with such devotion. All things seemed to praise God; the great solemn mountains stood silent; the clouds moved soundlessly across the blue of the sky. Not a sound could be heard, save when a man coughed softly, or when the little bell tinkled. On account of what happened, I recall one of those Sunday mornings in particular.

I had noticed, standing among the officers of one of the battalions drawn up in the church parade, an elderly man wearing ordinary blue civilian trousers and a military khaki shirt and helmet. He wore a leather belt but no coat. I no sooner saw him than I said to myself: "An old soldier!" And as I vested for the Holy Sacrifice the question came flashing across my mind again and again: Who can he be? What war was he in? When I turned after the Communion to address the men, there he was standing, well in front with the officers. He listened very attentively to my sermon, which was on the text, "Son, give me thy heart." Toward the end I said a few words about Our Lady, because it was the Sunday within the octave of the Assumption. I told the lads to run to their Mother in all their trials; to be Knights of Our Lady, to think of her especially during their long hours of sentry duty at night, and never to let a day go by without saying her beads. Then, after I had given my blessing and had turned to unvest before my little portable altar, my "old soldier" came forward and introduced himself. He was a judge from my home province, and he would be glad if I would permit him to say a few words to the men. I was very pleased that he should do so. A word was said to the officers in charge, and the men were called to attention.

The judge stood up on the rifle box that I had just vacated, and there in God's beautiful out of doors, with the great green mountains looking up to their Creator in silent humility, this old Catholic gentleman spoke to the lads in a wonderfully clear voice of their Mother and his Mother. It was very edifying to hear this educated Catholic layman speak so. He concluded with a few words about the Mass. "I have assisted at Mass," he said, "in many large cathedrals in different countries; but, I think, never with such devotion as I have this morning here in the open air before your little altar placed on the rifle boxes, and God's beautiful sky and sunlight above us. After all, gentlemen, it is the Mass that counts, the changing of the bread and wine into the Body and Blood of Christ. God could do it and God did do it. " When the old man finished I could not but say gratefully, "God bless you, judge," for I felt that his words would do very much good.

VII ⌒ A Little Indignation

The time passed quickly for me, though I think for most of the men it went slowly; they seemed always restless, always longing to get to the front. They used to come to me often with their little grievances. They seemed to think that their troubles would disappear once they reached training camp overseas. I remember one Sunday, after I had finished Mass and the last company had marched off the field, two soldiers came forward from somewhere and saluted. One of them, the taller of the two, acted as chief spokesman. "Father," he said, "we have not heard Mass today. We were ordered to go to the Protestant service." Excitement flashed in his eyes. "The service is just over, Father, and we slipped over here to tell you." It was strictly against K.R.&O. to order Catholics to a non-Catholic service. The lads did not belong to my battalion but to a construction battalion that had but lately come to camp. Headquarters of this battalion were not far away, so I did not wait for my breakfast but obeyed the first impulse and went immediately to the training square of the No. Construction Co.[34] The church parade was over and the chaplain had just finished packing his books and was preparing to leave the field with the adjutant. I asked the chaplain if the Catholics had been ordered to attend the service. "Yes," he said, and then went on to explain that it was a universal church service and that all the men had been ordered to attend.

I asked him to look up a book entitled K.R.&O. I told him that it was a serious offence that had been committed; that my men had a right to attend their own service; that there was no such thing known in the army as a universal church parade. When they saw they had made a mistake, both chaplain and adjutant were very apologetic. Shortly after this, when the battalion was to leave for overseas, the chaplain wrote me a note asking me to hear the confessions of the Catholics. I think they came to a man; two other chaplains came to help me. This construction battalion was composed mostly of men who had moved quite a lot over different parts of the world and had grown a little slack in the observance of their religious duties. Big things were done for Our Lord that night. Perhaps many would have passed the summer without even coming to Mass had not this great indignity been offered them.

So the days passed quickly, and then one evening word came that we were to leave—but only for another camp. There was great rejoicing at first, for the lads thought that orders for "Overseas" had come.

VIII ⮂ We Break Camp

Movement orders finally came, but not for overseas. The battalion was repositioning but only to the military camp at Sussex, New Brunswick. A celebratory bonfire occurred, and Murdoch's description of the soldiers and their behaviour is touching. However, in contrast, the slow train ride to Sussex did not highlight soldierly innocence. Multiple stops along the route saw liquor gain entry to the troop train. By the time the train reached their hometown of Chatham, many of the soldiers were very drunk. Murdoch felt sick at the spectacle. A public holiday had been proclaimed and the soldiers' families had all turned out in their Sunday best only to find a train filled with drunks. This was at odds with their good behaviour at Valcartier. Undaunted, Murdoch devised a plan. The next Sunday he proposed a solution. If the men would sign a pledge card not to drink (exclusive of the daily rum ration in the trenches, for this was considered medicinal), he would place their names on a silk cloth within his portable altar. They and their commitment would be recalled at every Mass. About two hundred men accepted the proposal.

The autumn dragged on, the days grew colder, and finally movement orders for overseas arrived. Here Murdoch experienced one of the disappointing realities of army life. Although he had summoned all the area's Catholic priests to come out and assist him in hearing the men's confessions, his plans came to naught. The call to commence preparations to leave came earlier than expected, and the men had orders to pack immediately. No confessions would be heard and no Mass celebrated. The immediate demands of the army completely trumped the chaplain's plan for religious services. – RH

It was Sunday, October 1. It was the most beautiful day I have ever seen. There had been a heavy frost during the night, and in the morning the hills, which had been green all summer but had lately begun to put on their autumn tints, were glorious in bright scarlet, yellow, and russet, with still here and there a dark green patch of spruce. The white frost was on the ground and a covering of ice one-eighth of an inch thick was formed on the basin of water in my tent. The air was cold, clear, and invigorating. The men were all in excellent spirits. I said Mass for my own men and then walked about two miles toward the entrance to the camp to say Mass for the other soldiers who still remained in the different areas. The Sabbath day stillness seemed more intense than ever.

Perhaps it was on account of the very small number left in the camp. When I turned around after I had said Mass, I could not but pause in admiration of the wonderful beauty of God's works. I took for the text of my sermon: "O Lord, Our Lord, how admirable is Thy name in the whole world." I told the lads that as Our Lord had made all things beautiful, we ought to keep our souls beautiful in His sight, and that one of the surest means of doing so was to come to Holy Communion. Then I preached on the Blessed Eucharist. When I reached our own lines after Mass, nearly all the tents had been taken down and rolled up. I had breakfast at one of the men's cookstoves. We were to break camp at twelve o'clock. I think I was the only one who was sorry to leave. Things had gone very well during the summer; there had been many consolations in the ministry. Many men who had passed long years away from the sacraments had come into the white bell tent pitched in the open space in the valley and, kneeling there, had been reconciled after many years' estrangement from God. I had watched the men in the evening and had noticed how cheerful they were, how much like boys they were in the tricks they played on each other.

One evening, shortly before we were to leave, a great bonfire had been lighted. All through the day the men had worked at the base of the slopes cutting down dry trees and carrying them out. The fire was built in the square where the men drilled and took their physical exercises in the mornings. It was a thrilling sight to watch the little tongues of fire darting in and out among the pile of dry twigs, increasing in size and speed till they developed into one great waving pillar of flame that tore its way upward through the gigantic pile of dry old trees, hissing, crackling, and roaring as it went. The flames must have reached forty feet in height, and at times the sparks swarmed down on the tents like bees to a hive, and the soldiers had to beat them out. The band marched around the flaming pillar and played, keeping always within the circle of light made by the fire. Many soldiers followed in procession, some of them performing comical acrobatic feats as they went. There was an almost new tent floor up near the colonel's tent, which some of the lads thought would make excellent fuel for the fire. Presently about eight of them were carrying it toward the flames. The quartermaster, who had charge of the movables of the camp, saw them approaching and immediately advanced from his place near the fire, angrily shouting orders to them to put down the tent floor. They did, though not till the indignant quartermaster was very near them. Then they turned and ran quickly away. The quartermaster, who was a heavy man, did not pursue them. He turned toward the fire but only to find that a number of rough tables and chairs had gone to satisfy the hungry flames! He was very angry. The lads had become like little children, and I think their souls had become like the souls of little children.

And now we were going back to civilization! Our journey was one of about four hundred miles through many small towns and cities to a camp near the seaboard, where we were to wait a few weeks before embarking. We left Valcartier at the time appointed, and all that day and most of the evening our route lay along the noble St. Lawrence. In the morning we came into our own Province of New Brunswick, from the northern part of which our battalion had been recruited.

In many towns at which we stopped liquor was procured, and soon there were evidences that many of the men had taken too much. And when we drew near the town from the environs of which the majority of the lads had been recruited, a great number gave signs of almost complete intoxication, so that parents who stood among the great crowd that had gathered to see the lads as they passed through were greatly humiliated. I felt sick at heart, for a public holiday had been proclaimed and people had come from the whole surrounding countryside to see the battalion for the last time before going overseas. It was a gala day. They had waited all morning, and then many of the men who arrived were in every stage of intoxication! It was very humiliating to the poor parents, and the men had been so good all summer!

When the train pulled out, I went back to my seat in the Pullman. Two thoughts were working in my mind, so that my head felt a little dazed and I did not hear the officers talking around me. Neither did I perceive when they spoke to me. One thought was a very human one. I felt terribly disheartened, and I wondered if the people thought that the men had been drinking so during the summer, and I fell to wishing that they could only know all about the men in camp. The other thought was that I was grateful to God for having chosen me to minister to them. For surely they needed a priest!

IX ᕱ The Panel of Silk

The following Sunday, when all my Catholic soldiers were assembled at Mass in the church of the town where we were encamped, I spoke of what had transpired during our journey from Valcartier. During the week I had thought out a plan, and I had bought a few packages of blank visiting cards and a number of lead pencils. I had cut the pencils in two and had put a part in every pew, also a blank card for every person that would sit in the pew. In the course of my little talk I spoke of how fine a thing it would be if they could take the pledge, given in such a way, however, that they might be free to take the rum served in the trenches, which, under those circumstances, could be considered medicine. Those who would take the pledge would write their names on the blank cards; the cards would be gathered up after Mass; the names would be typewritten on a panel of silk; the silk, bearing the names, would be used as a lining for my little portable altar, and whenever Mass would be said, a special remembrance would be made for the lads who had taken the pledge. When we gathered up the cards after Mass, they numbered almost two hundred. They were typed on the panel of silk, and the panel of silk, with the names, still rests in the little altar. All through the war they have been remembered. Many of those names appear elsewhere on small white crosses "where poppies grow," so that now they are no longer mentioned in the memento of the living; but there is another part of the Mass when they are remembered—with "those who have gone before us, signed with the sign of faith, and who rest in the sleep of peace."

X ❧ Movement Orders

We did not stay very long in our new camping ground. For a few days the men seemed quite content. Everything was new to them; but soon they began to wonder how long it would be before we would leave. The nights often were very cold in the tents, for it was now late in October. We began to feel sure that orders for departing must come soon as no preparations were being made for going into winter quarters. On Sunday I had announced confessions for the following Wednesday. On the day set, four priests came to help me, but just as the men were being formed to go to the church, word came that we were to leave that evening for overseas. The men were dismissed and soon there was a scene of general disorder; but on all sides were happy faces. All seemed glad to go. They had been looking forward to it for so long a time. I was obliged to tell the priests who had come so far that there would be no confessions. I kept the hosts that the Sisters in a nearby town had made for me, as I hoped to hear the men's confessions on the boat on the way across the ocean.

All night long we stood around, waiting for the train to come to take us, but there had been some delay, and so it was not till early in the morning that we left. Our journey was not a very long one, but we were obliged to wait at many different stations till trains passed us. As the movement order had called for a night trip, no dining car or buffet had been attached. The men went hungry all day. The last trip had been one of overindulgence. This was one of abstinence.

We had no breakfast and no dinner, yet the men seemed quite content and joked pleasantly over the fact that they were hungry. At one country station where we were side-tracked, the bugler jumped out on the platform and blew the call: "Come to the cookhouse door, boys!" But as there was no cookhouse door to go to and no "Mulligan battery"—the name given to the field kitchen, with its steaming odours of Irish stew—they greeted the call of the smiling bugler with derisive laughter.

At four o'clock we were all aboard the SS *Corsican*, and at five we pulled out from the dock, the band on the upper deck playing "Auld Lang Syne." Many relatives of the lads, who had arrived in the little seaport town, waved their goodbyes from the dock as the boat swung clear from its moorings and steamed slowly down the bay. The boys swarmed up the rope ladders and cheered; many little tugs far down on the water darted about, shrieking shrilly their farewells. We were off to the war.

XI ∾ The High Seas

Padre Murdoch and the 132nd Battalion left Halifax on board the Corsican on October 26. They arrived in Liverpool, England, ten days later on November 5. As battalion chaplain, Murdoch heard confessions and said Mass throughout the voyage. His sympathies and sentimentality are revealed when he relates his experience of seeing "holy" Ireland—to him a land of peace and quiet, a moment bordering on a spiritual experience. England was a different story. England was all business, all ordered like a great machine set to work with one mind and a determined intent. Once in England, the troops took a train to the southeastern destination of Liphook. Once there they marched through the mud and the drizzle to the sprawling military site known as Bramshott Camp. After a week of unremittingly overcast skies, rain, and camp life, Murdoch says he understood why English writers spoke so often of "depression." – RH

The doctor and I had been allotted a stateroom together, but I was subsequently given one down below, where I said Mass the first morning and heard confessions every evening. The chief steward was a Catholic and he was very kind. I had permission to say Mass in the second-class saloon, which was the largest on the boat, and nearly all the men came to Holy Communion. Our first Sunday out I said Mass for the lads below. As I proceeded with the Mass the seas became very rough, so that the book fell off the altar three times; the chalice, however, never moved. Many became sick, and the Red Cross section was busy. On the first day out we donned our cumbersome lifebelts, which we wore all the way across the Atlantic. I took mine off only while saying Mass. They hung on the berths at night. During the day the men walked up and down the upper deck; sometimes there were drills, etc. We saw no vessels. Every day we plunged forward through rough seas, and in the afternoons, as I sat in my little stateroom hearing confessions, I could hear the dull pounding of the waves on the sides of the vessel.

I was very pleased with the example the Catholic officers gave the men. Every one of them came to confession and Communion on the way over. One, the old quartermaster, who was confined to his cabin with a severe attack of la grippe, could not come to Mass with the others, so I gave him Communion in his cabin toward the last of the voyage. The second morning afterwards, however, as I walked back and forth making my thanksgiving, I stopped quickly and peered out over the sea. I could see very faintly, across the water, a long, serried line of hills that looked greyish blue in the early morning—the hills of Ireland! I ran quickly to tell the quartermaster, who had been born in Ireland and had still a true Irishman's great love for his native land. He was not there. I was surprised, as the doctor had told me that he had given orders that he was not to leave his cabin till after we reached port. As I went out on deck again, I noticed, up forward, leaning over the gunwale and looking toward Ireland, a great muffled figure. He wore one khaki great coat, and another, thrown loosely about his shoulders, gave him a hunched appearance. It was the quartermaster! I went forward quickly: "Captain," I said, "didn't the doctor tell you not to leave your stateroom till we docked?" He didn't say anything for a second or two, and I noticed a mist had come into his eyes. Then he pointed far across the grey waste of waters. "Ah, Father," he said, "but there's Ireland!"

XII ❧ By Ireland

All day long we sailed by Ireland, and she seemed strangely peaceful and quiet. Perhaps it was the great contrast with the sea, the wide tumbling waste of waters that, night and day, was always restless; or perhaps it was a benediction resting over the whole country. Anyhow it seemed that way to me as often as my eyes rested on the hills and fields of holy Ireland. Since that morning I have seen many different countries. I have come back to my own land over the same great distance of waters, and it was in the early morning that I saw it first, yet that strange spiritual peace that seemed to rest over Ireland was decidedly lacking. That early morning scene still comes back to me; and all through the day, whenever my eyes rested on the hills of Ireland, I felt that I was making a meditation and that I was being lifted in spirit far above the little things that bother one here below.

Down below us on the water, with the swiftness almost of swallows, darted here and there the long grey anti-submarine boats. Seven or eight of them had come to meet us. Later on in the day appeared the minesweepers, low, short steamboats painted for the most part red and carrying one-yard sails. The sails were of dark brownish-red colour. They worked in pairs.

XIII ∽ England

That evening we moved slowly up the Mersey and at nine o'clock anchored out in the stream in full view of the city of Liverpool. We could not see it very well, for throughout the city the lights were dimmed and windows were darkened. All along the Irish coast the impression was one of peace and quiet, a spiritual something. But England seemed to give one the idea of a great machine, working slowly, steadily, untiringly. One was spiritual, the other material. That was my first impression of England as a nation, and that impression remained with me during my stay in the country. Every time I returned on leave from France I found it always the same. England, as a nation, seemed to be wonderfully organized, and that whole organization seemed to run smoothly, powerfully, and heavily. Each individual had his special work to do in that colossal workshop called England. He knew how to do that, and he did it, quietly, methodically, and well. But, taken away from his own work, he seemed to lack resource—the resource and initiative of the men from the New World.

We entrained early in the morning. For most of us it was our first experience with the compartment cars of the Old World—little compartments running the width of the car, a door opening from each side of the car, with two seats running from one side to the other, each holding from three to five people, who sat facing each other. We passed through many quaint towns and many large cities, and it was evening when we came into the quiet little station of Liphook. We were due there at two o'clock, but there had been many delays along the way. Sometimes the lads had pulled the rope and had stopped the train; and each time a stolid brakeman had opened the door of compartment after compartment, asking solemnly, "Oo pulled the reope?" Of course no one gave him the information he asked, whereupon he closed each door and went patiently on to the next compartment.

XIV ❧ In Camp

I have often remarked that English writers use the word "depression" much more frequently than do writers on this side of the water, and I have often wondered what could be the reason for this. I had not passed one week in England before I knew. A few days in an English military camp will give one an idea of what depression is.

The military camp to which we were sent was Bramshott—a great collection of long, low, one-storey huts, built row on row, with a door at each end, opening into muddy lanes that ran the whole length of the camp. It was raining mildly the evening we arrived, and we marched in the darkness for three miles along soft muddy roads, and now and again we splashed through a puddle, though we tried to avoid them.

There seems to be an especially slippery quality about the mud of England—to say nothing of that of France—that makes it very difficult to retain one's balance. My cane, which according to military regulations I always carried, for the first time now proved useful. Day after day as the soldiers of the camp drilled in the soft, muddy squares, their movements resembled sliding more than orderly marching. Sometimes thick pads of the soft, yellow mud clung heavily their feet; very often a gentle drizzle of rain fell, and nearly always the sky was dark grey and sombre, so that one wondered no longer why the word "depression" should be so frequently used in English literature.

But notwithstanding the mud and the dark skies, many of us grew to like England. There were many quaint, winding roads hedged in places with hawthorn bushes or spruce or boxwood. These led us into delightful little country villages with their old freestone churches, sometimes covered with ivy that often ran for a long distance up the old Norman tower.

England was not all grey skies and gloom. There was both natural and spiritual beauty to behold.

XV ∾ The Cenacle

To Murdoch's great surprise and disappointment, his beloved 132nd Infantry Battalion was destined never to reach the trenches. Within three weeks of arrival in England, it was broken up into drafts of reinforcements to replace losses at the front. Murdoch was now a chaplain without a battalion. He was temporarily stationed at

Bramshott as assistant to its Roman Catholic chaplain, Father Knox. He relates several tales of devotional life and personal encounters from this period. First, there was the convent ("Cenacle") and its Sisters in nearby Grayshott. Soldiers could walk there on Sunday afternoons for a service of Benediction (prayer and adoration of the Sacrament), sandwiches, and socialization. He also relates the tale of a young Spanish immigrant to Canada who was then a Baptist minister's orderly and a lapsed Catholic. Murdoch was scandalized when he learned that the soldier was from the 132nd Battalion. Indicative of the lack of ecumenicalism of the period, Murdoch relates: "I was responsible to God for this man's soul, and apparently he had lost his faith." Murdoch will resume this man's story later in his narrative.

It must be noted that in Murdoch's world, the main denominational competition (and occasional adversary) was the Church of England. As he relates, the Anglicans were "recognized as the official religion of the British Army." This provides the necessary background to his tale of Tim Healy and the Garrison Church Hut service blackboard. Tim Healy's famous namesake was a prominent Irish Nationalist politician much in the news at the time Murdoch was writing The Red Vineyard.

Finally, Murdoch tells the story of the open-air service of dedication to "the Sacred Heart of Jesus," which involved three thousand Catholic soldiers from across Canada. – RH

Not more than three miles from the camp was situated the convent of the Sisters of the Cenacle, a beautiful three-storey building of red brick and stucco hidden away among great hemlock, spruce, and cypress trees. It is a kind of rest house, where at certain seasons of the year retreats are given for ladies, who come from different parts of England and pass a week at the convent. All during the war there was an open invitation to the Catholic soldiers of Bramshott Camp to visit the convent on Sunday afternoon and assist at Benediction of the Most Blessed Sacrament.

There were three or four different ways of going to Grayshott, near which the Convent of the Cenacle was situated. One of these was a footpath that led first through a moor, covered in summer with purple heather, then through bracken, almost as high as an average man, and bunches of green gorse bushes that blazed light yellow at certain seasons with flowers resembling in shape the sweet peas'. It was a quaint little path, passing on its way "Wagner's Wells," a chain of what we on this side of the Atlantic would call ponds, in a low, wooded valley. In summer these were very pretty when the full-leafed branches of the trees hung low over the Wells and the water was almost wholly hidden by tiny white flowers that rested on the surface. All during the war, on Sunday afternoons, a long, irregular line of khaki-clad figures went leisurely along the footpath to Grayshott, passed scenery strange though pleasing, mounted quaint rustic stiles till they came to the convent of the Sisters of the Cenacle.

The first Sunday I visited the convent there were so many soldiers present that the little chapel could not contain all. I learned afterwards that this had happened so frequently that, in order that all might be present at Benediction, the good Sisters had asked for and obtained a general permission to have the services on the lawn just in the rear of the chapel. Benediction was given by a little Belgian who was doing chaplain's work among the Canadians at Bramshott, while Father Knox, a recently converted Anglican clergyman, led the soldiers in singing the hymns. Little red hymn books, which the English government had supplied the Catholic soldiers, were passed around to each soldier. It was a beautiful sight there on that English lawn, as all knelt grouped together, officer and soldier, priest, Sister, while the white Host was raised to bless us all. Then the lads sang strongly and clearly that beautiful hymn, "Hail, Queen of Heaven," that was sung so often during the war under many different conditions. The Irishmen sang it as they advanced to take a difficult position that the English had failed to take at Festubert.

The Sisters dispensed hospitality; large teapots of tea and plates stacked high with thin slices of bread and butter, and baskets of thick slices of yellow cake with currants in it. Then in the evening the soldiers walked back to camp through winding footpaths and over stiles. I am sure there are many men scattered over the country who will remember gratefully the Sisters of the Cenacle at Grayshott. It must have inconvenienced them greatly, yet Sunday after Sunday, all during the war, soldiers went to the convent, and always the Sisters treated them most hospitably.

On Sundays, when the number of men present was not too large, Benediction was given in the Sisters' chapel. It was a very pretty little chapel, and on the altar, day and night, the Sacred Host was exposed for perpetual adoration; and always two Sisters knelt to adore. On the Gospel side of the altar stood a beautiful statue of the Blessed Virgin that was almost covered with the military badges worn by soldiers of the different battalions. In some way known to women, the good Sisters had draped a mantle about the statue, and to this was pinned the badges of these modern knights.

After Benediction the lads would all come to a large room where tea would be served. Often among the little khaki-clad groups a Sister of the Cenacle would be seen standing, or sitting, listening to the stories told of the country far away across the seas. The Sisters wore a black habit, a small purple cape that reached to the elbows, and a white cap covered by a black veil, except for a one-inch crimped border around the face. Sometimes, when it was time to leave the convent, a certain group would step forward to say goodbye to the Sisters and to ask their prayers. These would be men ordered to leave during the week as a draft for some battalion in the trenches. And the lads "would be remembered in the Sacred Presence there, where remembrances are sacred, and each memory holds a prayer." Day and night, as the Sisters knelt before the Lord and offered their continuous prayers for a world that seemed to have forgotten Him, special prayers were said for those whose badges hung on Our Lady's mantle.

XVI ∽ The Battalion is Broken Up

We were not in England three weeks when orders came for a draft of men to reinforce a battalion that had suffered severe losses at the front. In a few days, 150 men left for France. We thought at the time that reinforcements would soon come to us from Canada, but not much more than a week passed till we were called on for another draft. This time the order was that 350 men be sent to the 87th Battalion. This second order came as a shock to us all. Many of the officers had been in the battalion for almost a year; they had watched it grow strong and numerous and had helped to form the thing most essential in a battalion, an "esprit de corps." I had never thought of going to the front except as a unit. The idea of our being broken up had never entered my mind, but before Christmas came, our battalion had lost its identity as 132nd Battalion, and the majority of the men had gone to join different units at the front.

It was impossible for me to be with all my men, as there were no two drafts in the same brigade; still, I thought that I might be permitted to go as chaplain to the brigade in which was the largest number of men, so I obtained permission to go to London to explain matters to the senior chaplain. He was very kind, but he said I must await my turn; there were other chaplains whose battalions had undergone the same process of annihilation as had mine. These must go first; work would be found for me in England till my turn would come to go to the front. I returned to Bramshott Camp a somewhat wiser man as to the workings of things military. But as I sat in the cold first-class compartment, with my feet on a stone hot water bottle (seemingly this is the only way they heat the cars in England), my mind was busy with many things. One was that I never should have offered my services as chaplain had I foreseen the catastrophe that had befallen us. I had counted on being with my men till the last. Before leaving for overseas many of the mothers of the lads had come to me and had told me what a great consolation it was to them to have the assurance that a Catholic priest would be with their sons. Now I was not going with them; still, I had been convinced that the lads would be well cared for spiritually. At Bramshott I became assistant for a time to the camp chaplain, Father John Knox.

XVII ∾ The Little Spaniard

I had not been given very much information at headquarters as to how soon I might be sent to the front, for they did not know how soon the call might come for chaplains. In a few days the remnants of my battalion left Bramshott for a camp at Shoreham-by-Sea—all save a few, who stayed as officers, servants, or clerks in different branches at headquarters.

One afternoon I was sitting before Father Knox's tiny fireplace in his little room, talking of the Sunday church parades, when a very young soldier entered, saluted, passed Father Knox a letter, and then stood at attention. I did not notice the lad particularly, as Father Knox read the letter in silence, for my eyes were on the small heap of glowing coals in the grate before me, and my mind was busy on a scheme to get all the men in the camp at two church parades on the following Sunday. As Father Knox began to write the answer, he looked up from the paper and asked, "Catholic?"

Then for the first time the lad began to speak, hurriedly, and with foreign accent. His eyes took on a queer strained expression; his head seemed to crouch down to his shoulders. It transpired that he was a Spaniard and had been brought up a Catholic, but after going to Canada had been accustomed to go to Protestant churches. He was now orderly to a Protestant minister and had received a few books from him including a copy of the New Testament in Spanish, so at present, his religion was the "Lord Jesus." I had already turned from the fire and was watching the lad. It was the first time I had ever heard a Catholic speak so, and I felt a great pity for him. But quickly the pity gave place to other emotions, for in reply to Father Knox's question as to what battalion he came over with, he said "One Hundred and Thirty-second"—my own battalion. Slowly a dazed, nauseating feeling chilled me. Such a thing to happen! I was responsible to God for this man's soul, and apparently, he had lost his faith!

I questioned him a little, only to learn that now he was orderly to a Baptist minister and that it was he who had given him the New Testament in Spanish. I appointed an evening for the lad to come to see me. He came and we talked for a long time, but he seemed to be strangely obsessed. The more we talked, the more I noticed the queer strained expression in his eyes, and when he left me that night I feared I had not done very much toward reviving his faith. It was many months before I saw him again.

XVIII ❧ The Garrison Church Hut

The days passed quickly. New battalions from home came and took up quarters in camp and to their surprise were broken up and sent in drafts to France. Every night Father Knox or I remained on duty in the little garrison hut, that the lads might have an opportunity of going to confession before leaving for France.

The garrison church hut had been built by the military authorities for the use of all religious denominations. It was used on Sundays by the Catholics, or, as the army equivalent has it, RCs, at seven o'clock for the Communion Mass for the men. The Protestant denominations had the use of it all the rest of the day. There was a little altar on which the Anglicans offered their Communion service, but we never used this. Father Knox had an altar of his own, on rollers, which was moved out in front of the other one before Mass and wheeled back after Mass.

Just outside the entrance to the hut had been erected a large blackboard for announcements of services. Always on Saturday night this board held the order of Anglican services. We had never interfered with this, as the Anglican is recognized as the official religion of the British Army. However, one Saturday evening as I came out alone from the hut, I happened, in passing, to glance at the board. The customary announcements were not there; instead was written in bold white letters the order of Catholic services for the morrow. Not only was the notice of the camp service given, but the Benediction at Grayshott Convent was mentioned also. For a few seconds I stood gazing at the sign, in great surprise. Soldiers passing along the little lane paused to read and then passed on. I knew Father Knox could have had nothing to do with it. Then, as I stood there in the night looking at the announcement board, I smiled. "Tim Healy," I said, "Tim Healy!"

Tim Healy was a lieutenant who had come over from Canada with an Irish battalion. Like many another it had been broken up, and Tim was waiting anxiously his turn at the front. He had been born in Ireland and was a near relative of the great Tim Healy. The following afternoon I saw him at the Convent of the Cenacle. I went across the room to where he was sitting and waited till he had finished his tea. Then, without any preamble, I said, "Mr. Healy, did you erase the announcements on the board outside the church and put the Catholic order on?" Tim forced an expression of innocent wonder into his face, which, I thought, was a little too elaborately done, but almost simultaneously appeared a pleasant twinkle in the eyes of him. "No, Father," he said, "I didn't," then he smiled broadly, and his eyes twinkled merrily. I looked at him in great surprise, for I was almost certain that he had done it. But Tim had not finished, and as his eyes continued to twinkle said quietly, "But I sent one of my men to do it. I hope he did it well." "Oh, yes," I said grimly, "I think it was done well—if not too well." However, nothing ever came of it.

XIX ∼ The New Sacrifice

Things went much the same at Bramshott. Spring came, and for the first time I saw the primroses, which are among the first flowers to bloom in England. They do not belong to the aristocracy, for one sees them everywhere: along railway embankments, along the roadsides, near the hedgerows—everywhere patches of the pretty little yellow flowers smiled the approach of spring.

Then one day when the spring birds, nesting in the great old English trees, were cheering up the poor war-broken lads that lay on their little cots in so many military hospitals throughout the country—Vimy Ridge had been fought, and many of the lads who had sailed with me had fallen that victory might come—word came that I was to join the Fifth Canadian Division, which was then preparing to go overseas.

It was a beautiful day when I left for Witley Camp where the Fifth Division was quartered. The birds were chorusing their glorious melodies from hedge and tree and field; but along lanes that should have worn a peaceful country setting went clumsily great motor lorries in different ways connected with the war. Witley Camp was only six miles from Bramshott, so it did not take us long to speed over the Portsmouth road through the beautiful Surrey country.

I took up temporary quarters with my old friend Father Crochetière and slept on a table in his office. I was not very long there when another old friend dropped in to see me in the height of Father Hingston, SJ [Society of Jesus, the Jesuits]. Both priests welcomed me very kindly and told me I was just in time to help in the remote preparation for a stirring event. They spoke with great enthusiasm, and it was not long before I was made aware of the cause. A Solemn High Mass was to be celebrated in the open air the following Sunday, and the Catholic soldiers from all parts of the camp were to attend in order to be consecrated to the Sacred Heart of Jesus. There were more than three thousand Catholic soldiers in the camp. The following Sunday morning I was up very early to help in the preparations.

It was a beautiful morning. The sun was up, clear, bright, and warm. The air was very still. Though preparations, both military and religious, had been most carefully made, there was discernible in the manner of the priests who had worked so hard for the bringing about of this great religious ceremony some signs of anxiety. They feared lest there be a hitch in the deliverance of orders, so that all the men might not be present. There was no need to fear, for at nine thirty, three thousand Catholic soldiers drew up in the grove of pines on the border of the lake at the northwest corner of the camp, and all anxiety disappeared. There were French Canadian lads from the Province of Quebec; Irish Canadian Rangers from Montreal; Scotch laddies, with feathers in their caps, from Ontario and Nova Scotia; Indian lads from Eastern and Western Canada.[35]

An altar had been built against one of the very few oak trees that stood in the grove of pines, and above the cross that stood upon it, a large picture of the Sacred Heart of Jesus was nailed to the tree; surmounting all was a canopy of larch and ivy leaves. Daffodils, tulips, and larch stood out brightly among the candles on the white altar. All about the carpeted elevation on which the altar had been built stood many potted plants. As the parade was drawn up beneath the trees, on the carpet of dry pine needles and the last year's oak leaves, bands of different battalions played and the kilted laddies made music with their pipes.

Father Crochetière sang the Mass, with a priest, Father McDonald, who had come over as chaplain to a Scottish battalion, as deacon and the writer as subdeacon. The choir of thirty voices, which sang the Royal Mass so beautifully, was under the direction of Lt. Prevost of the 150th Battalion. And so under the British oak where "Druids of old" once offered their pagan sacrifices, the Holy Sacrifice of the New Law was offered, and Canadian lads knelt to adore. And there by the quiet lakeside, the miracle of God's wonderful love was wrought, and the promise made by the Divine Master on the border of another lake, the day following the multiplication of the loaves and fishes, was fulfilled. For many of the soldiers had waited till this late Mass to go to Communion, and under the beautiful sunlight that filtered through the trees they knelt to receive the "Bread of Life."

After Mass a short sermon was preached in English and French by Father Hingston, SJ, chaplain to the Irish Canadian Rangers, in the course of which he explained clearly and beautifully what the ceremony of consecration meant. Then Colonel Barre, commanding the 150th Battalion, read the Act of Consecration to the Sacred Heart of Jesus in French, and Major McRory, officer commanding the 199th Irish Canadian Rangers, read it in English. Each soldier was then presented with a badge of the Sacred Heart.

And just as of old the multitude who followed the Divine Master were blessed before they departed, so, after the Consecration to the Sacred Heart had been made, the lads knelt while Benediction of the Blessed Sacrament was given, and then all was over. "He blessed them and sent them away."

As I stood that day by the little altar near the lakeside, while bands played and the lads fell in preparatory to departing, I could not help thinking of the many different places where they had worshipped since they had left Canada; and though I could not foresee the strange scenes they would inevitably meet on the red road of war, which they would shortly travel, still I felt sure that one day would stand out in their memories in bold relief: the day they made the Act of Consecration to the Sacred Heart of Jesus, the day when they knelt before God's altar built in the open air under the trees by the lakeside—and Jesus passed!

XX ⌒ Through English Lanes

In May of 1917, Murdoch was transferred from Bramshott to nearby Witley Camp. Here he joined the twenty thousand men of the 5th Canadian Infantry Division as they prepared for France. At Witley, he joined two other Catholic priests, Fr. Crochetière and

Fr. Hingston. Next, after a year in the army, Murdoch finally went on a brief five-day spiritual retreat with the Carthusian monks of Parkminster. There he experienced what he described as "a strange peace everywhere," and the retreat master struck him as a man "who had stepped aside from the great noisy highway of the world to listen in silence to the voice of God." The timing was fortuitous, for just a week later Murdoch received orders to proceed to France. – RH

The early summer in England, especially in Surrey, is very beautiful, and as the work was light, we had many opportunities to walk through the lovely country roads. But even prettier than the highways were the lanes that led off from them and went winding, with their hedges, through copse and field and quaint little red-brick villages, each with its century-old, ivy-covered church that had come down from the good old Catholic days. In some of them a statue of some saint still stood, and in many were ancient holy-water stoops and baptismal fonts.

Often, gigantic chestnut or oak trees, grouped near a quaint old gate, told us of the entrance to some baronial estate or castle; but nearly always our only view of the estate was a piece of road with very carefully trimmed box hedge or a great blazing hedgerow of rhododendrons and a small white board, attached to a gatepost or tree, which informed the passing wayfarer that there was "No Thoroughfare."

It was very pleasant to steal away from the camp and the sounds of shouted orders and practicing military bands and bugle notes to the quiet country where the birds sang blithely and the strange notes of the cuckoo's solitary call from some distant tarn or wood came sweetly to the ears; one forgot, for the moment, the thought of war and all associated with it.

I remember one afternoon, I had taken a walk with Father Hingston and Father Crochetière down a shady lane that wound, for the most part, through a high woodland when we came suddenly to a small village of seven or eight houses. To our right was a long box-hedged footpath, winding through a field or two till it was swallowed up in a grove of tall, full-leafed beech and oak trees that stood presumably before a rich country seat. But we did not take the footpath to the right. Instead, the priests—both had been here before—turned to the left, and presently we had passed through a little gate into a very small but lovely rose garden. A tiny path, with a tiny boxwood hedge not more than a foot high, led from the gate to the door of an old-fashioned, white house. Just before the door was built a latticed portico, over which climbing roses grew. We were admitted by an elderly housekeeper and were asked to go upstairs. There we found a priest whose age might have been forty-five and whose hair was just beginning to turn grey about the temples. He was about medium height, rather slight, with an ascetic face. He was sitting in a low room that was very bare save for a table on which were some morning papers. Across the hall was a room in which was a great old-fashioned fireplace with an inglenook. The priest's name was Father McCarty, but he spoke with a decidedly English accent. He was a member of a religious community known as the Salesian Fathers. Knowing that he had such a very small parish, I asked him if he found the time heavy on his hands. He replied that he did not and that although he had only three or four families in all, including the rich household of Capt. Rusbrook, whose large estate we had passed on entering the village, he was quite busy, as he was writing the life of the founder of his order, Don Bosco; he also from time to time helped the chaplains at Witley Camp.

XXI ❧ At Parkminster

There was a different spirit in Witley Camp than there had been at Bramshott, for in the whole division—twelve battalions of infantry and three brigades of artillery, etc.— was the one feeling of expectation of soon going overseas. Any day the orders might come. Father Hingston had made a retreat in London, and Father Crochetière had just returned from five days' rest and prayer at the wonderful monastery of the Carthusian Fathers at Parkminster. I decided to go there.

The following Monday, late in the afternoon, I drove up the winding drive, through hawthorn hedges, to the gates of the monastery. Everything seemed very quiet; no one appeared in garden or window. A bell-rope hung outside the blue-grey door. I pulled it quickly. From somewhere within came a great clanging and almost simultaneously a clatter of heavy boots on stone flags. Inside, a bolt shot back, and immediately a white-garbed, white-bearded old brother stood before me, smiling in the opening. He shook hands with me and bade me enter. "We have been expecting you, Father," he said, with that gentle courtesy that one finds in a religious house. He took my grip, notwithstanding every protest, and led me along the rough, stone-floored corridor to the guest house, where I was given a large, airy corner room, plainly though adequately furnished. Snow-white sheets were on the bed—I had not seen sheets for a long time.

The old, white brother told me to sit down, that presently the Retreat Master would come. Then he left me. I went over to a window and looked out. Just below was a large garden with rose-fringed walks, enclosed by a very high stone wall. Outside the wall, green fields, fringed with dark trees, stretched far away. Beyond these, rolling Sussex downs, looking greyish-blue in the summer haze, rose to meet the skyline. A strange peace was everywhere, and save for a slight nervousness that seemed to have come to me with the great silence of the house, I was glad that I had come.

In a little while a knock sounded on the door and the Retreat Master entered. He was not very tall and rather slight, and though his hair was grey he was not old. There was nothing very distinctive in his face, now rough with a three-days' growth of beard—the rule of the order is to shave every fifteen days—and there was not much colour in his cheeks. The eyes were small, grey, and almost piercing. But there was that same indefinable atmosphere of peace about him. It seemed as if he had stepped aside from the great noisy highway of the world to listen in silence to the voice of God. Yet, as he talked, the Father seemed to take a childish interest in all that I told him of my experiences in a great military camp with officers and men of the world. But away below the wonder that rippled over the surface of the spirit of the monk there seemed to be great depths of silence, and as I tried to fathom these depths, I felt a strange helplessness come over me. I could not understand this man who sat smiling simply and cordially and at the same time seemed to be enveloped in an atmosphere not of this world.

Before he left for the evening, the Retreat Master pointed to a card that hung on the wall. "The Order of Retreat," he said. "You will be able to follow it?" I assured the Father that I would, and then he was gone for the night.

My retreat passed very quickly—I had only five days—and during that time I forgot all about war and preparations for war. Every day for about half an hour the Retreat Master came to my room and talked a little. He told me many things about the monastic life that I found very interesting. Each monk, he explained, lived in a little brick, two-storey house, which was attached to the great main corridor that formed a quadrangle about the church. The lower storey was a kind of workshop in which was a lathe and different kinds of carpenter's tools, and to it the monk descended in his free time to do manual work. A small garden, in between the different houses, was allotted to each monk, where he worked for a while each day and grew vegetables for his own frugal board.

One day I told the Retreat Master that I had read a description of Parkminster in one of the late Monsignor Benson's novels, *The Conventionalists*. The monk smiled reminiscently. He recalled the day that Mr. Benson—he was an Anglican at the time of his visit—in company with another minister, had called. Mr. Benson had seemed very much interested. The other had made some strange remark. Monsignor Benson had never visited the monastery as a priest, nor had he ever brought anyone there to join the community. The monk assured me of this, and he had been Guest Master for many years. Yet when I had read *The Conventionalists*, I had been almost convinced that the story related was a personal experience. It may have been to some other monastery that the young man had gone, although Monsignor Benson had said Parkminster.

Shortly before I left the monastery, the Retreat Master came to have a last chat. "When you reach the front," he said, "tell your men that we are praying for them day after day, night after night." I felt a strange feeling of security on hearing these words, but as I left the monastery gates and turned to say farewell to the old monk, I felt a distinct sinking of my heart. "Perhaps," he said rapturously, "you'll be a martyr!"

XXII ⚭ Orders for France

Murdoch was sent to No. 2 Canadian Infantry Base Depot on the French coast at Étaples, a British Empire staging area for troops and supplies for the front. Étaples was also the site of many of the military hospitals. Murdoch gives a vivid description of peasants working their fields, of the natural beauty of the sunsets, of the dirtiness of the streets, and of the overall busyness of wartime Étaples. He describes the congestion of market days, the sight of nurses from the military hospitals buying fresh food, and the omnipresent "Estaminet" signs advertising, in English, that "Eggs and chips" (fried potatoes) were served. At Étaples, where there could be as many as a hundred thousand men training, Murdoch's primary priestly employment was that of hearing confessions. This work could be very pressing when a large draft of soldiers was departing for the front—it might well be the soldiers' last opportunity to confess and to receive the Sacrament!

Murdoch found it "wonderfully edifying" to hear the confessions of the Irish lads, although he reserved special praise for the New Zealanders, "those quiet-voiced men" with "piercing eyes." Here we encounter another aspect of Murdoch's outlook reflective of the time— his tendency to attribute specific traits to particular nationalities or ethnic groups. While the Irish were extremely deferential to Roman Catholic priests, so too were the New Zealanders, but additionally, as part of their nationality, they also exhibited certain physical characteristics. As Murdoch relates it, New Zealanders were "nearly all tall, lithe men, dark-haired, with long, narrow faces and eyes that had a strange intensity of expression." Apparently if a man was short and round-faced, he was clearly not a New Zealander! – **RH**

Not a week had passed after my retreat when one morning a runner from divisional headquarters came into my hut, saluted, and passed me a paper. I was ordered to France. This was good news, for I had now been in the army over a year. The battalion had been recruited to full strength early in 1916, and I had hoped to be in France before the end of that year. It was now June 1917.

The following morning, I left Witley Camp for London, where I was to receive further orders and equip myself with bedroll, trench boots, etc. At headquarters in London, I learned that I was to go to No. 2 Canadian Infantry Base Depot, at Étaples. From there, after a while, I would be sent to the trenches.

Étaples is a quaint little fishing village on the Canche River, about two miles from its mouth. Before the war it had been a famous resort for artists; quite a colony had lived in the little town. Apart from its quaintness and the picturesque costumes of the townsfolk, its chief interest for artists lay in its beautiful sunsets. It was a glorious sight to look down the Canche, widening between the jack-pine-crested sand dunes, as it flowed nearer the sea, to the great golden sun sliding down toward the merry dancing blue waves of the Straits of Dover, slowly turning red and redder as it sank among the long pencils or banks of reddening clouds fringed with gold. When the sun would sink into the waves, the water would be crimsoned for miles, and for a long time after the great red disc had disappeared, the distant sails of the fishing boats made a very pretty picture as they moved silently over the waves.

Étaples, besides being quaint, was a very dirty little town. At any hour of the day one might see a good housewife come to the door and empty a tub of soapy water that had served its use into the cobbled street, where it was mingled with other soapy waters that ran continuously along the gutters. Every morning, piles of garbage appeared in the streets before the houses.

During the war almost every house bore a sign nailed to the door upon which was written or printed the word "Estaminet," which signified that within one might purchase wine, beer, coffee, and other refreshments. Sometimes accompanying the sign was a smaller one, bearing the English words "Eggs and chips." All the narrow, cobblestoned streets that ran from every direction into the village stopped at the large market square. Market days were twice a week, and then it was difficult to find one's way through the crowds who came to buy from the black- or white-hooded country women, whose market wagons, mostly drawn by donkeys, were laden with everything imaginable from farm, house, and field. It was a striking scene there in the old market square before the town hall. Soldiers from almost all the Allied armies could be seen there, while nurses from the great military hospitals, about one-half mile from the town along the road that followed the Canche toward Camiers and the sea, moved quickly, nearly always two by two, carrying small market baskets.

XXIII ⁓ At No. 2 Canadian Infantry Base Depot

At the No. 2 Canadian Infantry Base Depot I had the most wonderful opportunity of the war to study the Catholics of the allied armies—Irish, Scotch, Welsh, English, New Zealand, Australian, and Portuguese. For here were depot camps for all these troops. Often there would be as many as 100,000 men training at one time, but after every engagement, drafts would be called for up the line. Then they would be given their full equipment from the large ordnance stores at Étaples, and in the evening they would come to confession and Communion. There were two large Catholic recreation huts, with a chapel in each. On Sundays, folding doors were opened and the whole hut became a chapel; hundreds of soldiers came to assist at the different Masses that were said in each hut.

In the evening, great numbers came to confession, and always crowds assisted at the early weekday morning Mass. Every evening, priests would be on duty in the little chapels hearing confessions and, if soldiers had been called urgently and were leaving for the front, giving Communion.

It was my lot for the most part to hear confessions in the Catholic hut to which came not only my own Canadian lads, but the Irish of the famous 16th Division: Connaughts, Leinsters, Munsters, Irish Guards, etc. It was wonderfully edifying to sit evening after evening and hear the confessions of these Irish lads. They would usually begin by saying, "God bless you, Father!" They came in extraordinarily large numbers every night and always stayed a long while to pray. The faith seemed to be part of their very being. Though they did not parade it, these lads seemed scarcely to breathe without showing in some way the love for their faith. When they met the Catholic chaplain in the street, they did not give him the salute they were supposed to give him, in common with all other officers. They always took off their hats. They were the only soldiers who ever did this. I asked an Irish Catholic officer about it one evening. "Why, Father," he said, "they think the military salute not good enough for a priest. It does all very well, they think, for a general or a field marshal or the King of England, but it's not enough for a priest. They must take their hats off, although they break a military rule by so doing." "God bless them," I said warmly.

The Queen of England visited the hospitals and military depots of Étaples while I was there. Happening to be near the Irish depot when she was about to pass, I stood among the great crowds of soldiers that lined each side of the road. In about three minutes the Queen would come along. Suddenly I heard the high, effeminate voice of an English officer of superior rank calling out: "Tell that man to put on his coat. See here, you!" Looking in the direction toward which the colonel called, I saw an Irish soldier, minus his tunic, go galloping in his heavy military boots through a path that widened accommodatingly for him and closed behind him, so that progress was almost impossible for the aristocratic colonel, who perhaps wished to identify the man.

I remember one evening after I had finished confessions in Oratory Hut and had come back to the tent in my own lines, finding a young Scotch officer sitting at the little deal table waiting for me. After talking for awhile, he told me that for some time he had been wishing to become a Catholic and that if I could spare the time he would begin instructions whenever I wished.

We began that night, and a few weeks later I baptized him in the chapel of Oratory Hut. An Englishman—I think his name was Edmund Hanley—stood sponsor. During the ceremony the chaplain of the Portuguese soldiers came in and knelt reverently. When all was over and we had offered congratulations, the Portuguese priest shook hands with the neophyte; then he came over to me and gave me both his hands warmly. Although he could not speak my language, nor I his, still we were brother priests, and I was sure he knew the joy I felt over this new sheep coming into the fold of Christ.

XXIV ∾ The New Zealanders

Of all the lads of different nationalities who visited the little chapel in the evening and who came so often to Holy Communion in the early morning, I think I liked the best the New Zealanders. They were nearly all tall, lithe men, dark-haired, with long, narrow faces and eyes that had a strange intensity of expression—perhaps one might call them piercing. They were quiet-voiced men and spoke with rather an English accent. They were the gentlest, finest men it was my good fortune to meet in the army. They were excellent Catholics, many of them daily communicants. The Maoris, the aborigines of New Zealand, were treated by the white men with the same courtesy that they showed one to another. The Maoris were the most intelligent-looking men of

the yellow race I had ever met. In fact, it was only by their colour—
which was almost chocolate—that one could distinguish them from
the New Zealanders themselves. Those of the Maoris who were
Catholics were excellent ones.

I recall one incident that impressed me very much with New
Zealand courtesy. I had come to a segregation camp, just outside the
little village of Étaples, to arrange for the Sunday church parade of
the soldiers on the following day. The soldiers who were quartered
in the segregation camp were men who had come in contact with
those suffering from contagious diseases. They usually stayed in
this camp about three weeks. If after this period no symptoms of
any contagious disease appeared, they returned to their different
units. The day I speak of, three officers were sitting in the mess
when I went to announce the services, two Englishmen and one
New Zealander. I told the officer in charge that I should like to have
the Catholic men paraded for Mass the following day, suggesting to
him to name the hour most suitable. He, an Englishman, said eleven
o'clock. I was about to say, "Very well," when the New Zealand officer
interposed gently but firmly. "You will have to make the hour earlier
than that, Captain," he said. "You know the Father will be fasting
till after his Mass." The English officer looked at me quickly. "Why,
Padre," he said, "it did not occur to me that you would be fasting.
Certainly, we'll have it earlier. How about nine o'clock?" Nine would
suit perfectly, I assured him. As I was to say an early Mass for the
nurses at seven thirty, I would just have time to move my altar to
the dunes, where I was to celebrate Mass, before the soldiers would
arrive. The Mass was finished very early that Sunday, and there
was no long fast. I was very grateful to the New Zealander for his
thoughtfulness. As I have said before, they were the gentlest, finest
men I had ever met.

XXV ∿ The Workers

There was one thing about the natives of Étaples that impressed me particularly, and that was the respect each artisan seemed to have for his work. In the little village were candle makers, bakers, boot makers, makers of brushes, etc., and all these workmen seemed to be interested in their work and to have a great respect for it. They worked slowly, patiently, and always thoroughly. I noticed the same spirit in the fields. Just beyond the hill and the giant windmill that overlooked the village, unfenced green fields sloped downward to green valleys, then up over the hills again. Through this open countryside wound the white roads of France, and always the great main roads were arched by ancient elms. Unlike England, not even a hedge divided the property of owners. Here, every day, crowds of farm labourers, mostly women and girls, came early to work. One noticed a total absence of all modern farm implements. The women still used the old-fashioned reaping hook that was used long before the coming of Christ. What they cut they bound carefully into tiny sheaves. The women, for the most part, were dressed as the woman in Millet's picture *The Angelus*, from hood to wooden shoes. Here, again, the work was done patiently, quietly, and thoroughly. The modern idea of saving labour seemed never to have come to them.

Sometimes when not very busy I would take a walk through the long white roads, leading into a white-housed, red-roofed village, the Norman tower of the little church piercing the treetops; then out again through more green, unfenced fields to another little village two, or three, or sometimes four miles away. Often while on these walks, I used to think of the rugged strength of these sturdy French peasants who went so steadily and quietly about their work. They were strongly built people, well developed, and their faces were deep red—I suppose from so much work out of doors.

XXVI ❧ Orders Again

*At the end of September 1917, Murdoch received orders to proceed
to No. 7 Canadian General Hospital (CGH). It was a mere two
miles distant. As was the usual army procedure, the outgoing hospital
chaplain, Fr. Coté, was proceeding to the front. Murdoch provides a
concise description of the layout of these hospitals with their ward huts
and ambulance lanes. His description of the hospital trains loaded
with wounded is both vivid and moving. He further provides an
outline of the medical evacuation system that moved the wounded
from the trenches to the hospitals on the French coast. Murdoch
especially highlights the fact that it was women who drove the
ambulances that moved the wounded from the trains to the hospitals;
by the autumn of 1917, men were in short supply, and the rear areas
were scoured for every available man. Note also the vast scale of the
war as indicated by Murdoch's reference to the eight local hospitals,
two of which were Canadian, namely, No. 7 Canadian General
Hospital with beds for 2,500 wounded and No. 1 Canadian General
Hospital outfitted for 2,000 wounded. Even given these large bed-
capacity figures, it must be recalled that the Étaples region was but
one of several hospital concentration sites along the French coast. – RH*

I had come down to my tent one evening a little later than usual
to find a D.R.L.S. letter from the Chaplain Service awaiting me.
D.R.L.S. meant "Dispatch Riders' Letter Service." I opened it
quickly, as a letter from headquarters, brought by a dispatch rider,
might contain very important orders. This was an order to report
for duty at No. 7 Canadian General Hospital the following day.
I looked at my watch. It was nearly nine o'clock. It was very dark
outside and the rain was beating on my tent. No. 7 was at least two
miles distant, but I must see the chaplain before he would leave. I
put on my trench coat and stepped out into the rain.

As I drew near the hospital, I was obliged to pass by a German
prison camp. I suppose my thoughts were wandering that night. At
least the first thing I realized was seeing through the rain the bright
blade of a bayonet thrust at my breast; then I heard the voice of
the guard: "Quick! Are you friend?" I stopped suddenly. I had not
heard him challenge me the first time, which he surely must have

done. I realized in an instant my position. "Yes," I shouted, "friend."
"It's a good job you spoke, sir," warned the guard, and then he said,
quickly, "Pass, friend."

Although I had realized my position, I had not felt the slightest
alarm, but now as I walked along in the darkness, a strange fear
took possession of me, so that I shook almost violently. I have been
challenged often by sentries since that night, but it has never been
necessary to inquire more than once, nor have I ever been halted so
suddenly by a pointed bayonet.

I found the outgoing chaplain, Father Coté, packing his
bedroll, and as he packed he gave me all the advice necessary to
an incoming chaplain. The following morning he went up the line,
and immediately after lunch I left No. 2 C.I.B.D., where I had been
most cordially treated by both officers and men, and came to No. 7
Canadian General Hospital.

XXVII ⌘ Hospitals and Trains

No. 7 Canadian General was only one of a group of hospitals
situated along the highway that led from Étaples to
Camiers. There were seven or eight large hospitals in all,
though only two were Canadian, the others being British. Although
I was quartered at No. 7, I had also to attend the other Canadian
Hospital, No. 1. There were about 2,500 beds in No. 7, and about
2,000 in No. 1. At one end of No. 1 there was a marquee chapel-
tent, and at the rear of No. 7 there was a low wooden chapel called
"Church of Our Lady, Help of Christians," but this was used mostly
by the British Catholics.

The military hospital in France usually consisted of a number of
long, low, detached one-storey huts, built in rows, each row behind

the other. Between the rows ran little lanes just wide enough to permit two ambulances to pass. There was a door in each end of every hut, so that it was very easy to go from one hut into the other. Each hut was a ward; in some hospitals they were numbered, in others they were lettered. Down each side of the aisle, running from door to door, was a row of beds—low iron beds covered with army blankets. In most of the hospitals there were no counterpanes, but there were always clean white sheets and pillowcases. At one end of the ward were two small cubicles, one of which was the nurses' office, the other a kind of pantry and emergency kitchen, though nearly all the cooking was done in the general kitchen, which was a special hut.

Into these large, quiet wards, far away from the roar of the heavy guns, the crackle of machine guns and rifles, the wounded lads came, carried by train and ambulance. Many who will read these lines have seen the troop trains, with their hundreds of khaki-clad lads leaning out from car windows, cheering, singing, and waving, as they were carried swiftly by on their way to seaport or training camp. Perhaps they have watched long companies of soldier boys march up dusty roads, while flags waved and bands played and people cheered, to the lines of cars waiting for them. If so, they will recall the great buoyancy of the lads—their gaiety as they passed on their way to training camp or port of embarkation for overseas. This lightheartedness accompanied them across the sea and went with them up through France as they journeyed in other troop trains to the front. And whenever thirsty engines stopped at water tanks, or when a halt was made to exchange a tired engine, little French children assembled and gazed wide-eyed at the soldiers who had come from across the seas. They wondered, too, what those words meant that someone on the troop trains always called out and which brought such a thundering response. Many trains went up along the same way through France and stopped, as others had stopped, and always some voice called out those words, and always hundreds of voices roared back, "No!" So in time the French children learned them, and whenever the trains slowed into a station, the little ones would run to the cars and one of their number would call out, "Har we doon-hearted?" Then, mingled with the laughter of the khaki-clad lads, would come thundering the answer, "No!"

After awhile trains bearing soldiers began to come down from the line. But when the engines stopped at watering tanks or stations, the little French children that gathered about them noticed certain differences between these trains and the ones that went up to the front. Everything seemed very silent, save for the slow panting of the engine. On the side of every car was painted, in the middle of a large white circle, a red cross. No groups of laughing faces appeared at open car windows, though now and again the white, drawn face of someone lying in a berth peered out through the glass. Sometimes a white bandage was tied around the head, and sometimes on the white bandage was a dark red patch. No one called out, "Are we downhearted?"

Trains kept coming down from the front somewhat irregularly, silent trains with red crosses painted on white circles on the sides of the cars. Then one day there was a slight change in the appearance of these hospital trains. The red cross was still there, but painted near one end, on the side of the car, was an oblong of red, white, and blue about three feet long and two wide. The little children knew well what this was—the tricolour of France. But they did not know what the oblong of red, white, and blue painted on the side, at the other end of the car, represented. The disposition of the colour was different, and the formation of the coloured parts was not the same. There were more stripes in this oblong, and the stripes were narrower and red and white in colour. In an upper corner was a small blue square with many white stars on it. Then one day someone told the little children that this was the flag of the Americans who had come from so far across the seas to help their fathers and brothers in the war.

As I write these words I recall the passing of the trains of France. Those that went up took lighthearted lads who leaned from car windows and sang and cheered as they went through French villages. And the trains that came down, with red crosses on them, had for their passengers quiet lads who lay in berths, bandaged in every conceivable way. But although they suffered much, and although occasionally a low moan escaped through pain-drawn lips, those wonderful lads were still "not downhearted."

They passed through many different hands after they were wounded, and always they were well treated. First, stretcher-bearers picked them up and carried them to the regimental aid post, which was usually a dugout in one of the support trenches. Here they received treatment from the Medical Officer of the battalion and his staffs. Then they were carried by other stretcher-bearers down the trenches to the field station, from which places motor ambulances took them to the advanced dressing station where bandages were rearranged or improved. Then they went to the clearing station, where they remained for perhaps two or three days until there was a clearing for the hospital to which they were to go.

Ambulances took them to the Red Cross trains, and stretcher-bearers carried them gently to berths in the cars, and then they began their long journey to the base hospital—the big, quiet hospital far away from the roar of the guns. From time to time Medical Officers passed down the aisle of the car, and sometimes a Red Cross nurse, clad in light grey uniform, gave medicine to the wounded lads or examined a dressing. The journey from the casualty clearing station to the base hospital often took many hours. It was usually evening when the long line of Red Cross cars came slowly into the smooth siding that had been built since the war. The bugle call would sound and many hospital orderlies and stretcher-bearers would assemble, as, one after another, the big green ambulances, each one driven by a woman, came swiftly down to the siding. Gradually their speed slackened, and they moved slowly down the line of hospital cars, in the sides of which doors opened. Then gently and carefully the wounded lads, wrapped in thick brown army blankets and lying on stretchers, were lowered from the cars and carried to the open ends of the ambulances, where the stretchers were fitted into racks running their full length—two above and two below. As soon as the stretchers were securely strapped, the machine slowly moved off to the hospital, which was just a few hundred yards away.

XXVIII ❧ DI's and SI's

Murdoch found hospital chaplaincy fulfilling as well as challenging. He was often preparing both dangerously ill (DI) and seriously ill (SI) Catholics for imminent death by administering the last sacraments. The autumn of 1917 was the time of the horrible Battle of Passchendaele, and casualties were very high. The hospitals were filled to the very limits of their capacity, and the doctors, nurses, and chaplains were pushed to the brink of their ability to cope. Murdoch's description of the severely gassed soldier gasping out the words of his last confession provides a glimpse into that time. So too does his tale of fear at potentially missing a request to minister to a dying soldier when he was "advised" to take an afternoon off. There is also the record of his chat with the anaesthetist who was unsure if he was capable of enduring much more.

Thankfully, all was not bleak; there were rays of light amidst the shadows. Murdoch was cheered by the Irish wounded who identified their units not by the British Army's designation but by their Catholic chaplain's name. Moreover, as Murdoch's story of uniting the two brothers who were in different hospitals shows, simple acts of kindness meant a great deal at such times of stress and challenge. – RH

I remember the day I arrived at No. 7. The quartermaster allotted me a burlap hut in the officers' lines, just large enough to contain a low iron bed, a rough table made of boards from an old packing case, a chair (which was not there), and a little stove when it was cold enough for one. I hung my trench coat on a nail and asked the two men who had brought my bedroll to place it where the chair should have been. I gave just one look around the hut then went out again and up to the Registrar's office, first to No. 1, then back to No. 7.

Every morning a list was posted outside the Registrar's offices, on which were printed the names of the DI's and SI's, those dangerously ill and seriously ill. For obvious reasons, the Catholics of both classes were always prepared for death immediately. I found a number of Catholics in a critical condition, and I administered the last sacraments to them. It was long after six o'clock when I finished my work. I was leaving No. 7 feeling a little tired, for I had covered quite a lot of ground on my visits, when I heard "Padre" called by one of the nurses, who was coming quickly behind me. I stopped until she came to where I was standing. She asked me if I were the new RC chaplain. On being answered in the affirmative she told me she had a list of men of my faith who should be seen by their chaplain immediately. She passed me her list as she spoke, and in a second or two I was comparing it with the names written in the little black book that I had taken from the left upper pocket of my tunic. I had seen them all: all had been "housled and aneled," had been prepared to meet God. I told her so, quietly, and I showed her my little book. She compared the names, then she looked at me keenly. "My!" she said. "How you Catholic priests look after your men!" Then she was gone again.

XXIX ❧ Down the Hospital Aisle

Although the emergency cases were attended at all hours by the chaplain, it was in the afternoon that the general visiting was done. Each patient, when he had entered the hospital, had attached to the buttonhole of his shirt, or overcoat if he was wearing it, a thick waterproof envelope containing a card on which was written a description of the wounds he had received and the treatment that had been given them in the different stations through which he had passed.

Sometimes, though not often, there was a smaller card attached to the large one—but we shall speak of this card later. The nurse in charge of the ward kept the cards of her patients in her office. As the religious denomination of the patient was always given on his card, together with the number of his bed, it was very easy for me to find my patients once I had written down the names from the cards.

The first question that I usually asked the men, after I had inquired about their wounds, was how long it was since they were at Communion. Nearly always it was a few days or a week, as most of them had gone to Holy Communion before going into the trenches, though sometimes it was a month or two; and sometimes a man looked up at me steadily and said, "Ten years, Father," or perhaps fifteen, or perhaps more. Then I would say, quietly, "It will soon be time to go again, won't it?" Usually the man smiled, but generally he agreed with me. When I would meet a man a long time away, I would make a note in my little book so that I might make some special visits to him. Often, I had the great joy of seeing men, a long time away from the sacraments, return to God.

One afternoon I stopped at the bed of a bright-eyed young Canadian whose face lit up on seeing me, for he knew I was the priest. He had lost one of his arms above the elbow, so I began to talk to him of the wonderful artificial limbs that were being made for those disabled in the war. The lad just smiled quietly—he was not the least bit downhearted—as he said, "They can't help me much in my line, Father." Then he fumbled with his hand in the little bag in the small white locker that had been placed near his bed, and when he found his pay-book he asked me to open it and read the newspaper clipping that was there. The headline said, "Pat Rafferty Enlists," and underneath, in smaller print, was a second heading: "Champion Light Weight Boxer of Western Canada Goes to the Front with the Battalion." Then there were two short paragraphs, and below them was a picture of a young man in civilian dress. I examined it a moment, and as I looked at the original, I felt a wave of pity well up within me. Yet the brave young soldier smiled.

It was not only Canadian soldiers who came to the hospital, for men of all the English-speaking armies were brought there. I always enjoyed a talk with the Irish wounded; they had such a warm friendliness and reverence for the priest. It really was not necessary for me to procure the number of their beds once these men knew that it was the priest who was coming down the aisle, for I could have found them by the eager, smiling faces that watched me as I came. They always got in the first word; before I quite reached their beds I would hear their truly Irish greeting, "God bless you, Father," and then as I would shake hands, they would ask me eagerly how I was—I had come to see how they were. They always wanted a medal—they pronounced it more like "middle"—and it was a little one that they wanted. One day I spread out on the palm of my hand eight medals of assorted sizes and told a great giant to help himself. Among the medals was the tiniest one I have ever seen. The great finger and thumb did not hesitate for a second but groped twice unsuccessfully for the tiny medal; finally, the third time they bore it away, while over the large face of the Irish lad spread the delighted smile of a child. When I asked one of these lads which battalion he was in, expecting of course to be told the First or Second Munsters, or Leinsters, or Dublins, etc., but that is what I never heard. This is what they would say: "Father Doyle's, Father," or "Father Gleason's, Father," or "Father Maloney's, Father."

One afternoon, just when I entered, my eyes fell on a bright face looking up over the blankets. I knew he was a Catholic, an Irishman from the Munster Fusiliers, though I judged from the manner in which the large blue eyes regarded me that he was not so sure about my religion. I thought that there was also a hint of battle in the glint of his eye, so I walked quickly over to his bed, without the faintest flicker of a smile, and said, "Let me see now, you're a Baptist, aren't you?" The blue eyes of the Munster lad blazed as he looked up at me. "No, sir, I'm not! I'm a Roman Catholic!" he said, and as he panted for breath, I said to him quietly, "Well, now, I'm glad to hear that. I'm a Roman Catholic, too!" Then swiftly the vindictive look faded out of the blue eyes of the Irish lad and a smile floated over his face as he said, somewhat shamefacedly, "Excuse me, Father—I didn't know, Father—I'm glad to see you, Father," (pronouncing the "a" in Father like the "a" in Pat), and a big red, brown-freckled hand was shyly offered me. It was only three days since Father Gleason gave him and all his comrades Holy Communion, but he would be pleased, if it would not be too much trouble to His Reverence, to go again in the morning. I wrote his name in the little book and promised to come in the morning with the Blessed Sacrament.

XXX ∿ The Two Brothers

I had been visiting the two brothers for over a week—indeed one of them for over two weeks—before I knew they were brothers. One was in No. 1 hospital, the other in No. 7; one had been wounded in the chest or shoulder, the other in the knee. I carried messages one to the other, and they looked forward eagerly to my coming, for it was three years since they had seen each other. They used to anticipate with great pleasure the day when they would be convalescent and could see each other. Then one evening the lad who was wounded in the knee told me that the following morning there was to be an evacuation for England and that he was among the number. Although he was glad to hear this good news, still he regretted very much not being able to see his brother before leaving. "It is so long since I've seen him, Father, and he is so near," he said wistfully.

I looked at the young fellow for a few moments, wondering silently what I could do to bring about a meeting of the brothers. First, I thought I might obtain permission for the ambulance to stop at No. 1 on its way to the siding and that the young fellow might be carried in on a stretcher. But on second thought I felt it would be very difficult to obtain such a permission. Finally, I decided to ask the adjutant for permission to have him taken up to No. 1 on a wheel stretcher. The adjutant was very kind, granting my request. That evening the two brothers met for the first time in three years and passed two hours together.

This little act of kindness did not pass unnoticed, for I learned afterwards that it had met with the warm approval of many in both hospitals—I suppose because it was just one of those little human touches that everybody loves. But I could not help thinking of the numerous other meetings in the early morning, or often at any hour of the day or night, when through my ministrations two others were brought together, sometimes after a much longer separation than that of the brothers. One would be some poor broken lad who sometimes was a little bashful or shy about the meeting; the other was Jesus of Nazareth, the Saviour of the world. Not many concerned themselves about these meetings, but—there was "joy among the angels."

XXXI ⬧ An Unexpected Turning

It was now November. The days were passing very quickly, for I was kept busy; convoys were coming daily. Passchendaele was being fought. I had to visit the DI's and SI's very often, for many were being admitted. One morning I stopped just long enough to prepare an Australian for death. He had been wounded through the throat and could not swallow, so that it was impossible for me to give him Holy Communion. I absolved him and anointed him quickly, then I told him I must pass on as I had many more to visit. It was almost impossible for him to speak, and he did so with great pain, but as he gave me his hand and his dying eyes looked at me, he made a great effort. "Cheerio," he whispered. Truly these wonderful lads were not downhearted!

During the month of November thousands of patients passed through the hospital. Everybody was working extremely hard. Sometimes during the night, convoys arrived. The anaesthetist, who sat next to me at mess, told me that he was beginning to feel that he could not continue very much longer; for days he had been giving chloroform almost steadily, as there were very many operations. We were both longing for a little lull in the work so that we might get a few hours' rest.

There were many places where the officers of the hospitals used to go. There was The Blue Cat at Paris Plage, a famous seaside resort about three miles from Étaples, where they went to have tea and bathe in the sea. There was the village of Frencq, where a little old lady kept a small coffee house and made omelettes that were famous. Then there were two officers' clubs and an officers' circulating library at Étaples. I had been to the library at different times while at the base. There was a large reading room, exceptionally well lighted for it was a part of an old studio. Tea was served every afternoon from three thirty to six o'clock, at which a number of old English officers assembled. It was very amusing to listen to them relating past experiences, in which often a good dinner was not forgotten. They treated the soldier-waiter as if he were one of their own personal servants, calling him often, and although there was but one syllable in his name (it was Brown), they managed to twist the last letter into a rather complaining inflection. I watched Brown a number of times, and although he came "on the double" and stood head erect, looking at his nose, as all good butlers do, still I thought I detected on more than one occasion a merry light in his bright brown eyes, and he seemed to be exerting a little extra willpower in keeping his lips composed.

Then one day there came a lull in the rush of work, and being advised by one of the officers to take a little recreation, I obeyed. I recall that afternoon particularly. I went to the officers' circulating library, which was at the rear of the town hall, where I passed the afternoon very pleasantly looking through a delightfully illustrated edition of *Our Sentimental Garden*, by Agnes and Egerton Castle, whose home I had visited while at Bramshott. The quarto volume contained many drawings of their pretty garden from different angles. It was very restful sitting in the quaint old studio, through the great windowed wall of which streamed the autumn sunlight. Toward five o'clock, tea was served by my old friend, the butler humorist. Then as the sun went quietly down into the sea, far out, I walked back to No. 7, feeling very much benefited by my visit, meeting hundreds of soldiers, nurses, and civilians on the way.

It was dusk when I entered my little burlap tent. I lit the lamp, and as I did, the light flashed over an open letter on my newspaper-covered desk. All the feeling of exhilaration that had cheered my return walk left me suddenly, and an overwhelming, foreboding cloud came over my spirits, for the letter said: "Please come quickly, Padre, there is one of your men dying in Ward 3, bed 17." It was signed by the adjutant of No. 1 hospital, and the hour of the day was marked on the letter. It had been sent at 2:30. It was now 6:00 P.M. I turned down the lamp and went quickly out of the little hut praying, as I ran up the road, that the lad might be still alive. I walked down the ward, not noticing the friendly faces that turned to greet me, as was their custom. The red screens were around the bed. I moved them gently and stood quietly by the lad's bed. An orderly moved a little to one side.

"He's dead, sir," said the orderly. "Died just a minute ago."

I put on my purple stole, gave the lad conditional absolution and anointed him conditionally. Then I stood for a long while looking on his still white face, wishing with all my heart that I had not left the hospital that day. Then the orderly made a little movement, and I turned and went down the aisle of the ward, repressing a great desire to burst into tears; it was the first time, through my neglect, that I had ever missed a call to the dying. In passing I talked to a few patients, but there seemed to be a strange numbness in my brain, so that I did not follow the words spoken by the occupants of different beds where I stopped; one or two ceased speaking and looked at me keenly. J

ust as I was about to leave the ward, little Sister Daughney came in. She stopped and spoke to me, and her words were as sweetest music to my ear.

"Ah, Father," she said—Sister was from Ireland—"I sent for you this afternoon for the lad who has just died. He would have been glad to see you, Father, although there was no need; he said he had been anointed and prepared for death just six hours before up in the CCS."

I looked at the little sister talking so quietly and in such a matter-of-fact way, while thundering in my ears was the desire to break forth into a great *Te Deum Laudamus*. She spoke to me of two or three new patients who might develop more serious symptoms, then passed on to other duties, whilst I went up the lane to my little marquee chapel to kneel before the tabernacle and make known to God my fervent gratitude. And so, after all, I had passed a very pleasant day.

XXXII ∾ Private Belair

The days passed quickly, for they were well filled, and sometimes at night the call would come; my door would open quite abruptly, awakening me, and the light from a small flashlight would dazzle my surprised eyes, while a voice called, "RC chaplain?" I recall one night in particular. I had been awakened by the orderly calling, to find him standing at the head of my bed, his flashlight focused on a message written on white interlined paper that he held before my eyes. The words read: "Come quickly, Father, Wd 14, bed 7, Belair, gassed." It was signed Sister Kirky, who weighed almost three hundred pounds. In twelve minutes, I was dressed and standing in the ward by Private Belair. I was a little surprise to find him sitting up with just his tunic and boots removed. He sat in such a way that his arms rested over the back of his chair, which he faced. He was panting terribly and was evidently suffering greatly. Every little while, when he seemed to have sufficient strength, he would begin to pray in whispered Latin, "*O bone Jesu,*" then his voice would die out in a trembling whisper and the prayer would become inaudible.

"Oh, Father," he whispered, "I am—so glad—you came. All my life—I have prayed—to have the grace." Then he began to pray again, and I made ready to hear his confession. It did not take long for it cost him terrible agony to speak. Then I anointed him. I had not brought Holy Communion, being so eager to reach him that I had not taken time to go up to the chapel called Church of Our Lady, Help of Christians. My own marquee chapel had blown down a few days previous, and I had removed the Blessed Sacrament to the above-mentioned church. I told the sick man I was going to bring our Blessed Lord, but that it might take a little while, as very likely I should find the church locked and should have to find the key.

Although the ward had been but dimly lighted, it was extremely dark on coming out, for it was raining, and in my haste I tripped over a tent guy rope, taut by the rain, and fell on my hands and knees on the cinder walk. Then I walked on more carefully, rubbing tiny particles of cinders from my stinging hands. Just as I reached the chapel I was challenged by the guard. This time I answered quickly: "Friend. RC chaplain No. 7 Can. Gen. Hospital." I stood to be recognized. Then the guard spoke but this time softly, and he peered at my rain-wet face. "Ah, Father," he said, "it's you!" It was one of the Irish lads from the Sixteenth Infantry Base Depot who was one of the guards for the German prison camp opposite. He may have seen me saying Mass at Oratory Hut, or perhaps he had spent a few days at the segregation camp.

The door of the little church was locked, and I did not know where to find the key. I knew that an English Redemptorist, Father Prime, chaplain to No. 26 British General Hospital, said Mass here every morning; perhaps he might know where the key was kept. It was half a mile to Father Prime's little hut at No. 26, and I went very quickly, praying all the while for the poor gassed soldier that he might have the great privilege for which he had prayed so much. Father Prime was very easily awakened and seemed glad that it was not a call for him to go out in the rain. He had the key and presently I was hurrying back to the little church. The Irish lad, still on guard, as I returned bearing the Bread of Life to the dying soldier in the hospital, knelt on the rainy ground, and I could just tell that he was bowing his head as the Saviour passed. The poor fellow was still alive, though panting in great pain. He received Holy Communion most devoutly. I felt that I was in the presence of an exceptionally good man. In the afternoon he died.

XXXIII ∾ A Little Nonsense

Murdoch rounds out the story of his stay at No.7 Canadian General Hospital (CGH) with a tribute to the nurses, a reference to blood transfusions, and "a little nonsense." Although termed "sisters," the nurses of the Canadian Army Medical Corps—often affectionately nicknamed Bluebirds due to their powder-blue work uniforms—were not in religious orders but were professionally trained nurses.

Murdoch praises them for their devotion and hard work. He also records that it was not unusual to see one of their members sent away for a mandatory rest. As for blood transfusions, a new medical procedure pioneered, in part, by Canadian doctors, Murdoch relates the sacrifice involved by an orderly-donor in the early days of the procedure.

Murdoch's "nonsense tale" is another matter. By 1916, the British Army on the Western Front had two interconnected problems—men who would fake illness to get away from the trenches (malingerers) and others who were experiencing a new condition termed "shell shock." How to tell which was which and what to do about those suffering from legitimate psychological injury was a work-in-progress. As Murdoch's story relates, at No. 7 CGH it appears that the working assumption concerning these cases was that most such men were malingerers. In effect, they were one type or another of fakers who simply needed "encouragement" to return to the ranks. Today, thankfully, PTSD is better understood and more empathetically treated. As The Red Vineyard progresses, we will learn that Murdoch himself experiences first-hand the reality of psychological injury. – RH

It was hard work visiting the wounded, listening time after time to each one as he described the nature and history of his wounds, which in many cases were so similar. Often on leaving one hut to enter another, I have paused to look longingly out to the estuary of the Canche, where the sun would be sinking slowly, and breathe the strong, aromatic air coming from the sea and the marshes that grew from the river mud—then in again to great wards of poor broken lads and the antiseptic odours of the hospital.

Although the spirits of the lads, on the whole, were bright and merry, and those who nursed them brought sunshine to their work, still one would scarcely think of entering any one ward with the intention of being entertained. Yet frequently I have gone into a certain ward of No. 7 Canadian General with no other intention than that of being amused. For in this ward were the malingerers, that is, the men who were trying to "put one over" on the doctors. The soldiers called them "lead swingers." The ingenuity of some of these men was really extraordinary. I have seen a case come through three or four different posts, diagnosed as measles, until finally the doctor in the stationary hospital saw that the man had used a preparation of some oil to bring out the rash and had raised his temperature with cordite.

The first day I went into Wd. —, I was somewhat puzzled. I had not known that this was the ward of malingerers and so was surprised to find so many healthy looking men in hospital. The nurse in charge looked a little surprised when I entered and said smilingly, "Well, Padre, what are you doing here? Nobody ever dies in this ward." "Well, Sister," I said, "as far as I can see now, everyone has the appearance of being quite spruce." Then she said quietly: "P.U.O.," nodding her head a little after pronouncing each letter. Then she went into her cubicle to continue her work. That evening at dinner I asked the doctor who sat nearest me what was meant by "P.U.O." He smiled, then said: "It means, Padre, 'Praxis of Unknown Origin'" and kept smiling as he continued: "We sometimes meet a case that really puzzles us, but nearly always, when you see 'P.U.O.' on a medical history sheet, you can count on its being a case of malingering." He did not say very much till we had nearly finished our meal, then he said, "Wait, Padre, after dinner and we'll see Boots."

This was a nickname for the doctor in charge of Ward —, one of the jolliest MO's in the mess. We found him in the anteroom, three or four others grouped around him; but instead of the customary broad smile on his good-natured, fat face, there was a look of real indignation. He was explaining to his smiling listeners something about a few cases that had been sent to him, and as we drew near I caught these words: "Dey had da hitch"—the doctor was a French Canadian—"and dey were sent to my ward—height of dem! Sent to me, and dem wit da hitch!" Everyone was laughing and trying unsuccessfully to suppress it.

Then a young doctor interposed: "And what did you do, Boots?"

"Do?" echoed the other. "What did I do? I just took dare papers and sent dem up to the skin disease hospital. Dere's no room for men wit da hitch in my ward."

The mere thought of the indignity seemed almost too much for the good doctor, so he paused for a little and his face grew red as he looked around on his smiling audience. Then he said, "Da idea of sending men wit da hitch to me!" He had closed his lips tightly and was nodding to himself at the insult that had been offered his ward by having men with the itch sent to it, when the doctor who had spoken previously spoke again: "Yes, Boots, the idea of sending sick men to your ward!" Boots looked at him quickly, and suddenly the dark clouds were dispersed, and the light of his broad sunny smile spread over his good-natured face. "Dat's hit," he said. "What do dey want to send sick people to me for?"

The others laughed and moved on, and presently I found myself making arrangements with captain "Boots" to visit his ward when his "patients" would be undergoing treatment the following morning. The only condition the good doctor imposed was that I would not laugh. This I promised.

The following day, as I walked down the aisle of No. —, I realized how hard it would be to fulfill the condition the doctor had made for my visit. The men were undergoing "treatment"; some held the handles of a galvanic battery in their hands while their bodies squirmed and twisted, but never for one instant did they drop the handles; others had their feet on steel discs in tubs of water, while others underwent electrical treatment in different ways. The doctor moved from bed to bed, inquiring with simulated solicitude as to the state of each patient, offering a word of encouragement to some poor fellow who writhed under the current that passed through hands and feet.

"Dat's right, my lad," the doctor would say encouragingly, "just keep your feet on de disc." Perhaps it did not occur to the good doctor that the man was powerless to take his feet off the disc! To another he would say, "Dere, now, my lad, we'll soon have you in perfect health again"—and I would wonder how the strong, rosy-cheeked lad would look when in perfect health.

I was not surprised to hear two or three lads inform the doctor that they thought they felt well enough to go back to their battalions again. The doctor would always agree with them. One fellow said, within my hearing, "He might as well give us the chair at once!"

I remember coming out of the ward that first day, and when I was out of view, I stood in the lane and laughed and laughed. The fat doctor had been so funny and also the poor fellows, squirming and twisting under treatment that was not at all necessary for them.

I made many subsequent visits to No —. Whenever I would feel tired out from the more serious work of visiting the wounded, I would step down the lane and listen for awhile to Doctor "Boots" passing up and down the aisle giving his electrical treatment.

XXXIV ⁓ Transfusion

A lthough the little wooden chapel called Church of Our Lady, Help of Christians was nearer No. 7, I always said Mass in the chapel at No. 1. It was wonderfully edifying there in that little marquee chapel. I don't know who had had it erected, for it was standing when I went to No. 1, but I do recall the devout congregations of walking wounded in their hospital suits of light-blue fleeced wool; the hospital orderlies who came so reverently; the white-veiled, blue-clad nurses who came in large numbers. Two Masses were said on Sunday so as to accommodate the different shifts of sisters, and every Sunday evening there was Benediction and a short sermon.

I remember one morning noticing that the hospital orderly who served the Mass trembled while answering the opening responses. He was a tall, well-built young fellow with light hair, and usually his face had the glow of excellent health; but when he passed me the cruets, I noticed that his face had almost the pallor of death and that although it was a cold morning in early autumn, little beads of perspiration stood out on his white forehead. After Mass I asked him if he were not well. Then he told me quietly that he felt extremely weak, having given a quantity of his blood just a few days before to save the life of a wounded soldier who was dying from loss of blood. The wounded man was now recovering. It was not the first time he had given his blood, and, he said, as he smiled painfully and with the appearance of great weakness, he felt that it would not be the last time. As he moved about slowly and wearily, extinguishing the candles and covering the altar, I felt a great admiration for this generous lad, and I thought truly there are other heroic ways of giving one's blood than shedding it on the battlefield! It was quite a common occurrence in different hospitals to go through the process of transfusion of blood. The most necessary condition was that the blood of the donor be adaptable to the system of the patient.

XXXV ～ The Ministering Angels

The nurses—"sisters" we called them—throughout all the base hospitals were most attentive to the wounded, without the slightest display of any maudlin sympathy; they worked hard and long and one never heard the least complaint from their lips. It was a common occurrence at No. 7 to see a nurse being ordered away for a complete rest, made necessary by the terrific strain of her work.

The Catholic nurses were, on the whole, very faithful in the practice of their religious duties, many being weekly communicants. To communicate daily was not practicable for many, as they were on duty during morning Mass. Often, I have seen a nurse come with five or six of her patients to Holy Communion, some backsliders she had rounded up. Often, while giving Holy Communion to a soldier in the ward of a non-Catholic nurse, I had been annoyed by the lack of any special preparations on the part of the sister for the administration of the Sacrament. But one morning I found a spotlessly white cloth spread over the small locker, a clean graduate glass of fresh water, and a spoon. There was also on the locker a folded white towel for the lad to hold when receiving Holy Communion.

It pleased me very much to see such care taken to prepare for the coming of Jesus, and it was with deep gratitude that I went to thank the sister in charge, after I had given the lad Holy Communion. "Sister," I said, "how did you know how to prepare everything so well? It was so clean, and everything necessary was there." The good little sister seemed pleased that I had even noticed the preparations. Then she said, "Well, Padre, I knew just what was needed for I studied nursing in a Catholic hospital." As I went out of the ward the thought struck me how fine it would be if only all the non-Catholic sisters would prepare for the Saviour's coming as had their sister nurse, and as I thought I formed a little plan.

The following day I was notified by a non-Catholic sister to bring Communion to a boy in her ward, and there and then I tried out my plan. "Sister," I said, "yesterday morning I was called to Sister ___'s ward to administer one of my lads who is dangerously ill, and I was very much surprised to find the table arranged as if it had been done by an RC sister." "How did she have it arranged, Padre?" she asked. Then I told her just how things had been prepared. The following morning when I brought the "Bread of the Strong" to the poor wounded lad, I found, as on the previous day, everything spotlessly arranged for the visit of the Guest.

After that, whenever a non-Catholic sister told me that a Catholic lad had need of my ministrations in her ward, I told her how well the last sister had prepared locker, etc., and invariably the following morning, when I went in silence to the bedside, I found that all things had been made ready.

XXXVI ❦ More Orders

Suddenly, in early December 1917, Murdoch was ordered to the front. His relatively well-ordered life at No. 7 CGH came to an abrupt and unexpected end. He learned of the change not by receiving orders but by his replacement walking into his hut. Murdoch had to go. First to Étaples, then to Calonne-Ricouart, and finally to the 75th Battalion. Regrettably, his orders had not been forwarded to the battalion, and he initially received the cool welcome of a suspected spy! A week later he was redirected to Chaplaincy Headquarters, but Fr. French, the officer in charge of all Canadian Roman Catholic chaplains in France, was absent. Finally, Murdoch was sent to his ultimate destination. He was to be the RC chaplain to the entire 3rd Canadian Infantry Brigade.

Unlike most Protestant chaplains, who ministered to a battalion of one thousand men, Roman Catholic chaplains were assigned to brigades of four battalions of roughly four thousand men. Murdoch's task was to minister to all the Catholics distributed throughout the four different battalions of the 3rd Brigade. These men were usually geographically scattered across a broad area in their individual battalions. What made matters more difficult was that for purposes of food and shelter, Murdoch was attached to the 16th Battalion. The 16th Battalion had only eighty Catholics. His predecessor had been attached to the 14th Battalion, which had several hundred Catholics. In short, as for the practicality of his ministry, Murdoch was attached to the wrong battalion. However impractical for the chaplain, the logic of the army was both inscrutable and unquestionable. Murdoch simply had to obey.

Murdoch describes his drive to the front in great detail. As well as mentioning the increasing devastation, he also makes poignant note of "what had," from a distance, "seemed to be trees" but that were in actuality the crosses of a military cemetery. He describes the scene as "a great forest of little low crosses" where the upturned soil constituted "the little green tents where the soldiers slept." – RH

D ecember came. During the first week of that month, I prepared my hut to stand the cold of the winter months and began to look forward to a time of relative repose after the past five months of strenuous work. The fighting was not to be so intense during the winter, therefore there would not be so many casualties. I had been given a fine little coal stove, and I was beginning to enjoy coming into the hut at night to be greeted by its cheerful red glow. There were worse places to dwell in, I told myself, than a burlap hut with a coal fire burning in it. I was looking forward to peaceful winter evenings with books to read, or perhaps a few hours writing, when one evening just before dinner a knock sounded on the door and an officer stepped into my hut. I had never seen him before. He looked at me somewhat strangely for a second or two, then asked if I had not been expecting him, "for," he said, "I am Captain Hawke, the new RC chaplain to No. 7 Canadian General Hospital. You are to go up the line."

For just a second a faint dizziness came over me, and the vision of bright coal fires faded from before my mind, and I thought, with considerable falling of spirits, of winter in the trenches. I shook hands with the new chaplain and then I told him I had not been expecting him, and that so far no orders had come to me to report at the front. Just as I spoke, however, another knock sounded on the door, and before I had time to open it an orderly entered and passed me a DRLS letter: I was to report at the 75th Battalion the following day.

So on the morning of December 11, 1917, I left No. 7 with real regret. I had always found the doctors very friendly, and they had shown me many kindnesses. I had grown to love my work in the hospital and the peace and quiet of the little marquee chapel at No. 1 Can. Gen. after the day's work was done. Now, I must break new ground!

It was a cold morning when I took my place on the seat of the ambulance alongside the driver. The waiters crowded about the door of the mess—the doctors had not yet come from their huts—and one of them, an old Scotchman wearing a glengarry, who had already seen service up the line, stepped forward and patted me on the back and wished me "guid luck." Then the ambulance leaped into high gear and we were off to the station.

There were certain formalities to be gone through at the military station at Étaples: certain papers had to be shown to the RTO [Railway Transport Officer] and instructions received from him. It did not take long to give my instructions. I was to take the train on No. 9 track. I was to detrain at Calonne-Ricouart; there I would receive further instructions. There was a great crowd of troopers on my train who leaned from car windows and sang merrily as the train passed through French villages. Then, I remember, as we stopped at one village, I heard in the distance the sound of the guns, and always as we advanced came clearer and clearer the deep booming. For the first time I heard sounds of the actual conflict of the World War.

An officer whom I had met on the train accompanied me to the staging camp, which was but a short distance from the station at Calonne-Ricouart. I presented my papers at the little office. The orderly room clerk looked at me quickly. "Why, sir," he said, "you're in luck! The Seventy-fifth Battalion is just a few yards up the road. Better stay here for lunch, then I'll send a runner with you."

I may have been lucky in finding the Seventy-fifth, but there my luck ended for a few days, for when I entered headquarters of the

Seventy-fifth, which was in an old château, I was told that there had been some mistake. They had a chaplain, a Presbyterian, who was then away on leave. The RC chaplain of the brigade was quartered with the Eighty-seventh. The adjutant treated me politely but with a little suspicion. He asked me for my papers. Then he requested me to be seated. I did so but with a feeling of vague uneasiness; now and then an orderly clerk looked at me quietly though searchingly and then continued his writing.

I wondered where the mistake had been and where I was really to go; but most of all I wondered at the suspicious glances that were flashed at me by different ones who came into the room. I waited for a long time, almost two hours; once or twice I was questioned by the adjutant, and after each visit I wondered why he was questioning me so. Then the colonel came in, and he had not questioned me very long till I became aware that I had been suspected as a spy. I was asked to remain in the orderly room till more word might be received. I felt very much like laughing at my predicament, for I knew that it would not be very long before headquarters would learn my history. In about an hour I was told that I might take the battalion chaplain's billet and that I was to stay with the Seventy-fifth till orders would come. There had been some misdirection of orders.

XXXVII ∾ Held for Orders

I remained a week with the Seventy-fifth before any further orders came. The battalion was resting after the terrible fighting at Passchendaele. After dinner in the evenings, we would gather before the little open coal fire in our mess—the second-in-command, who was a lieutenant-colonel, the doctor, the quartermaster, transport officer—and chat pleasantly. They were very friendly, though at times experiences were related, I think, for no other end than—in the language of the army—to put my "wind up." I tried not to let them see how well they were succeeding. I found the Medical Officer, Dr. Hutcheson, to be the friendliest of the officers. He was an American, a young man with grey hair, whose hometown was not very far from that of Irvin Cobb.[36] The way he came to talk of Cobb was on account of one of his stories that he happened to be reading. I learned through the papers later on that Dr. Hutcheson had won the Victoria Cross.

There was another officer in the mess with which I was quartered who kept us all in a continual state of anxiety. He was a lighthearted, merry, boyish fellow and just a wee bit reckless. It was on account of the cane he carried. Of course, all commissioned officers in the British Army are supposed to carry a cane or a hunting crop, but not the kind of cane the young officer in question carried. The cane was in reality a miniature breech-loading shotgun, which took a very small cartridge of very small shot. He had already wounded one man slightly.

One day while taking a walk out through the country from Calonne-Ricouart I saw for the first time the transport section of a battalion of the French army. It was drawn up on the roadside; all the wagons, limbers, etc., were painted a greyish-blue color. The horses were busy with their nosebags, and the soldiers, in blue uniform, were standing in little groups about limbers, taking their dinner, which consisted of cold beef, white bread, and red wine. They were all small men, most of them with long, black, silky beards. They chatted among themselves, and all along the village street French women and children looked out from windows; I noticed tears in the eyes of some of the women.

It was a scene that had been enacted many times in the history of France. It was very interesting to watch those blue-clad soldiers of the Old World standing in small groups in the little lane. Perhaps, I thought, in the many wars of France there have been many such halts in this tiny village. I was walking along musing so, when for one reason or another I turned my eyes from the transport column and looked down the road. Coming toward me on horseback was a trooper of the Canadian Light Horse. He was a large, clean-shaven man under his wide-brimmed hat. He sat with perfect ease in the saddle and looked quietly over the French transport section as he went. There seemed to be some indefinable atmosphere about the man that made one think of great, illimitable spaces of unrestricted freedom of movement. A few seconds previous I had been thinking of the romance of old France, but I had not been prepared for this inset. A breath, strong and clear, of my homeland came to me, and I felt proud of my countryman.

I used to say Mass every morning in the little church of the village, the pastor of which was a very delicate looking young French curé. Two black-bearded French soldier priests said Mass before me. Then at seven thirty, when the Masses were finished, the parish priest taught catechism to the children of his parish. Later, in many places where we came to rest, I saw early in the morning little children assembled in their parish churches for catechism.

XXXVIII ∾ The Front at Last

I had been with the 75th Battalion about six days when one evening the adjutant gave me a letter that contained orders to proceed the following morning to Camblain-l'Abbé. It was well on toward evening when the large motor lorry, on the seat of which I sat next the driver, pulled into the village of Camblain-l'Abbé. The old stone church stood on a hill, looking down over the town, and at the base of the hill in a long, level field stood row upon row of one-storey Nissen huts, in which were the headquarters of different branches of service of the Canadian Corps.

The lorry stopped at the end of a large plank walk, down which I was directed to walk till I should come to the headquarters of chaplain service. This did not take very long, for presently I was standing before one of the huts, on the door of which appeared the letters CACS (Canadian Army Chaplain Service). I knocked on the door and stepped in. Three military chaplains were sitting in the office; one who bore the insignia of lieutenant-colonel was signing some papers for a young chaplain who was a captain. The third chaplain, a major, sat in a far corner eating nut-chocolate bars. I looked from one to another. I did not know any of them. I had been expecting to meet Father French, who was the senior Catholic chaplain of the Canadians in France. I made myself known, only to find that all the chaplains were Anglicans and that Father French was absent on duty and would not be home for two or three days.

That night I dined with many of the staff officers of the Canadian Corps and slept in the quaint little presbytery of the French curé on the hill. The following evening toward sundown, in company with Lt. Colonel McGrear, chief chaplain for the Church of England, I went to Carency, where I became attached for quarters and rations to the Sixteenth Canadian Scottish, which was one of the battalions of the Third Canadian Infantry Brigade of which I was now RC chaplain. My other battalions were the Thirteenth, Fourteenth, and Fifteenth. All, with the exception of the Fourteenth, were kilted battalions, and each one had its own band of bagpipes. I was somewhat disappointed to find myself attached to the Sixteenth as the Catholic chaplain who had preceded me had been quartered with the Fourteenth in which was an average of four hundred Catholics; in the Sixteenth the average was about eighty. There was some military reason for my appointment, so all I could do was to obey orders.

We left Camblain-l'Abbé and the motor went quickly over the well-kept road. Soon the town, with all the houses still intact, was left far behind, and presently, not far ahead, I saw a large signboard attached to two posts about fifteen feet high. At the top, in large black block letters, were the words "Gas Alert," and beneath were words to the effect that from now on all troops must wear their gas masks "at the alert." This meant that instead of carrying the mask at the side, with the bag closed, it must be tied about the chest, with the bag open, so that in a moment the mask might be raised to the face.

A little nervousness came over me, for now on all sides were signs of great devastation—broken and torn buildings, crumbled walls, fields deeply marked with shell holes; and the road became rough, for it had been mended in many places after being rent by shells. Less traffic appeared along our way; everything seemed quiet. On our right, in the distance, I noticed what seemed to be a square forest of miniature trees, which, as we drew nearer, became regular in shape and equidistant from one another. As we came still nearer, I noticed low mounds, "row on row." What had seemed to be trees were crosses—a great forest of little low crosses—and between the rows and rows of crosses were the long lines of "the little green tents where the soldiers sleep."[37] We passed two or three other military cemeteries, then the ruins of a small village or two, where many soldiers looked out from cellar windows or low huts built of pieces of broken stone and scraps of corrugated iron, with a piece of burlap hanging and weighted at the end for a door. Dugouts were built into the hill that sloped up from the roadside. The silence of the whole countryside seemed uncanny. We came up a little hill where, on our right a few hundred feet back from the road, were perhaps a dozen corrugated iron stables, open at the sides but with a partition the whole length of the hut running through the middle. In the foreground was the basement of what had once been a long, narrow dwelling-house. Here we stopped, for we had come to headquarters of the Sixteenth Battalion, or, to give them their full name, the Sixteenth Canadian Scottish. They were a kilted battalion, hailing from British Columbia.

The colonel told me to remain in the motor till he returned from the orderly room, which I did. In a few minutes he came back with the adjutant and two soldiers. The adjutant welcomed me kindly; the two soldiers picked up my bedroll and began to carry it toward headquarters. I shook hands with the colonel as he said goodbye. Then I accompanied the adjutant to headquarters. I had arrived at the Western Front.

XXXIX ~ A Strafe and a Quartet

As Murdoch soon discovered, his room was a partitioned-off section of a bombed-out basement that served as battalion headquarters. Upon arrival, he met the commanding officer of the 16th Battalion, Colonel Peck, who in addition to being a highly regarded soldier, had recently been elected as an Alberta MP in the Canadian federal election of December 1917.

Murdoch next describes his first encounter with his batman, George. Every officer at the front had a batman as a personal assistant. Batmen were privates who had the task of looking after the personal needs of the officer to whom they were assigned. To be assigned as a batman was a desirable fate for it released the man from life in the trenches. Thus, we soon learn that it is George who makes Murdoch's bed, who secures extra blankets, and who brings Murdoch his breakfast. George also knows the ways of the front. He educates Murdoch as to the difference between an artillery strafe and an actual bombardment. George further advises that if Fritz's (German) bombers came over that first night, then the safest place for Murdoch to be was huddled in a nearby trench. – RH

My room was a partitioned off portion at the end of the cellar in which was headquarters; there was no fire in it and the month was December. Through cracks in the portion of the building that was above ground blew the cold, wintry wind. That night at dinner in "the mess," which was in the portion of the cellar adjoining my billet, I met a number of the officers—though the majority were still in the line—and they were among the finest men I had ever met. The commanding officer, Colonel Peck, one of the best-loved men on the Western Front, was a huge man with a black drooping mustache that gave him a rather fierce appearance, but there was a look of real kindness in his eyes. He possessed the Distinguished Service Order medal, and later he won the highest decoration of the British Army, the Victoria Cross. At that time, although we did not know it till later, he had been elected a member of the Canadian parliament.

When I returned to my billet, I found a lighted candle sticking to the bottom of an upturned condensed milk tin; someone had been showing me an act of kindness. I had no sooner entered than there was a knock on the door. A young soldier opened it and came in. He said he had come to open my bedroll and prepare my bed. I looked at the berth, which was a piece of scantling about seven feet long running the width of the room, to which was attached two thicknesses of burlap about a yard wide that were fixed to the wall. I wondered how I was going to sleep, for I was shivering then. Suddenly the young soldier ceased tugging at the straps, listened quietly for a second or two, then not looking at me but keeping his eyes fixed on the bedroll, he said slowly and solemnly, as if addressing some imaginary person in the bedroll: "All is quiet on the Western Front." He neither smiled nor looked at me but continued his work. For months I had read those words in the daily papers of England, but now there was something so comical in the lad's manner of saying them that I could not help laughing as he went on with his unpacking.

But it was not for long that "all was quiet on the Western Front." Suddenly I heard a far-distant rumble that had the rhythmic roll of snare drums, yet the sound was much stronger and it was increasing quickly in intensity and volume. Soon it was a great thundering roar with a minor rattle. The earth seemed to be trembling. I looked at the soldier. "A bombardment?" I questioned. "No, sir," he said quietly, "that's just a strafe over on the LaBasse front. Those are our guns. Fritzy'll open up after they stop. You should go outside and see it, sir." I stepped out, almost falling into a trench that was just outside my door. Away to the northeast for about a mile flitted short, sharp, yellow flashes of light. Although the rumbling of the guns was so loud, I judged them to be five or six miles distant. Everything was quiet about where I stood. It was a moonlit night and along the white road, as far as I could see, was a line of broken trees, with here and there the irregular walls of a ruined village. Presently there was a lull, then complete silence; in the clear moonlight, the devastated countryside gave one a weird impression.

Then "old Fritzy opened up," and although the rumble of his guns was not so distinct, I judged that he was giving us about as much as we had given him. I wondered how much harm would be done and whether many of our lads would be killed. Then slowly the firing ceased and presently again "all was quiet on the Western Front." I was just about to re-enter my quarters when I received another surprise. From a hut just a few yards away came sounds of singing. I listened: it was a low sweet song that I had never heard before—a quartet, and the harmony seemed perfect. I had never before heard such sweet singing. An officer came out of the mess and stood near me, listening in silence. Then he said: "That's pretty good, Padre." I agreed with him, but I confessed I had never heard the song before. "Why, Padre," he said, "the name of that song is 'Sweet Genevieve.' Strange you never heard it! Wherever men are congregated, one will hear that song. It's an old song, Padre. Strange you never heard it!" So I had heard two sounds that I had never before heard: one was the sound of a "strafe" on the Western Front; the other was the singing of "Sweet Genevieve."

XL ~ The Valley of the Dead

When I re-entered my hut I found that the young soldier had opened my bedroll and removed the few little articles that were in it. The bedroll was arranged for the night on the burlap berth. "You haven't enough blankets, sir," he said. Then he was gone, but in about five minutes he was back again with two thick brown army blankets. After I had thanked him, he looked around to see if he could improve anything before leaving for the night. Not seeing anything, he was just about to open the door when he turned and said, "If old Fritz comes over to bomb us tonight, sir, the safest place for you will be down in the trench. It's a moonlit night and Fritzy likes to be out in the moonlight." There was no bombing that night, but it was so extremely cold that I could not sleep. I spent the night changing from one position to another in the hope of getting warm, but I remained awake till daylight.

About seven o'clock the following morning I heard a fumbling at the latch of my door. I had just finished my prayers. I waited, for I knew the door was not locked; then as the latch was raised the door opened, assisted by the foot of the one entering. First there appeared a large granite iron plate of steaming porridge and a smoky hand holding it, then a granite iron mug of something steaming, and another smoky hand holding it. Then appeared the kindly soldier of the night before, his pleasant face a little begrimed but smiling, the arm of the hand which held the mug hugging to his side a small earthen jar of sugar with a spoon in it. I went to his assistance and soon we had the things spread out on an upturned ration box, which had been the seat. Now it was the table, and the bed was my seat.

"How did you sleep, sir?" asked the soldier. I told him. Then he said he must try to find something to make a stove. He went on to tell me that he and the cook had built one but that it was not working well. He held up his hands as evidence, and I looked at his face. "The cook is out there now," he said, "trying to cook the breakfast and swearing, for there's more smoke coming out around the stove than there is going up the chimney." I poured from the earthen mug a little of the hot diluted condensed milk over the steaming porridge, and the soldier told me to take all the sugar I wanted as there was plenty. He stood beside me for a while waiting to see if I would make any comment on the porridge. I had never been in the habit of eating any cereal at breakfast, but this morning I was very cold and also very hungry. I tasted the porridge; it was hot, piping hot. It tasted slightly of smoke, but that didn't matter. "It's fine," I said. "Not smoky?" he asked. I assured him that if it was a little bit smoky it made no difference.

He went out again, but I had not quite finished the porridge before I heard another fumbling at the latch, and in a moment he appeared again with another granite iron plate on which were two rashers of bacon and a large slice of toast; in the other hand was a large mug of hot tea. "Is this dinner?" I asked. The lad smilingly told me to eat all I could, that when a man loses sleep the best way to make up for it is by a good meal. He picked up the empty porridge plate and the empty mug, leaving the sugar bowl, and went out again; but in about three minutes he was back with a jar of compound jam, strawberry and gooseberry. "Has the cook stopped swearing yet?" I asked. "Yes," replied the lad, "I told him you said the porridge was good. He knew it wasn't, and when he saw your empty plate he smiled. He'll be all right now for awhile." "What is the name of this place?" I asked. "Carency," he replied, "in the Souchez Valley. Just across the road, on the other side of the valley, is where the sixty thousand French soldiers and civilians were gassed. Their own turpinide gas that they had sent over against the Germans came back on them. The wind had changed. There are some of the victims in the wood that have never been buried. The valley is called Valley of the Dead." He went on to tell me of the great battles that had already been fought in the area where we now were. I learned that we were almost at the base of Vimy Ridge.

"What is the difference between a 'strafe' and a 'bombardment'?" I asked him. "Well," he said, "a bombardment is usually all thought out beforehand, and a lot of preparations are made for it and it usually lasts a long time. A 'strafe' is just a firing that might start up any time, and it generally lasts only a few minutes. Sometimes a green hand in the line brings off a 'strafe' that might last half an hour with the loss of many lives and the cost of thousands of dollars. The first night in the line, every minute or two some fellow thinks he sees someone coming across 'No Man's Land,' and sometimes he 'gets the wind up' pretty bad and fires. Then old Fritz thinks someone is coming toward him and he fires back; then two or three of our fellows answer, and immediately old Fritz comes back stronger. Then the whole line opens up and the machine guns begin to rat-tat-tat, and an SOS flare goes up for the artillery, and presently the earth is rocking under a 'strafe' and everybody except one wonders who started it all."

As the lad then began to gather up the empty dishes, I made apologies for having eaten so much; always my breakfast had been just a little bread and jam. His only comment was, "Sorry, sir, I didn't have a couple of eggs for you." Long after he went out I kept thinking of the horrors of war; what catastrophes might transpire through the changing of the wind or through "getting the wind up."

After I had returned home from the war I was giving a series of lectures in a little town. In one of them I happened to mention the terrible tragedy of the turpenide gas.[38] Many among my audience found it hard to believe that there had been so many victims. The following day the priest with whom I was staying asked me many questions about the Valley of the Dead. A day or two later, as we were sitting in his office, one of his parishioners came in on some business. I was about to leave the room when the priest motioned me to stay. When the man had finished his business, he looked at me and said, "So you have been to the war, Father?" I said I had been there. "Well," continued the man, who had come a long distance, "I met a lad who was through it all, and he told me he found the gas worse than anything. He said he was in a place, one time, where thousands and thousands had been froze stiff by a strange kind of gas. He said that there was a church there, filled with people sitting in the pews, and the windows were all up, and this gas came right in through the windows and froze all the people in the pews. They're all there yet, and if you pay a quarter you can see them." The man was most serious. I did not dare look at the priest till he had gone. For a moment the priest shook with laughter, then he said to me, "Father, send for that returned man and make him your assistant. He can tell the story much better than you." "Well," I said, "considering that it was France, they might have made the admission fee one franc instead of a quarter." However, my story had not been exaggerated.

XLI ✑ New Friends

The next day, Murdoch met other members of the 16th Battalion: a goat—the battalion mascot; the battalion interpreter, who dealt with the complaints of the local French population; the cook; and his new roommate, "Wild Bill." As his first Sunday at the front approached, Murdoch experienced first-hand the realities, and the challenges, of being a brigade-level chaplain to four different infantry battalions. While the 13th, 15th, and 16th Battalions were all still in the trenches, the 14th was scheduled to relocate on Sunday. The result was that Murdoch lacked any prospective congregants. Thankfully, Fr. MacDonnell of the 72nd Battalion needed help covering his own scattered flock. In the end, Murdoch held Mass in a large YMCA tent. While Mass was lightly attended, a goodly number of men came afterwards to receive Holy Communion.

As Christmas approached, Murdoch coordinated his efforts with the two other chaplains in the area, Fr. MacDonnell and Fr. Murray. These men would do Christmas Mass for Murdoch's two battalions at Château de la Haie while Murdoch walked two miles to Petit Servans to celebrate Mass for his two other battalions as well as for the Catholics of ten other units in the area. In the end, Murdoch had a long but satisfying day. In retrospect, he noted, "I think it was the happiest Christmas I ever spent." – RH

Shortly after the young soldier left there was another knock on my door, and as I stood up to go to open it I heard outside the voice of a man speaking as if to a child. When I opened the door, there stood a kilted officer over six feet in height, with the pleasant face of a boy. He was accompanied by a billy goat, the mascot of the battalion. The officer greeted me warmly and then looked at the goat, saying, "Shake hands, Billy, shake hands with the new Padre." So Billy and I shook hands, or rather, I shook Billy's raised hoof.

In the afternoon I took a walk along the Valley of the Dead. Away in the distance I noticed a large balloon far up in the air and, seemingly, two men standing in the large basket attached to it. It was the first time I had ever seen a balloon, and I was a little surprised to find that it was not round but shaped like a sausage. It was a greyish-khaki colour. The sun was just setting far away behind the broken trees when I walked back from Neuville St. Vaast; the sky was pink with here and there a pencil of red clouds. Along the skyline flew three homing airplanes. As I turned to see if any more planes were coming, I noticed the large balloon being hauled slowly down toward the earth.

When I entered my little billet, I found the young soldier at work putting up a stove that he had found and patched with a piece of tin. I asked him what the great balloon was doing up in the air. He told me that it was an observation balloon, and that the two men in the aerial car were observing with field glasses what was going on behind Fritz's line. The airplanes that I had seen wending their way against the winter skyline were scout planes that had been patrolling the sky for hours. "Now," he said, "they are going home to roost."

Before the stove was finished, the Third Brigade interpreter—the men always called the interpreter "the interrupter"—came to visit me. He was the first Catholic I had met since coming to the Sixteenth. He seemed very friendly and kind. The badge of his office was a sphinx. It was Napoleon who designed this badge for interpreters—I suppose to remind them that although they would learn much that was occurring, it was part of their office not to divulge it. The interpreter's work was made very hard at times by the good peasants of France. Sometimes, while marching through a rich farmland, a soldier lad would "annex" a hen, or a head of cabbage, or some grapes, or apples, etc.; then the irate owner would seek the interpreter and oblige him to conduct him or her before the proper military authorities, where compensation would be demanded from the government.

The cook also came in to see me; he, too, was a Catholic and seemed to be a lad full of energy. I was surprised to learn that in private life he was a tailor. Before he left, he made arrangements for going to confession. Then, by some strange association of ideas, I asked him if his stove still smoked. It was going much better now, he said.

That evening after dinner as I sat wiping my eyes with my handkerchief, when it was not being applied to my nose—for besides giving real warmth, the new stove emitted a quantity of smoke—an officer knocked and came in, followed by two soldiers carrying his bedroll. I had been expecting him, for in the mess just before dinner I had heard the officers planning the allotment of sleeping space for the night. A number had been sleeping in their bedrolls on the floor of the mess, and now two or three other officers were coming back from leave. I had heard an officer say: "We'll put 'Wild Bill' with the Padre." The others had agreed to this.

I had been wondering who "Wild Bill" was. I did not think the officers were playing a practical joke on me, for I had always found officers most respectful to the priesthood. But now "Wild Bill" had entered, and as I looked through the slight smokescreen, my eyes rested on one of the gentlest-mannered men I have ever met. Without being in the least effeminate, he came quietly over and shook hands. I understood now why they called him "Wild Bill," for I recalled that at college one of the slowest moving lads I

had ever met had been rechristened "Lightning." I felt grateful to
the other officers who had billeted "Wild Bill" with me. He slept in
his bedroll on the floor, after he had spread a rubber ground sheet
over it. Gradually the room became sufficiently warm to sleep in.
The soldier had found some coal. And as the smoke died away I fell
asleep and did not awake until morning.

XLII ❧ A Little Burlap Room

The following day was Saturday, and I began to think of my
duties for the morrow. I had learned that the Thirteenth,
Fifteenth, and Sixteenth Battalions would remain in the
trenches till Monday. I called at the orderly room of the Fourteenth
only to learn that they would be moving Sunday. When I returned to
my billet I found a letter from Father MacDonnell, telling me to call
to see him at the Transport Section of the Seventy-second Battalion.
I did and found a little man, dressed in Scotch military costume—
tartan riding breeches, round-cornered khaki tunic, and glengarry
cap. The Seventy-second was a Scotch battalion from Canada,
but its chaplain was a Canadian from Scotland. He had been a
member of the Benedictine Monastery, at Fort Augustus, Scotland.
He was then busy composing a little work on the Holy Name,
for he was anxious to establish the Holy Name Society among
not only the Catholic soldiers, but also all other denominations.
This was accomplished later with the co-operation of the general
commanding officer of the Canadian Corps, Sir Arthur Currie. He
was not a young man—his hair was beginning to turn grey. I took
him to be about fifty years old. He wished me to work with him on
Sunday. This I did, saying Mass in a large YMCA tent, while he said

Mass some distance farther down the valley. I did not have many at Mass, but a good number came to Communion. Most of the men were in the trenches.

In the afternoon, toward three o'clock, I heard the inspiring strains of a military march coming up the Valley of Death. I knew the march well. It was "The Great Little Army," one of the most popular marches on the Western Front. I stepped outside and looked down the valley. A battalion of infantry was marching back from the line. "It's the Fourteenth," said a young soldier standing nearby. I watched them carefully. The Fourteenth was one of my battalions. I had heard of it before; it had been the sacrificed battalion in one of the big battles. The men had advanced without support in order to give the enemy the impression that we were stronger than we really were. They had suffered terrible casualties, but their manoeuvre had met with great success. I watched them till they disappeared round a turn in the road—Hospital Corner, I think it was called—and still I stood listening to the band. Very likely I would meet these lads on Christmas Day—which meant within the week.

I had no sooner returned to my "room" when the young soldier who had been so thoughtful of my interests came in. "Sir," he said, "the colonel and all the headquarters' officers have gone to Château de la Haie; the battalion is going there tomorrow. I think you should take the colonel's room before anyone else gets it." In ten minutes, all my belongings were in the room just vacated by the colonel. It was a warm room completely lined with burlap: ceiling, walls, and floor were covered with it. There was a small burlap-covered table and a low bench, about three feet long, also with a covering of burlap, but above all else, there was a tiny stove with two doors that slid back so that one could see the fire burning in it. Since then I have been in very much worse quarters on the Western Front.

The following morning, I said Mass on the little table, and the cook, who had now only four officers to provide for, came to Holy Communion. The next morning the interpreter, with a young soldier who was being called home to Halifax to care for his wife and child who had just passed through the terrible disaster, knelt reverently in the little burlap room to receive their Lord.[39]

XLIII ❧ Christmas at the Front

We had planned to have midnight Mass in one of the large moving-picture huts at Château de la Haie, for here in reserve were four full battalions: one belonging to Father MacDonnell; one to Father Murray, a young chaplain whom I met just before Christmas; and two, the Fourteenth and Sixteenth, belonging to me. My other battalions were only about two miles beyond these, the Thirteenth at Petit Servans and the Fifteenth at Grand Servans. But First Divisional Headquarters, which was then at Château de la Haie, reconsidered the matter. They thought the Catholic soldiers coming in at such an early hour might disturb others who would wish to sleep and, also, that there might be too many lights used, so that some aerial Santa Claus from across the line might wing his way above the camp, dropping a few Christmas bombs in passing. We then decided to have two Masses in the large hut at Château de la Haie and one in the church at Petit Servans. Fathers Murray and MacDonnell were to say the Masses at Château de la Haie, and I was to go to Petit Servans.

I found that not only had I to notify the men of my own battalions, but also all the units in my area. As there were about ten other units—labour groups, engineers, divisional trains, etc.— this took me quite a while. In fact, it took all Monday afternoon. But the following morning, which was Christmas, when I turned around after the gospel to say a few words to the lads, I felt more than repaid for any inconvenience, including my four-mile walk from Carency to Petit Servans before Mass, for the church was filled. All the seats were occupied and the large space in the rear was packed with standing soldiers—kilted laddies from the Thirteenth and Fifteenth, with their officers; soldiers from the engineers; members of the labour groups; stretcher-bearers from the First Field Ambulance. With a full heart I thanked the Christ Child for bringing together all my Catholic men. It was the first time in four months that I had been able to assemble such a large number. At the hospital, naturally, the groups were small. And as I looked at the sea of faces, so reverently attentive, many bearing marks of the terrible conflicts through which they had passed, I felt a twitching at the throat, so that it was a few seconds before I could begin to speak. It was a long while that Christmas Day before I finished giving Holy Communion, for nearly all the men in the church came.

On my way home I learned from Father Murray that the Fourteenth and Sixteenth had attended Mass in a body in the moving-picture hut at Château de la Haie and that great numbers had gone to Holy Communion. My Christmas dinner was a piece of dry roast beef, almost burnt, some potatoes, bread and margarine with a little apricot jam, and a cup of tea—that was all. Yet I think it was the happiest Christmas I ever spent, for, as I thought of that first wonderful meeting with those Canadian Catholic soldiers on the Western Front, I felt that in their midst those words, written so long ago, "There was no room in the inn," could not be said that Christmas Day.

XLIV ∿ Back to Rest

A striking example of a chaplain's perspective on the war is found in Murdoch's tale of his battalion going back to rest. His description of the men emerging from a land of death and trenches, then passing through wasted villages, and finally arriving at roads and open green fields is most evocative. The journey is punctuated by an ascending order of sound. It begins with a few soldiers quietly whistling, slowly transitions to the entire battalion singing, and then culminates with the arrival of the battalion's band playing various marching tunes.

On the battalion's march out for rest, Murdoch notes passing a roadside shrine. These life-sized depictions of the crucifixion were commonplace in France and Belgium. Later writers, those of the disillusionment school of Great War literature, would use these shrines as a means to highlight the irony and the apparent contradictions inherent in Christians waging a "war for civilization." Murdoch did not share this cynical perspective. He saw in the depiction another sufferer, someone who could identify with the soldier's plight and with whom, he trusted, the soldiers could identify in return. Rather than ironic contradiction, Murdoch states that "many a lad…understands it all much better now than when he first came to the front." – RH

Every morning for a week or two I was in the little church where I had said Mass on Christmas Day, and every evening while I was there men came to confession. Then one morning the young soldier who had been so attentive to my wants, and whose name I had learned was George, came into the burlap room in a state of evident excitement and said, "We're going back to rest, sir."

I did not know exactly what "back to rest" really meant, but I judged from George's sparkling eyes that it was something very good. "That's good news," I said. But one had to be a soldier of the line to realize what good news it really was. One must be actually in the trenches when the word comes to comprehend fully what those words "back to rest" mean.

"We're going back to rest, chummy," somebody says, and the word is relayed quickly down the front-line trench. And tired-faced lads, many of them with faint, dark rings around their eyes, smile broadly as they stand half crouching in the muddy trench. Onward the glad tidings go, whispered or uttered in low voices: "Out to rest, Bo; the relief's coming in tonight at half past ten. Hooray!" But the "hooray" does not express adequately the feelings of the speaker. It must do, however, as a loud cheer is not permitted in the front-line trench.

When it is dark, the relief comes in very quietly and takes over the different posts; then, as quietly, the lads go down the support trenches till they slope up to the great wide road that seems so spacious and airy after the deep, narrow trench they have been standing in for days. On they go, past long rows of broken trees that once were majestic, full-leafed elms, then through masses of ruined buildings and broken stone walls, with here and there a small corrugated-iron hut or shack, built just lately. At times, not very far away, a long yellow flash, followed by a thundering report, tells them that our heavies are at work.

Somebody begins to whistle, "There's a long, long trail a-winding" or "Over There," then others catch the lilt, and in a few seconds hundreds are whistling to the swinging, sweeping thud of marching feet. When they get a little farther on their way, the whistling ceases and a song is struck up, though not too loudly. Above them are the silent stars peacefully shining. Away behind them shrapnel bursts savagely and sprinkles its death-bearing message. But that is far behind, and now they are going out—out to rest!

Perhaps they march all through the night, carrying their equipment and their heavy packs on their backs, and as the dawn comes, they notice at every crossroad a great cross, and nailed to the cross the figure of the Crucified—white, blood-streaked, the thorn-crowned head bent in the agony of suffering, the face livid with pain and misery. And many a lad under his weight looks up. He understands it all much better now than when he first came to the front. Some breathe a little prayer. They are going out to rest—but they will be coming back again!

They continue their march till the morning sunlight begins to brighten all the land and the roar of the guns has become but a faint distant rumble, then, perhaps, they sit on the roadside or along the edge of a field, the grass of which looks so fresh and green after the rolling, shell-torn No Man's Land they have been looking over for days, where never a blade of grass could be seen, only the grey, shell-pitted earth, with here and there a line of white chalk, which made one think of a white-capped, angry sea. Birds begin to sing in field and green wood, and from many field kitchens and little red fires built on the roadside comes the odour of frying bacon.

Some of the lads take off their packs and go to sleep on the roadside, their faces grey with the dust from marching feet. Much traffic goes by—khaki motor lorries, general service wagons, dispatch riders on motorcycles. Then from the distance come the strains of a military march played by a brass band that is approaching; it may be "Colonel Bogey" that they play, or "Sons of the Brave," etc. It is the band of the battalion coming to meet the lads and play them back to rest. When everyone has eaten his bread and bacon and has finished his pint of hot tea, they fall in, feeling much refreshed. Then there is a rumble from the big drum and a rattle from the smaller ones, and the inspiring music of a military march breaks on the air. The lads straighten momentarily under their packs, and there is a new swing to their tired feet. Perhaps they pass through many fields lined with tall elms. Perhaps they pass many French peasants, old and young, going to work in the fields, who smile pleasantly. They may go through a quiet little village or two till they come to a more flourishing one in which is a large château. Then the band, which for the last fifteen minutes has given place to a few buglers and drums, strikes up the battalion's own march and the order comes ringing down the line, "March to attention." Then the tired lads know that they are coming into rest billets.

The organization in "rest" is done very quickly. One battalion takes over from another, and in a very short time enamel signs are hung out of billets that tell where are the different officers and orderly rooms. If there is a curé in the village, and if it so happens that the Catholic chaplain of the brigade is quartered with the battalion that has come to rest here, a little sign hangs from the curb's gate, bearing the words "RC Chaplain," for the soldiers' priest is nearly always billeted with the parish priest of the village; and on the church door a paper is tacked giving the hours of Mass, confession, etc. Sometimes there is no curé in the village; perhaps he has been called to join the soldiers of France; perhaps at one time the village has been heavily shelled and he has followed his people. In this case, often it's necessary to renovate the little shell-torn church, but this is quickly done. And in the morning, after Mass has been said, a tiny lamp burns in the church, which tells the soldiers that the Master has come and is calling them.

At twelve o'clock the soldiers' work for the day, when they are out in rest, usually finishes, and they receive any papers and magazines that may have come to them from friends across the sea. These are very welcome arrivals, and so are the boxes of good things that sometimes come from home. Then, as the lads sit under trees, or in front of tents, or in low hay lofts to eat their dinner, papers are opened and those who have received boxes or parcels from home pass around candies, cake, etc., to those who have not, and so a very pleasant hour passes.

The afternoon is usually given over to games and athletic sports. If different troops happen to be quartered together in the same village, the competition between the two becomes very interesting. Perhaps a baseball game is arranged between American and Canadian lads, while English lads look on, it must be admitted, with irritation. They cannot understand why one side should shout such things at the other; why they should try to rattle the pitcher. To them it seems quiet abusive, and judging from their talk, they are disgusted. "Call that a gaime," one will say, "when one side keeps on 'ollerin' at the blighter bowlin' that ball, so's 'e caunt throw well?" "Call that sport?" "Call that fair ply?" "I carn't see where the fair ply comes hin when they tike such bloomin' hunderanded wys o' tryin' to win." His mate agrees with him, and presently they move off to some other scene of amusement. Meanwhile, little French boys who have come to watch the baseball game go racing about the field, imitating some of the plays in the game that is so strange to them, and as they go sliding to some imaginary home plate, one can hear such expressions as "Safe!" and "Hat a-boy."

It was early in the morning when we left Château de la Haie, for we were not under observation and it was not necessary to move by night. We assembled on one of the squares near a long, tree-fringed avenue that was one of the approaches to the château. For some time before we fell in I heard from all quarters strange, unearthly noises, and in every direction I turned I saw, at quite a distance from each other, kilted figures walking up and down bearing their wide-branched bagpipes, each one emitting the weirdest wails imaginable; they were the pipers of the Sixteenth pipe band tuning up. However, when we started off, the sound was quite different, for the pipes and kettle drums make merry marching music. I know of no other music that can make tired men march so briskly and with such a swing as that of the pipes. I had never before marched with any unit that seemed to draw such universal attention as did the Sixteenth Canadian Scottish Battalion, and I think it was owing chiefly to the strange music of the pipes and the uncommon uniform of the kilted laddies. For as we entered village after village, doors and windows began to open, and old and young and middle-aged French peasants quickly filled them, smiling their admiration as the pipers played and the soldiers marched. Little "gamins," not content with regarding us, followed along at a trot, singing and cheering; the more enterprising among them picking up a block of wood and an old ration sack and, tucking them under their left arm while they spread out three or four pieces of sapling or old laths, gave an imitation of our brave pipers who played so valiantly. I began to think, after all, there might be some truth in the story of the Pied Piper of Ham[e]lin.

XLV ∾ Bruay

The battalion's rest destination was a small French village called Bruay. As chaplain, Murdoch shared a billet (housing) with the battalion's transport section, including the transport officer, the quartermaster (in charge of all supplies), and the paymaster. While officers were often billeted in various houses, with or without occupants, the ORs (other ranks, namely, the battalion's privates) often bedded down in sheds or barns. Once in a village, Murdoch arranged to share the local Catholic church with the elderly priest (curé) if he were present. Many villages had no priest at all. In France, all men of military age, priests included, had been called up to serve as active combat soldiers in the French Army.

In the middle of January, a full month after arriving, Murdoch finally had church parade with the soldiers of the 14th Battalion. The next week they were reviewed by the Canadian Corps Commander, General Currie, and then rotated back to the front. This time the battalion was sent to the French mining district of Lens and stayed at Fosse-dix. Here again Murdoch billeted with the local curé and his housekeeper. Murdoch describes his practice of "general absolution," as opposed to individual confession and Holy Communion, if the men were scheduled to enter the trenches immediately. This urgency left insufficient time for all of the soldiers to make individual confessions. Murdoch also self-effacingly describes his nervousness preceding his first trip to the actual front. – RH

Our destination was Bruay, a mining town of about twelve thousand souls in the department of Calais, or, as the French write it, "Pas de Calais." We marched into the town at about two o'clock and fell out at the square. My billet was in a miner's house. It was a very nice room with a stove in it, and as there was a coal mine just across the road, I did not want for fuel. The transport mess, which was composed of the transport officer, quartermaster, paymaster, and chaplain, was billeted in a large house not very far away. We had a dining room all to ourselves, but our cook operated on the same stove as did old Madame, who was the head of the house. We were obliged to pass through the kitchen on our way to the dining room, and I found it a very pleasant passageway, especially in the evening, for then it was crowded with happy faces. Old Madame and our cook both moved about the glowing stove where numerous pots and saucepans, boilers and frying pans, hissed and bubbled and sizzled, chatting away as they worked; for our cook was a French Canadian. Four or five soldiers sat about in the dim lamplight, and numerous children played up and down. Two young French boys, one about sixteen, the other fourteen, snow-white from head to foot, were often there, for old Madame had quite a large bakery on the premises, and these two lads, together with an old man whom we seldom saw, did the baking. Now and again we saw two women, the mothers of the children, who attended the bakeshop, which was in the front of the house.

I asked George one day how the cook liked his stove. I learned that he liked it very much but that he had his own little troubles, sometimes. When he would have some deep red coals just ready for making toast, old Madame would inadvertently throw a shovelful of fuel on the fire; or, sometimes, when the water in the kettle had just come to the boiling point and the cook was just about to make some tea, Madame would judge that the kettle needed replenishing and would immediately pour in about a pint of cold water; or, sometimes, a saucepan or some dish that needed quick cooking was moved by Madame from the front to the rear of the stove. "He finds it a little exasperating at times," said George, "but he's delighted with the billet."

We passed a very pleasant time in rest billets. Every morning we were awakened by the pipe band playing up and down the streets of Bruay. The tune they played was that of an old Scotch song, "Hi Jonny

Coup, are ye sleepin' yet." I said Mass in the ancient church of the town, and while I did so the old curé taught catechism to a large number of children. While I made my thanksgiving, a soldier-priest from one of the ambulances said his Mass. He wore a moustache but no beard, as did many of the French soldier-priests. It seemed strange to see a priest, robed in the vestments of Mass, wearing a black moustache.

There was an Irish chaplain at No. 22 hospital, and I arranged with him to say Mass for the Thirteenth and Sixteenth at Bruay the following Sunday while I went to Houdain to say Mass for the Fourteenth and Fifteenth and some details that were quartered there. The church at Houdain was a beautiful old stone structure built on the crest of a very high hill that overlooked the town. A long road zigzagged up the hill, breaking the steep ascent. The first time I went to the church, the old curé, a large red-cheeked man, pointed out the different villages far over the countryside. In one, the village of Amette, he told me St. Benedict Joseph Labre had been born, and in another—I think it was Cauchy—General Pétain, of the French army. I was interested to learn that I was so near the birthplace of St. Benedict Joseph Labre, since my parents had given to me the same names, Benedict Joseph.

I had a large crowd at Mass, and for the first time I had the pleasure of seeing the Fourteenth Battalion on church parade. They were a fine crowd of lads; many came to confession that day. Every evening from five till six I was on duty either at Bruay or Houdain, so that anyone who wished to come to confession might have the opportunity.

I remember one evening at Bruay, while awaiting the arrival of a soldier whom I was going to baptize and make a child of God, seeing a little girl with a shawl thrown over her head praying before a statue; near her, on the floor, was a bag made of some netted material with quite a large mesh. In the bag were two large rolls of French bread, and of course through the mesh the bread touched the floor, but the child paid no attention to this. She was rapt in prayer. I could not help looking at her from time to time, she reminded me so much of the pictures of little Bernadette that were so common in France—except for the two rolls of bread lying nearby in the dust. The little one prayed for nearly an hour, and I don't think she turned her head once—not even to look at the bread!

XLVI ⌒ Fosse-dix

We were in rest nearly two weeks when orders came to go back again to the line. We left one morning immediately after breakfast and were reviewed on the march by General Sir Arthur Currie, commander of the Canadians. Along the way we were greeted by the same outspoken admiration as on our passing out. On a veranda in front of a little estaminet, an old Frenchman, wearing the glazed, peaked yachting cap that was the most common headgear among men in this part of France, tried to dance the "Highland Fling," to the great amusement of half the people in the little street and the voiced encouragement of the passing soldiers.

Fosse-dix was a very small village; it cannot be found on the map, but Sains-en-Gohelle can be seen, of which Fosse-dix was a suburb. We were to wait here a few days in reserve before going into the trenches; the Fifteenth and Sixteenth were here and the Thirteenth and Fourteenth at Bully-Grenay. I was billeted with the curé of Fosse-dix, and I found him a very pleasant little man and one of the most zealous priests I have ever met. From three neighbouring parishes the pastors had been called to the Colours; so this little priest, who was none too robust—otherwise, he, too, would have been called—tried to attend the shepherdless flocks, and succeeded remarkably well.

It was a mining district we were in: all over the countryside could be seen the high smokestacks of the blast furnaces. This was the part of France said to contain the most natural wealth, and the Canadians were proud that they had been chosen to defend it.

On Sunday I was to say two Masses: one at Fosse-dix at nine o'clock, the other at Bully-Grenay at ten thirty. So on Saturday I went around to arrange for these, taking nearly the whole day to visit the different units in the area. Bully-Grenay, unlike Fosse-dix, had been almost totally demolished by shellfire. The church had been damaged in places, though not too seriously; but when I came in sight of the curé's house my heart turned sick. Nearly the whole of the second storey had been blown off, but the brave old priest still lived in the lower storey. I picked my way through little piles of broken stone and plaster, with a few pieces of splintered wood amongst the debris. I knocked at the door and the old pastor himself opened it. He was a stout, white-haired, kind-faced man who smiled brightly as he shook my hand. "Ah," he said, "I have not seen you before! You are a new arrival. Is it not so?"

I assured him that I had just lately come to the Third Brigade but that I had been on active service in France since early in the past summer. "Ah," he said again, and he stood back and looked me over from head to muddy boots. Then he called his old housekeeper, and when she had come he said, "He has but just lately come," and the old housekeeper looked at me quietly and smiled in a motherly way, then she went to prepare a bowl of hot coffee for the "newly arrived."

As the old curé and I sipped the black coffee, I asked him about his life—why he stayed there, etc. He told me that many times the little village had been shelled, and often the Germans had drawn very near its outskirts, but always he had stayed. They had struck his house on different occasions. Many of his people had gone, but there still remained about eighty, all told, those, with their families, who were in different ways connected with operations of the mine. Some of his flock were obliged to stay here, and—well, he must not leave them shepherdless. So the old pastor remained.

When we had finished our coffee, he rose to his feet. "Come," he said, and I followed him through a tiny passageway into a darkened room, for all the panes of glass had been shattered in the window frame, and the opening had been boarded across, save a small opening where a piece of translucent paper had been pasted. It was a few seconds before my eyes became accustomed to the semi-darkness, but when they did I was scarcely prepared for what they viewed. In the middle of the room, reaching almost to the ceiling, rose a great pyramid of bags of sand; in one side was an opening, and in this, on the floor, was spread a mattress and some bedding; this was where the old man slept.

As I walked up the sunlit street after I had said "*au revoir*" to the priest and his kind housekeeper, I was filled with profound admiration for the old pastor. I think it was the greatest admiration

I have ever felt for any man, and I quoted to myself: "The good Shepherd loveth his flock."

The following morning, as I stood in the shell-torn church of Bully-Grenay after I had officiated for the lads of the Fifteenth and Sixteenth at Fosse-dix, I found the church packed with the lads of the Thirteenth and Fourteenth. There was scarcely room in the church for them all. I said a word about the old pastor and—well, I don't think it was often that the collection plate was so well filled at Bully-Grenay as it was that morning.

I returned to the church in the afternoon to hear confessions and give Holy Communion, accompanied by Father MacPherson of the Fifth Divisional Artillery. We found the old pastor in the church teaching catechism to the few little ones of his flock. They sat on the high-backed chairs that are also used as kneeling-benches by the people of France. And whenever one or the other of us would come to the altar-rail bearing the Bread of Life to a group of soldiers, the old white-haired Shepherd, with his little flock, would kneel, while through the roof, which had been pierced in many places by shells, trickled the rain to drop on the floor beneath, carrying with it powdered plaster and flakes of calcimine.

XLVII ∾ The Little Curé of Fosse-dix

Every evening at four thirty the curé of Fosse-dix gave Benediction in his little church for the schoolchildren and any of the village people who could attend. After Benediction he usually said the beads, the Litany, and a few other prayers, and before he finished, my boys used to arrive for confession. As the confessional was in the rear of the church, facing the altar, I often saw the children coming down the aisle. First, an old Sister of Charity, her wide white coronet flapping on either side like two white wings, backed slowly down the aisle, the children coming two by two, facing her. Generally, as they came they sang a beautiful hymn to the Sacred Heart, but I can only recall the last two lines, which they always repeated. Translated, they would read: "Heart of Jesus, heart of clemency, save, save France in the name of the Sacred Heart!" The children would walk in perfect order till they reached the door where the old, fat Sister stood watching them. Although I could not see them then, I always knew when each couple had passed the good Sister; a scampering of feet and sometimes a little shouting were the signals.

One evening while the children were going out in the customary way, singing their beautiful hymn, I noticed five or six soldiers in the French uniform of grey-blue. They remained quiet while the children were singing the first stanza, but when they came to the lines I have quoted above, a great chorus sounded as soldiers joined with the children in imploring the Sacred Heart to save France.

Every evening, after coming from our mess, I stepped into the curé's room to have a chat with him. Sometimes I had a box of good things that had come from relatives back in Canada, for our Christmas boxes were only now beginning to arrive. I remember one evening opening a parcel while the little priest voiced his simple wonder at the strange things from across the seas. He had never seen chewing gum before, so I gave him a few sticks of Spearmint. In a little while I looked at him, but his jaws were motionless, and the gum was nowhere to be seen. "Where is your gum, Father?" I asked. He looked at me keenly, not understanding my question, so I repeated it. Again, he looked at me, but this time he answered me. "Why," he said, "I swallowed it!" Then, because I laughed heartily, I had to explain to him how the people of the New World use gum.

One day while I was absent, working among the soldiers, a shell came whistling over the village, bursting in the road near his garden, tearing several holes in the brick wall of his house. When I returned he took me out to see the havoc that had been wrought, pointing out with minute care every place where a splinter of shell had struck.

He seemed to be taking the whole thing so solemnly that I could not but become solemn, too; so I said to him, as I pointed to quite a large hole that had been torn through the frame of a ladder resting against the house, supposing he had been walking there, and that the shell had burst in the road about that time, and his head had been bent a little as the piece of shell went through the ladder—I looked at him, shaking my head ominously at the thought of what might have happened. He looked at me quickly. "Oh, if! If! If!" he said. "One could take Paris and put it in a bottle—*if* it would go in!"

He had a pass from a British general that permitted him to stop any military lorry going in his direction and take passage on it. It was always a mystery to the military chaplains how he had obtained it. During the day he was off searching for chaplains whose men were in the line and who could attend one or more of his shepherdless flocks the following Sunday. At different times throughout the early spring campaign, I was able to help him with his work, and I always felt glad of the opportunity, for he was truly a man of God.

XLVIII ~ Into the Line

The following Sunday at Fosse-dix I gave the men a general absolution and then Holy Communion, for they were going in the line immediately; after the service was over I asked them to leave me the addresses of their next of kin. Both Sundays, while at Fosse-dix, a young lieutenant served my Mass. The address that he gave me was that of a Mrs. Maxwell-Scott, London, England. I asked him if this was his mother's address, and he said it was. Then I said, by way of a passing remark, "I suppose you are a relative of Sir Walter Scott." To my surprise, he said he was. In the course of the week some little pamphlets arrived for the soldiers, and as I was examining them, I noticed that the name of the author of several was Mrs. Maxwell-Scott. The next time I met the young officer I asked if the author of the Catholic pamphlets was a relation of his. He smiled. "My mother," he said.

As not half my soldiers were in the trenches the first week, I did not spend all my time in the line. There were confessions and Masses to say for those who were out. But I recall quite vividly the morning before I went in the line for the first time. I felt a great uneasiness, so that I could not stay very long in the same place. I remember particularly the last hour before the time to go arrived. I took a clean sheet of paper, sat down at a table, and made my last will and testament. This I folded and placed in my pocket Bible. Then I sat quietly for a while in the little room till George came to tell me that a groom was at the door with my horse, and that I was to meet the officer with whom I was to go at the mess.

We rode over through Bully-Grenay, then up through Grenay, where we left our horses with the groom; from there on we walked through ruined buildings till we came to a great open waste, zigzagged with long white trenches. I had always expected to find the trenches brown, but here they were chalk-white. We passed Crucifix Corner, then left the road and walked through a field or two above the trenches. I was wondering when my companion would go down into them, for we could now see Fritz's line. We passed Loos, on our right, which was nothing but a few shattered walls standing, and the slag heap of a ruined mine; then on our left, a place called Hulluch. I was rather anxious to be down in the communication trenches; the countryside appeared very level and always we were drawing nearer the German front line. My companion, a veteran of the Boer War, did not seem to feel the slightest timidity. He had not spoken now for a few minutes and the silence was oppressive. As far as I could see, the whole countryside was criss-crossed with trenches; hardly a living person could be seen, yet in the twinkling of an eye the great gridiron before me could be alive with thousands of men now burrowing in the earth like foxes. I began to wish that I, too, were between two walls of friendly earth. Then the captain spoke: "We're under observation now, Padre. Fritz can see us walking along." "Then, why doesn't he fire at us?" I asked, but what I really wished to say was: "Well, why don't we jump down into the trench and walk along it?" but I did not say it. "Well," he replied, "we're a little too far for good rifle shooting, and shells cost too much to be wasted on just two men." I drew a long breath and felt grateful for the high cost of shells! Then I heard words that were like music to my ears: "Suppose we step down into the trench, Padre." I did.

XLIX ❦ Called Up

The winter of 1918 found Murdoch's 3rd Brigade relatively stationary in the Fosse-dix and Mazingarbe region of France. During this period, he had opportunity to meet two older and more experienced Catholic chaplains of the 1st and 2nd Brigades, namely, Fr. Lockary and Fr. Madden, respectively. He notes that Fr. Madden had already been awarded the Military Cross for bravery. Murdoch relates how he spent a week in the forward trenches with his unit. This included the nighttime experience of "freezing" for a Verey light as it lit up the darkness and his dangerous gambit of "peeking" over the top to view no man's land. Many "green" recruits had done this previously and not escaped the sniper's bullet!

The essentially static nature of wintertime trench warfare allowed Murdoch to minister to his men in a more conventional fashion. This included literally putting out his shingle to announce that confessions would be heard daily at 5 p.m. Murdoch's weekly report to his Roman Catholic military chaplaincy superior in France notes that during the week ending on February 3, he heard sixty-five confessions, while in the next two weeks he heard a total of eighty-five.[40] Hidden within these numbers is the story of "the one that was lost." Murdoch insisted that such men did not come to the priest out of fear but rather that "they had grown serious under hardship." Specifically, as a result of more than the usual amount of time without the distractions of ordinary life, men began to "think seriously of death and the fragility of human life." As Murdoch notes, their experience was of "the long vigil in the muddy front-line trench during the cold, silent hours of the night, when there was much time to think." This, rather than fear, is what accounted for the reinvigorated spiritual life of many men during the war. – RH

Although the Fifteenth and Sixteenth Battalions were in the line, the Thirteenth and Fourteenth were still in reserve and support, and every evening I was on duty at Bully-Grenay or Bracquemont to hear the confessions of these troops. I remember one evening while on my way from Fosse-dix to Bracquemont, where the Thirteenth was now quartered, hearing the strains of an accordion and a number of male voices singing some French song. I stopped and looked back. Down the little street came a strange procession. First, a young man, badly crippled from some hip trouble, limped rather quickly for one so stricken. High above him, from a pole that he carried, waved a large tricolour of France. Immediately behind him, still wearing his soldier's uniform, came a French soldier who had been wounded. It was he who played the accordion. Then behind him, and spread out the whole width of the street, was a column of young men of about seventeen or eighteen years of age. All were bedecked in gay colours—sashes of crimson or yellow or green, etc., around the waist and over the shoulders; streamers of different coloured ribbons waving from their hats or caps. As they advanced, they danced some strange continental dance that now and again called for the crossing of feet, and sometimes the resting of the hand on the shoulder of a neighbour. When they drew opposite me the singing and dancing stopped, and they fell into a regular marching step, while the wounded soldier played "Father of Victory" march on his accordion. They passed me, marching briskly and cheering irregularly. Doors flew open in the little village of Bracquemont as they entered, and mothers and sisters ran to them to see the young lads as they passed.

When I came out from the church that evening the lads were just coming back from the next town. Again, they were singing their song and dancing their fantastic dance. Just as they neared the church, the Thirteenth pipe band came behind them playing merrily. Hearing it, the lads quickened their step till it was almost in time with the Scotch music. On they went, keeping ahead of the band, which was obliged to slacken its pace a little, but it did so accommodatingly. I stood near an old man watching the procession. Alongside us were three middle-aged women who smiled as it passed, but I saw tears on the cheeks of one woman while she smiled. The old man told me that this was the procession of the young men who had just received their call to the colours. Tomorrow they would leave. On my way back to Fosse-dix I was wondering why it was that a lame man carried the flag; then suddenly it came to me that on account of his lameness he could not go to the war, and that very likely for this reason each class, when called, showed him the courtesy of appointing him to lead the procession.

L ⌁ Bully-les-Mines

The following week the Thirteenth and Fourteenth moved up to the front line from reserve, and we went to Mazingarbe, only about four miles distant from Fosse-dix. Here, again, I was billeted with a curé, a comparatively young man, who was very distant in manner, though most kind in helping me with my work and seeing that I had everything I needed. His church had been hit several times, and part of the sacristy had been blown off; the parish was being shelled periodically. Mazingarbe was the name of the town, but as there were two churches in it, within a mile of each other, the parish in which I was billeted was namely Bully-les-Mines.

Here I met for the first time Father Madden, OMI, chaplain to the Second Brigade, and Father Lockary, chaplain to the First Brigade. They gave me very good advice concerning the performance of my duties, for both had been at the front for many months. Father Madden had been there longer than Father Lockary, and he wore the little purple and white ribbon of the Military Cross. I found my work very easy the following Sunday.

On Monday morning, fully equipped with "steel lid," trench boots, pack on my back, I started for the trenches, where I remained till the end of the week. We had a little trouble getting up to headquarters, for Fritz was shelling them when we arrived; but we managed to make it between shells. Headquarters was in the basement of what was once a hospital at St. Pierre.

The first night in the line I slept in a cellar that had been roofed over. On going from headquarters to this cellar, I was accompanied by an orderly. Suddenly I heard a report like a pistol shot, and then a hissing, as of an extra-large sky-rocket tearing its way up through the air. My companion caught me by the arm and told me not to move. Then the hissing object turned, burst into a brilliant light, and began to descend very slowly, lighting up the battle front for almost a mile. Then the light went out and we went onward. "A Verey light," said the Corporal. "'Old Fritz' must be getting 'windy.' He's been shooting off a lot of Verey lights on this front. Always stand perfectly still, Padre, when you see or hear a Verey light." I had a companion in the cellar, the Medical Officer of the Thirteenth, Captain Cochrane, who was a Catholic and an American. All the wounded from the line were to pass through his hands. We did not have very many wounded.

My first visit to the front-line trench was made the second day of my visit. I went with the orderly officer for the day, Lieutenant J. McIvor, MC, who was the only Catholic officer in the Sixteenth. The chalk trenches were so similar, and so high, that I could not tell when I was in the front line. Mr. McIvor had been looking at me for awhile, then he whispered, "We're in the front line now, Father. Old Fritz is just across the way." It seemed strange: above us shells, going and coming, passed, making sometimes a soft, sweeping sound, at others, a shrill, whining noise. Everything was intensely quiet in the trenches. We were so near the German line that the occupants could be heard coughing, although I did not have the unique experience of hearing them cough. I stood up on the fire-step and peeped out over No Man's Land. Not a blade of grass could be seen, nothing but the grey earth that had been churned and riddled and tossed about by every missile of war. A little to my left a long green spar like a flagstaff stood up in No Man's Land; a little beyond this, and behind Fritz's line, was a partly demolished town. I saw all this in a second or two, then I felt a hand on my shoulder and a whisper came to my ear: "Not too long, Father." I stepped down from the fire-step. As we went back toward battalion headquarters, I asked the officer the name of the town I had seen. "Lens," he said.

LI ∾ The One That Was Lost

The winter passed quietly, each battalion of my brigade moving from reserve to support, from support into the line, then back to reserve again. And always in those little churches up near the line, whenever there was a chaplain, confessions were heard from five o'clock every evening. Here the work was most consoling, for my soldiers, moving about the village in the evening time, used to find their way to the church and there make a little visit or go to confession and Holy Communion. Often some would stay a long time praying. They had left mothers and fathers, wives and children, but the sanctuary lamp, burning softly, sent to them the silent signal, as it did at home, that "the Lord was in His holy temple." Often as I sat in the confessional in those little churches of France, I thought of God's wonderful ways, of the ineffable graces that flowed so continuously to the souls of those lads. And many times, when the evening's work was done and the last soul shriven, I have left my confessional and walked up the aisle to the altar-steps, and, kneeling down, have thanked God with a full heart for having made me a priest.

On one of those evenings, after I had finished hearing confessions in the church at Bully-les-Mines, I noticed an old soldier sitting in one of the middle pews. He must have been nearly seventy; his hair was quite grey. I waited in my confessional for a short time, thinking perhaps he might wish to come, but as he did not, I stepped out from the box and began to walk up and down the aisle; and the old soldier stayed on. At last I stopped at his pew and asked him if he wished to go to confession. He said, "No," and then went on to tell me that he had been to prayers the night before and that he had come back again thinking there would be more prayers. But he repeated that he did not wish to go to confession. I told him there would be the Way of the Cross the following evening, which was Friday. The curé was having Lenten devotions twice a week. I was just about to leave the church then, as there was no one else to go to confession, when the old soldier spoke again. "Father," he said, "would you like to talk to me?" It seemed rather an unusual way to ask the question. Usually men said, "Father, I'd like to speak to you a minute." However, if this man had anything he wished to say to me, I was there to hear it and also to help him by any advice I could. So I said that I would like to talk to him, if he wished. I then sat down beside the old man and slowly he began to speak. "Father," he said, "I don't want to go to confession—I haven't been to confession for forty years. I've led an awful life, Father. All that time I have been trying to do without God. Lately, though, Father, I have begun to think that I can't do it. Since I've come to France I've seen a lot, and I've been thinking a lot. I've come to the conclusion that there is some power directing all things. For even to run a peanut stand there must be someone behind it to direct things. I believe in God, Father—but I don't want to go to confession."

He stopped speaking for a second or two, and we sat in silence. Up before the tabernacle the little flame in the sanctuary lamp leaped a few times. Then he spoke again: "But, Father, I have led an awful life!" He began then and there to tell me the history of his life. I listened quietly, and as he continued telling me of forty years' estrangement from God, I prayed with all my strength to the Sacred Heart of Jesus for grace to bring this poor lost sheep back into the fold. Surely the Sacred Heart would hear my prayer; "I will give to priests," He had said, "the power to touch the most hardened heart." For a long time, I sat there and the old man continued to talk. Now and again I would ask a question by way of encouraging him in his recital. At last he finished, and his head moved a little from side to side, very slowly, as he said, "Father, I've led an awful life!" "Yes," I said, "and now if you will come with me into the confessional and ask God's pardon from the bottom of your heart for all those sins, I will give you holy absolution."

It was late that evening when the old man stepped out from the confessional, but before he did he said to me, "Father, if ever you wish to make known all that has gone on this night, either by writing or word, you have my permission to do so, for it might help some other poor soul." All through his confession I had been praying for grace to know what to do next. I wished to give him Holy Communion, for one never knew when a missile of death might drop—just about that time a giant enemy shell had crashed into the village so unexpectedly that I saw a red-faced officer of the line turn a sickly white. And yet the old soldier had been such a long time away from the sacraments. But before he left the confessional, I had decided what to do. "Now," I said, "you will just go up to the sanctuary rail and pray a little and then I will give you Holy Communion." A few moments later I tiptoed softly out of the church and left the old man happy with Jesus of Nazareth, the Saviour of the world.

Frequently, since I have come home, when I relate some of the wonderful ways of the Master with these soldier lads, people say to me, "Ah, Father, they came back to the sacraments because they were afraid." To me, who have witnessed these miracles of God's grace, such words always sound harsh, and I then try to explain to the people what these men really went through. I describe the long vigil in the muddy front-line trench during the cold, silent hours of the night, when there was much time to think. Perhaps for the first time in years some men began to do a little serious thinking. Under ordinary circumstances, when the voice of conscience speaks, one has a thousand ways of deafening the ears. In the trenches there was no means of silencing the still, small voice. All things conspired to make one think seriously of death and the fragility of human life. It was these thoughts mostly that brought so many men back to God. He spoke to them and they heard.

I remember once having explained this state of things to an old woman who had said to me that the men came through fear. I had done my best to convince her that the reason the men came was that they had grown serious under hardship. She looked at me calmly and knowingly and said, "That's it, Father! They were afraid!"

LII ⟋ A Vague Unrest

The spring was drawing near, and a certain vague feeling of unrest was over the troops. Word was being passed about that old Fritz was preparing for something. On our side there were no visible preparations for a spring offensive.

And so the lads were restless. Very often, when the wind was favourable, large enemy toy balloons floated high over our lines, and as the long piece of smouldering hemp attached to each balloon burned up to a knotted cord, a package of propaganda articles was released and a great flock of fluttering leaflets came slowly down through the air, falling at last among the troops in the back areas. Usually these articles told of a big offensive that was to begin and went on to say that as the Germans had no hatred for the Canadians, and as they saw no reason for the Canadians taking part in this war, they advised them not to take part in it any longer. I remember one batch of leaflets gave us just seventy-two hours to get out of the war. Although we laughed at such propaganda, we were undeniably restless. For instance, we were especially watchful till the seventy-two hours had passed. We knew Fritz was going to strike, but we did not know when or where.

Just about the middle of March we moved out to Hersin, a little town about three miles from Fosse-dix, to rest. I was billeted with the curé, a most lovable man, to whose house was attached a large garden. There were a few peach trees in the garden and they were already in bloom. While at Hersin I was able to help the curé of Fosse-dix by going to one of his adopted parishes, Bouvigny, about five miles from where I was billeted. While taking breakfast with him, he showed me a small photo of the interior of the church of Bouvigny after a recent bombardment. Half the church seemed to be filled with broken beams and pillars, and looking out from the debris, untouched in any way, was an almost life-size statue of the Blessed Virgin. I was struck by the serene, calm expression of Our Lady, but this seemingly miraculous preservation of statues and crucifixes was a common occurrence on the Western Front.

Just before I left, a number of airplanes hummed by overhead, and casually I asked the curé if he had ever been up in an airplane. He surprised me by saying he had, during some great public event at Paris. When he had reached solid earth again after his flight, a society lady, standing nearby, had said, "Now, my Father, you will know the way to heaven!" He had replied, "Yes, Madame, and whenever you wish to know the way to heaven, I will be very pleased to teach you it." That was the last time I ever saw the little curé of Fosse-dix, for on Thursday, March 21, something happened, and we were ordered back suddenly to Mazingarbe. I remember the date very well for it was the Feast of St. Benedict and my birthday. The unrest was no longer vague.

LIII ∾ The Great Offensive

March 21, 1918, was Murdoch's birthday but also the day of the massive German spring offensive. Attacking on a sixty-mile front, the Germans sought to drive a wedge between the British and the French Armies on the Western Front. Bolstered by hundreds of thousands of additional troops freed from the Eastern Front by the Russian collapse, the Germans drove the British back. Chaos ensued. Murdoch records what happened with his brigade. For days they had to "stand to," that is, be prepared to march to battle at a moment's notice. Finally, on the twenty-seventh, they began to move.

Murdoch describes the fatigue of marching and of falling asleep while still walking. Arriving exhausted after walking all night, they learn that they are in the wrong place! Murdoch was lucky, for he then got to ride in a truck. Travelling toward Arras he saw, for the first time, a mass of French refugees fleeing from the advancing Germans. To see civilians suffer in this manner made him "sick at heart." Betraying his North America origins, Murdoch remembers the words of the American Civil War Union leader, General Sherman, "War is Hell." It is worth noting that Murdoch applies this phrase

*not to the soldiers, whom he expected would bear the brunt of war's
cruelty, but rather to the civilian refugees of France. Murdoch relates
a conversation with an elderly French refugee who thought they were
English. When assured that they were Canadians, the elderly veteran
of earlier wars exclaimed, "the soldiers of Canada are good soldiers."
The refugees were therefore sufficiently confident that the next day
they reversed their flight and returned to their homes. Murdoch also
references the many roadside "Calvarys," large statuary depictions of
Christ's crucifixion, that the refugees encountered during their flight
as possible sources of comfort and inspiration. – RH*

"**O**ld Fritz" had struck at a vital part of the Allied front,
planning nothing less than a separation of the French
and British Armies. He was attacking on a sixty-three-
mile front. He had "opened up" with a terrific bombardment; it was
no ordinary barrage but one he had been preparing for weeks. He
had begun the bombardment at five o'clock, A.M., and before noon
had broken through the British line in many places.

For four or five days we waited in Mazingarbe; the whole First
Canadian Division was now standing to arms ready to go whenever
they might be needed. Every morning from four o'clock till nearly
seven the Third Brigade was "standing to" on the square, fully
equipped for battle; for it was always just before dawn that attacks
were made. Fritz did not attack on our front, but on Wednesday, the
twenty-seventh, orders came for us to march.

I left Mazingarbe at about two o'clock for our assembly area,
which was Château de la Haie. I arrived there about four o'clock
to find every battalion of the Third Brigade quartered in the huts
about the château. On learning that we were going to be here till ten
o'clock, P.M., I immediately went around to all the orderly rooms and
announced confessions. There was a tiny house on the grounds that
had once been a private oratory; the stretcher-bearers were quartered
here, but on hearing that I wished to have the use of it, they very
kindly gave it over to me for four hours. I heard confessions here for
the time allotted, then when it was time for the occupiers of the hut
to prepare for departing, I stepped outside, still wearing my purple
stole, and stood under a tree, near which were tethered horses. There
was a long line of soldiers waiting. Each man walked up, told his
little story, received absolution as he stood there under the stars,

then passed on a few paces to say his penance, while the next in line moved up. For a long time I stood there while soldiers, going and coming, passed along the road near which the men were in line.

At midnight long lines of hooded motor lorries glided over smooth roads from three different directions towards Acq. On coming to the point where the roads crossed, they came slowly to a stop; then thousands of soldiers who had been sitting or standing along the roads began quickly to "embus." We waited for almost an hour, till the last lorry had moved off, then I fell in with the transport section. I could have gone in one of the lorries, but I wished to go with the transport section as then I might be in a better position to watch the movements of the whole brigade.

We went south, marching all through the night. It was a beautiful moonlit night. We went uphill and downhill, and always before us moved the long irregular line of the transport. There were vehicles of almost every description—limbers, general service wagons, "mulligan batteries," the "pill cart," which was a two-wheeled affair with a red cross painted on either side of the hood, mess cart, water cart, etc. We passed through one silent moonlit village after another, sometimes halting to rest awhile. Now and again an upstairs window opened cautiously, and a night-capped head peeped over the windowsill at the long line of the transport resting in the village street. Toward the dawn we were passing through a beautiful countryside in which were many old stone châteaux, built far back from the main road, with green fields bordered by high trees before them.

For the past six or seven days we had not been having very much sleep, and as daylight began to break, I began to feel very weary; once or twice while actually marching I fell asleep, only to be awakened by falling against the man marching before me. Often during the night, as we reached the crest of some hill, we could see the yellow flashes of shrapnel as it burst in the air, and always we were drawing nearer. But with the dawn we seemed to have drawn away from the war area, for now there was neither sign nor sound of the enemy guns. Whenever we stopped to rest, men would crawl into the ditches or lie down near a hedgerow or an open field and go to sleep. Once in a sunken road I noticed a number of cyclists sleeping; they were leaning against the high banks that sloped upwards and away from the road. There was just enough slope to the banks to see that they were not standing. Their faces were almost black from the road dust. On two or three bicycles were strapped large wicker baskets, and in each basket hopped about two or three carrier pigeons. These were to be used in an emergency.

In an open field a number of men from the transport sections were preparing breakfast, their horses drawn up on the side of the road, busy with their nosebags, and the odour of frying bacon was wafted on the morning air. We did not breakfast, as we had no rations with us. Two general service wagons with rations for the whole battalion were to join us farther on.

Once, on leaving a quaint little village grouped about a small, perhaps century-old stone church, we caught a glimpse of a wide stretch of green countryside. We had been ascending a hill for quite a distance before coming to the village. The ground mists had cleared, and the sun was out. From different directions, but converging toward the same point, were a number of white roads along which were moving or resting the long, irregular lines of transport sections from many different battalions. Just for an instant everything seemed to be changed. I thought I was back in my own peaceful country and that I was looking at a wonderful assembling of gypsy caravans. Up in the clear air a small bird soared singing its blithe, carefree song. It was the first time I had ever heard a lark. The joyous melody seemed but to emphasize the fantasy. Then suddenly my dream vanished, and I was back to France, sitting on the roadside on the twenty-eighth day of March, 1918, tired, sleepy, and hungry, wondering at about what time we would meet the oncoming German army!

When toward noon we entered a little town called Couturelle, word was passed along the line that we were going to halt here. I had just finished saying to George that I should not care to have to make the march over again when I noticed the quartermaster of the Thirteenth Battalion come galloping up the road, smiling and calling out: "We've come to the wrong place." He waved his crop to me as he passed, saying: "We have to go back to the Arras area, Padre!"

I looked in wonder at George. We had left the Arras front last night toward midnight. I had just said I should not care to make the march over again. Now we were to do so!

We came to a halt in an open part of the village, and there we had lunch; perhaps I should say breakfast. After the meal I went down to the little church to make a visit. When I came back all the men were sleeping. I then lay down in the ditch, put my haversack under my head, and although it was the twenty-eighth of March, I was soon sound asleep. In about two hours we were awakened.

LIV ∾ Agnez-lès-Duisans

I did not walk back to the Arras front. I went in a lorry. As we drew near our destination, I was surprised to see so much traffic—but it was all coming toward us. At every crossroad we were stopped by the traffic police, just as one might be stopped in a large city. It was the first time I had ever witnessed a retreat. Great stores were in Arras belonging to the military and the British Expeditionary Force canteens. Most of these stores were being removed, and the city of Arras, as well as the country villages near it, was being evacuated.

Up to this time I had seen the effect of war on combatants only. Now I was continually passing scenes that made me turn sick at heart, for all along our way came little groups of French peasants— mostly old and young women, and children, though now and again an old man was passed. Sometimes a yoke of oxen, hitched to a large farm wagon, were guided to the right of the road by a woman or young boy. And sometimes an old woman led a cow or calf, while an old man pushed a large wheelbarrow full of bedding. Once, while we stopped at a crossroad, I tried to study the faces of those who passed. On no face did I see the marks of any great strain or fear. All were attired in their Sunday garments. None of the children cried or seemed hysterical. All had a good colour, and their large eyes looked solemnly about at the strange scenes surrounding them, but not one of them hopped or jumped or smiled at us. The expression in their faces was one that I noticed in those of the older people. I can only describe it as one of stolidity. Here were these people leaving homes where perhaps whole generations of them had lived, going they knew not where, leaving behind them many things of value; but they must sleep on the way and the nights were cold, therefore they had all brought bedding along with them. For the first time since I had enlisted I recalled a short and succinct definition of war given by General Sherman. "General Sherman was right," I said grimly.

Presently we came into a little village, at the entrance of which was a large Calvary on the roadside, the great white figure drooping from the cross in agony. Tomorrow would be His day. Perhaps it was the continual passing of these wayside Calvarys that gave patience to the peasantry. I was glad when the driver told me that this was our destination.

The lorry stopped before a large camp of Nissen huts. A gentle mist had been falling for the last hour or two, but now it was developing into quite a drizzle. I walked across the muddy square, then down a little lane through rows of huts till I found my billet. In one part of the hut the rain was leaking through the roof, but I did not mind this. There were no berths, but we had our bedrolls and all that was necessary was to roll them out on the floor. I had been sleeping on floors now, from time to time, for over a year, and I cannot say that it ever inconvenienced me very much. Just as I was leaving the hut to go to the church to make a visit—for it was Holy Thursday—two Scotch Highlanders accosted me. They wished to know to which battalion I belonged. When I told them, they became very friendly and told me that they had just come from the front. Fritz had pushed them back a little that morning, but they had been holding him since dinnertime. This was good news, and I hoped that Fritz would continue to be held.

I had been praying before the lighted repository in the village church for a few minutes when I heard footsteps coming, then I felt a hand touch me on the shoulder, then a military chaplain walked by me into the sacristy. I followed him. When he turned, I recognized him immediately. It was Father Christopher Sheehan, an Irish chaplain whom I had met at St. Michael's Club, London, just about a year before. He had come to London to receive the Military

Cross from King George of England. "Don't you know me, Father?" he asked. I smiled and told him his name and when and where I had met him, also what I was doing there and when I had come. When I had finished his brown eyes lighted up pleasantly as with the enthusiasm of a boy he began to tell me that I was "in luck." For he was billeted at a convent school and had charge of all the livestock on the premises. Then Father Sheehan went on to prove that I was "in luck," and as he enumerated all the articles he had at his disposal, I quite agreed with him. The Sisters had left him bottles and bottles of preserved pears, peaches, and strawberries, many different kinds of vegetables, and a large number of hares, etc. His eyes sparkled with delight at the thought of being able to share his good things with someone. He looked at his wristwatch; it was nearly six o'clock. "Dinnertime," he said. "Father, come!" I followed him up the road, thanking God that I had fallen in with this warm-hearted Irish priest. On the way he told me that the lad with him was an excellent cook. I think the way the good things disappeared that evening was sufficient evidence of my appreciation of his culinary art. Yes, gentle reader, it was Lent—but, then, you know it was wartime!

Just as we had finished, George came in, but he was scarcely in till he found himself seated at the table that Father Sheehan and I had just vacated, and presently the cook and George had set to work. They went at it earnestly, carefully, and methodically, giving it all attention. The cook had prepared an enormous quantity of potatoes; an ordinary vegetable dish would have been too small to hold them all, so they were piled high in a large white milk basin. Father Sheehan and I had decreased the pile considerably, but now under the skillful treatment of George and the cook, the remainder disappeared with extraordinary rapidity. It was good to watch the lads; they worked with such dispatch and so whole-heartedly. It was a wonderful example of the adage, "What you have to do, do it well," and I felt loath to leave when Father Sheehan asked me to come with him to one of the classrooms.

LV ∾ The Refugees

ather Sheehan, opening the door of the classroom, stood back for me to enter. I did, and then fell back in surprise, for the little classroom was almost filled with French civilians and piles of bedding. The seven or eight little children looked wide-eyed at me, but they smiled brightly when they saw Father Sheehan. The older people greeted me simply, as is the way of the French peasant with the stranger. They were refugees from Dainville and were stopping at the convent overnight. Tomorrow, Good Friday, they were to continue their sorrowful journey. They were mostly women, though there was one old man among them who did most of the talking. He seemed somewhat apologetic as to his position. "Do you think," he said to me, "that if it were not for these women and children I would be here? I, sir, would stay to meet the enemy. In 1870 I was a soldier in the army of France, and I was a prisoner of war, but now I must look after these women and children." I expressed my sympathy with the old soldier and asked him a few questions about the Franco-Prussian war of 1870. When I had finished, he looked at me keenly. "You, monsieur, you are an Englishman?" "No," I answered, "I am a Canadian, chaplain to the Canadian soldiers." The keen look in the old man's eyes became more intense as they searched my face. "Ah!" he said with a slow intake of breath. "Ah!" he repeated. Then he stood erect. "The soldiers of Canada are good soldiers, " he half shouted.

As I bowed my appreciation of his praise, he turned and spoke to the women, but his words were uttered so rapidly that I could not catch their sense. Presently he turned to me again, and there was a bright, hopeful look in his eyes. "Are the Canadians going to remain here?" he asked. I said I thought we were, for we had come to stop the German advance. I did not add "if we are able," for I wished to give him courage. "Ah!" the old man said again.

The next morning as I came down to the convent to breakfast, I met a great number of refugees, only this time instead of leaving their homes they were returning to them. Almost in the lead of the procession, pushing a wheelbarrow stacked high with bedding, came the old man that I had talked with the previous evening. He greeted me warmly, as did the women; the little children smiled. "We are returning home," the old man said. "I don't think the enemy will advance any farther now." As I left him and his companions and turned in toward the gates of the convent, I felt a great gladness coming over me. Yesterday these poor people were going out from their homes, but since then the Canadian lads had come and now were lined up between the homes of these French peasants and the enemy. These people knew the Canadian soldiers, so they were going back to their homes. I felt proud of my Canadian lads.

LVI ❧ Arras

It was Easter weekend 1918. Murdoch wanted to minister to his scattered flock who were billeted throughout the city of Arras, but headquarters would not permit it. Given the incessant German shelling, they gauged that it was far too dangerous to assemble so many men at any one location. Once he had visited the deserted, crumbling ruins of the city with Fr. Sheehan, Murdoch agreed with the wisdom of the prohibition. Instead, Murdoch held Mass in the village where he was billeted. At Agnez-lès-Duisans, in the absence of the curé, Murdoch functioned as the local parish priest. At the time, this brought back memories of his first New Brunswick parish in a French-speaking Acadian district called Balmoral.[41] – RH

That afternoon, accompanied by Father Sheehan, I went up to Arras to visit my brigade, for most of the soldiers were billeted in the city. Arras was being heavily shelled by the enemy. Long before we reached the suburbs, we could see the sudden spurts of black smoke rising in many places from large buildings, and as we drew nearer we could hear the dull, quick echoing crash as shell after shell shrieked its way into the great chalk buildings and exploded. Our own field artillery was busy on the outskirts of the town, returning the German fire. A fine mist of rain fell.

It is extremely hard to describe the strange, unfamiliar depression that came over one entering the city, for everything was silent, save when a shell shrieked horribly and then burst, while almost simultaneously came the sound of falling stone and mortar and the tinkle of broken glass. Nobody walked in the silent streets, and in the great empty, dilapidated buildings there was no movement, save now and then the flutter of torn window-blind or soiled curtain in some empty window frame. In one part of the city, blood was mingled with the rainwater that ran slowly along the gutter.

We came to the giant statue of Neptune, which faced us and divided our street. We followed the street that ran to our left, passed the monument, and presently were at the hospital of St. John, which was in charge of some French nuns—I think they were of the Augustinian Order. They had given over one large wing of their hospital to the Canadians, who were using it as an advance dressing station.

There was a really beautiful chapel attached to this hospital, and there was an English military chaplain quartered near it, who said Mass there every morning. I arranged with him to have the use of the chapel on Easter Sunday to say Mass for my lads, but when on Saturday I went to Brigade Headquarters, which was in Arras, to announce the hours of service, I was told that there would be no church parades, as the shelling was so continuous that no congregating of the men above ground would be permitted. The battalions of the Third Brigade were scattered in different billets throughout the city. I was very sorry I could not have the men for Easter Sunday, but since it would have endangered their lives, I recognized the wisdom of the order. Before I left the city that evening there was not the slightest doubt in my mind but that the brigade officers had acted with great prudence, for I was the only one on the long road leading out of Arras, save occupants of an ambulance that came screeching up the road, passing me with terrific speed. When its sound had died away, I became more than ever aware of the shells that dropped so perilously near that I could hear the splinters falling on the cobbles just behind me.

LVII ⮞ Easter Sunday

Since I could not have a parade of my men at Arras, I decided to do what good I could at Agnez-lès-Duisans. We had early Mass for the civilian population, and as their curé was serving in the army I acted as parish priest that morning. Following my ordination to the priesthood I had been sent, as assistant priest, to a parish where French only was spoken. For three years I ministered to these people and when I had left them, I felt that I had a fair working knowledge of their language, though when I first went among them, I received quite a shock. During my classical course I had studied the French language for four years; my theological course had been made at the Grand Seminary of Quebec, where the great majority of the students were French Canadians. I had left the seminary thinking that I had an adequate knowledge of the French language; nevertheless, I took a whole week to prepare and memorize my first French sermon in the little parish. I entered the pulpit a little fearful, though when I found my words flowing with no great effort, I warmed to the work. I went down to the altar feeling that I had done fairly well; but after Mass, while receiving a Mass offering from a gentle old lady who had come into the sacristy leaning on a cane, I asked her very simply how I had preached. I shall never forget the kindly look with which the old lady regarded me, as she said, "It was all right, Father, all right! We all knew what you were trying to say." And I had been preparing for eight years! However, when I left these good people I think they used to know what I was saying. And this Easter morning, in faraway France, as peasant after peasant came to me to confession, I recalled these golden days of my early service for the Master when the first fervour of the young priest was strongly aglow and all the world was at peace.

On Monday morning I took Holy Communion to an old woman who an invalid and could not come to the church. Everything was spotlessly prepared and all the people knelt reverently when I entered the house bearing the Divine Guest. I tried to tiptoe softly in my big, heavy military boots, but as they were built for marching on long roads I did not succeed very well. It seemed very strange there in the soft, carpeted room: two or three women knelt near the bedside; the feminine touch was everywhere; for the first time since my enlistment, I felt the lack of cassock and surplice. Somehow, I felt a little awkward. She was an old woman, and her life must have been a very holy one. Simply and with great faith she received the Divine Guest, and I knew Our Lord would feel at home. When I was leaving, one of the women pressed into my hand a five-franc piece. It was the first I had ever seen; but when I wished to return it, the woman seemed determined that I should keep it. I did—as a souvenir.

LVIII ∾ The Ronville Caves

The Germans continued their heavy shelling of Arras. The ancient city had been built of chalk-stone blocks quarried from nearby mines. Murdoch learned that all the men of his brigade were billeted in the resulting massive underground cave system—the Ronville caves. There, he and Fr. Sheehan made arrangements to hear confessions and to administer Holy Communion to all the Catholics of the 3rd Brigade. Underground, as in the catacombs of old, for almost an entire day, confessions were heard and the Sacrament given. Murdoch describes the day as one of "consolation" wherein "great things had been done for our Divine Lord." As a Catholic priest, he felt "great joy." There had been only one significant interruption—when Murdoch was called away to give last rites to a man caught by shellfire at the cave complex's entrance. Even so, Murdoch notes that this man had confessed and received the Sacrament but an hour earlier. He had been spiritually prepared for death. The next day, Murdoch received word of a fellow Canadian Catholic chaplain's death a few miles distant. Fr. R. M. Crochetière, whom Murdoch knew from Witley Camp in England, had been killed by a shell. The following Sunday,

Murdoch assisted with funerals at the nearby cemetery. Of the nine soldiers buried that afternoon, two were Catholics who a few days earlier had been to the service in the caves. – RH

O n Wednesday morning while I was taking my breakfast in the mess of the Sixteenth Battalion, George came in with a cup of tea and some good news. All the battalions of the brigade were quartered in the Ronville caves—over three thousand men underground. This was, indeed, good news, for now I could do some work among the men, which I had been longing to do.

The Ronville caves were just beyond the railway station, under the outskirts of Arras. Nearly all the buildings of the city, including the Cathedral of Arras, were built of chalk. This chalk had been quarried from the depths of the earth, as near as possible to the city. When all the chalk necessary had been excavated, lo! there remained the chalk caves of Ronville—a series of caves at the end of short tunnels that branched off from a great main tunnel miles in length.

After breakfast I went down to the convent and found Father Sheehan seated in his dining room. Yes, he knew well the situation of the Ronville caves and would be only too pleased to accompany me to them. In a few minutes we were on our way to Arras. We went through the city, turned to our right just before we came to the railway station, passed over the iron overhead bridge crossing the railway tracks, turned a little to our left, and presently we were walking through a quadrangle, pitted deeply with old and new shell holes, toward the entrance of the caves. We passed through the opening and almost immediately were in complete darkness. We stumbled along for a little, I happening to be in the lead, then suddenly a long shaft of light shot silently ahead of me, illuminating the long white chalk corridor. Father Sheehan's small flashlight was at work. Then as we came around a curve in our road we heard from far down in the corridor a muffled complaint; our light was shining in the eyes of some poor oncomer; so immediately we were in darkness again, though far down the corridor, seemingly attached to the wall, a light as from a candle glimmered. We advanced slowly, Father Sheehan flashing his lamp intermittently on the ground just ahead.

I visited all the battalions except the Thirteenth and had arranged to have the men come to confession and Holy Communion the following day, when we almost collided with two kilted officers in the Thirteenth Battalion tartan. One was the chaplain of the battalion, then Captain Graham, MC (afterwards Major Graham, MC, DSO), a Presbyterian, a brave soldier, and a thorough gentleman; the other was a young Catholic officer who had but lately returned to his battalion after having been wounded. They had been looking for me. Captain Graham introduced the young officer, who was Captain E. Waud, and then left us. Captain Waud began very gently yet firmly to take me to task: "You have not been giving us an opportunity lately to go to confession, Father," he said.

I jumped interiorly, for this was the first time I had been accused of not giving the men every opportunity of approaching the sacraments, but I liked that young officer then and there. "Well, captain," I said, "no later than last Wednesday night I stood under a tree in Château de la Haie waiting for all the soldiers who might come; the Fourteenth and Sixteenth showed up well, but many of the Thirteenth did not show up." "Oh," he said, "we were at a concert that evening!" "Well," I returned, "I had announced confessions before supper, and if the men missed the opportunity of going by attending a concert it was not my fault. However," I continued, "I have just announced confessions for tomorrow at all the battalion orderly rooms, excepting the Thirteenth. I am on my way there now." The young officer seemed very pleased and promised to have all the Catholic soldiers of his company in New Plymouth cave the following morning at ten o'clock. "God bless you!" I said to him. "If all my Catholic officers were as eager to come to confession, and bring their men, as you are, my work would be made very much easier."

LIX ❧ The Banquet Hall

The following morning after breakfast, Father Sheehan and I went down on our bicycles to the parish church. Then each of us, wearing a white stole over our uniform, went to the little tabernacle and after genuflecting silently, took from it one small military ciborium full of consecrated Hosts. Then silently we left the church bearing our precious burden. When we entered Arras, which was now known as the "City of the Dead," we found, as usual, empty streets and the contour of many sections of the city fast disappearing under the unceasing bombardment of German guns.

We left our bicycles in care of the guard on the bridge near the entrance to the Ronville caves and walked through the quadrangle, which contained many more shell holes than it did on our previous visit. For this reason, our passage was made very quickly. The long main tunnel was much better lighted, however, lighted candles being attached at intervals on either wall. We turned to our right and entered a subsidiary tunnel, above the entrance of which was a signboard bearing the names of three or four different caves; New Plymouth was one to which the tunnel led. New Plymouth was wide and low and, although one of the smaller caves, could very easily accommodate comfortably five or six hundred men. At one end farthest from the entrance was what proved to be an excellent altar table. The chalk had been quarried in such a manner that what appeared to be a large chalk altar remained. Father Sheehan and I looked at each other in some surprise then placed our Sacred Burden on the altar, covered the two ciboria with a small white cloth we had brought, and lighted two candles, which we placed on either side—we had brought our pockets filled with small pieces of candles from the church. We then sat down on our steel helmets, placed on piles of chalk, for already we could hear the sound of many voices coming along the corridor. Presently a large crowd of men from the Fifteenth and Sixteenth entered the dimly lighted cave, removed their caps, genuflected before the altar, and then knelt in little groups on the hard chalk floor, silent in prayer—for the Lord was in His holy temple!

Quickly the men came to confession, and every ten or fifteen minutes either Father Sheehan or I stood up, went to the altar while some soldier said the "Confiteor," then as the little white cloth was passed from one soldier to another, they received with deep reverence their Lord. As each little semicircle of men received Holy Communion, they moved back into the more darkened portion of the cave where they knelt to make their thanksgiving.

We had been dispensing "the mysteries of God" for nearly an hour when a large number from the Thirteenth came in and knelt down near me. Just before them knelt their young captain. He had done as he had said; all his Catholic lads were with him. For a long time they knelt there on the hard chalk floor, and as now and again my eyes fell on the earnest faces of the lads as they prayed reverently, my thoughts would go back to the early ages of the church when the first Christians adored God in the catacombs of Rome.

In a little while I gave the young officer and his lads Holy Communion. At the time there seemed to me to be some earnestness about the young captain—as if this communion were a great and holy preparation for some event that I knew nothing of. While he knelt back in the gloom, silently returning thanks to God, I could not help associating him with the knights of old. Then when he had finished his thanksgiving, strengthened by the coming of the Lord, he left the cave at the head of his men, ready, like a true knight, for whatever was to come.

All day we worked in the Banquet Hall; all day long, with the exception of one or two short intervals, came the banqueters. At about half past twelve, a soldier came quickly into the cave calling loudly, "RC chaplain!" I stood up and went in the direction from which the voice had come. "Quick, sir!" said the soldier. "The MO of the Fourteenth says one of your men is hit and for you to come quick." Without delay I followed my guide down the tunnel till we came to the medical aid post of the Fourteenth. There, lying on a table with the doctor of the Fourteenth Battalion working over him, was one of the Catholic lads of the Thirteenth bleeding in many places from a number of wounds. He had stepped out from the cave for a minute and had been caught in the enemy fire. "Is it long since you've been to confession, lad?" I said. He looked at me through clear eyes, though he was in great pain. "Just about an hour ago, Father," he said. The doctor whispered in my ear, "He's going, Padre," so I put on my stole and prepared the lad for death. I always carried the Holy Oils in my pocket. Just as I finished anointing the dying soldier, one of his friends was admitted for a last word. "What will I tell your people at home?" asked the friend, who was a Protestant. "Tell them—" he laboured a little for breath—"tell them," he repeated, "I had the priest!" Shortly afterwards he was taken by ambulance to the Field Ambulance at Agnez-lès-Duisans, and the following morning he died.

I returned to New Plymouth cave and there I found Father Sheehan very busy, for the Fourteenth Battalion was now coming. We heard them quickly, however, as it was but a few days since they had come to confession at Château de la Haie. That evening, after the last man had left, Father Sheehan came over to me. "Father," he said, "wasn't it a great day's work?" I could scarcely speak for the great joy I felt. There had been such consolation throughout the whole day! Great things had been done for our Divine Lord, who had waited all day long in the dimly lighted cave, giving His deep, sweet peace to the souls of these lads of "good will." Centuries before, He had come to another cave, when "glad tidings" had been announced to the shepherds. "Yes, Father," I said, "it was one of the happiest days of my life." Then, simultaneously, we thought of the things of earth. It was time to go back to Agnez-lès-Duisans for, with the exception of one slice of bread and margarine between us, we had eaten nothing since early morning. It was now evening.

The following morning while at breakfast a letter from headquarters was given to me by the waiter. I opened it quickly. It read: "Capt. the Rev. R. M. Crochetière was killed in action, April 2nd, near Bailleulmont." This place was just a little to the south of Arras. Not a year before he had sung the great open-air Mass at Witley Camp when the Catholic soldiers had been consecrated to the Sacred Heart. Just yesterday he had gone home to the Sacred Heart to receive the reward of his stewardship. I sat back from the breakfast table and wondered who would be next. Then I went down to the convent.

Almost every morning I went down to the convent, for there was a lovely garden there where I could walk up and down under the trees and read my breviary. Often as I passed through the court before the main building on my way to the garden, I paused before a beautiful statue of the Sacred Heart of Jesus. The base of the statue was surrounded by a wide circle of green lawn, bordering which was a fringe of forget-me-nots, planted very likely by the good Sisters as a symbol of their devotion to the Sacred Heart. Every morning the children whom the Sisters taught before they went away came to the convent and asked a young woman—a kind of lay-Sister who came daily to do some work about the building—when the Sisters were coming back. "Very soon, perhaps—tomorrow, perhaps." And the little ones would stay through the morning and play till they were tired; then they would sit on the low benches and sing in their sweet childish voices the beautiful hymns that the Sisters had taught them.

The presence of the sky-blue, yellow-centred forget-me-nots always brought to my mind the love of the Sisters for the Sacred Heart; the sound of the children's voices in the morning always brought to my mind the love of the children for the Sisters. Just beyond the convent, on the other side of the Scarpe River, which here was only about six feet wide, was a group of Nissen huts that had up to a few weeks before been used as a Casualty Clearing Station, but at the beginning of the German advance, the patients and staff had been removed. Now it was being used by a Field Ambulance for dressing wounds or some emergency operation of casualties from the Arras front. Father Whiteside, an English chaplain, was on duty here, though usually he called me when any of my Canadian lads came in. Across the road from the Field Ambulance was a large military cemetery where regiments of weary soldiers rested softly, each under the shadow of a little white cross.

It was the following Sunday afternoon that I had my first burials in this cemetery. At two o'clock a procession of soldiers, mostly kilted laddies from the Thirteenth, came slowly up the long aisle of the cemetery: in the lead, following the pipe band that played the "Flowers of the Forest," walked nine groups of six men, each carrying shoulder-high one of their late comrades who had answered bravely the last call. One was an officer, the young knight who had passed his vigil in New Plymouth cave. While leading his men out of the

Ronville caves he had been mortally wounded, passing away a few hours afterwards. Of the dead, only Captain Waud and the young soldier from the Thirteenth whom I had anointed in the cave were Catholics.

And often as I passed through the court before the main building of the convent and paused to look at the sweet forget-me-nots fringing the lawn around the base of the statue of the Sacred Heart, I recalled the two who, among others, had remembered their Creator, and I felt now they were not forgotten: "Turn to Me and I will turn to thee," had said the Lord.

LX ❦ The Sheehans

Murdoch seldom explicitly mentions political topics in The Red Vineyard, *but there are one or two exceptions. This is one of those instances. Murdoch ventures to suggest reasons for the outbreak of the Great War! He does so by quoting a famous Catholic writer of the nineteenth century who, as it turns out, was Fr. Sheehan's cousin. This "seer and prophet" had predicted that "modern civilization" was to experience an "upheaval that will change the map of the world." His long list of causes included "the attitude of the Great Powers to each other, snarling and afraid to bite"; the attempt by contemporary philosophers to eliminate "the supernatural"; "the concentration of all human thought upon the fleeting pleasures of this life"; and the "denial of the life to come." By quoting this writer at such length, Murdoch clearly indicates his agreement. Present-day historians would not dismiss his list out of hand and are inclined to agree with at least some of his observations. – RH*

We waited at Agnez-lès-Duisans a few days longer, but "old Fritz" did not strike on the Arras front, though all the world knows that he continued to gain elsewhere. Two or three times during the week, Father Sheehan went up to Arras with a quantity of provisions to two Poor Clare Sisters who lived on in the basement of their ruined convent in order to pay court to their King.

In the evening we were kept busy hearing confessions and giving Holy Communion to soldiers in the parish church. One evening when we had heard the confessions of all the men present, I stepped into the sacristy to say a word to Father Sheehan, who was just going out to give Holy Communion. "Ah, Father!" he said in his gentle, friendly manner, "I am glad you came in. Will you please go down there to Pat and tell him not to go to Communion now. You see, Father, he was there this morning, and he's such a pious lad that when he sees the others going to the rails, he might forget that he was there this morning and go up again." "All right, Father," I said, but somehow or other I found great difficulty in suppressing a strong inclination to smile as I walked down the flagged aisle of the church. Pat—Father Sheehan had pointed him out to me—who was intently reading his prayer book, looked up kindly at me as I drew near. "God bless you, Father," he whispered as I stooped over him, and he disposed himself elaborately to listen. It actually pained me to keep from laughing as I prepared to deliver my message.

"Pat," I said, "Father Sheehan sent me to tell you not to go to Communion again. He is afraid that you might forget you were there this morning and go back again." Pat just looked at his book and shook his head as he smiled indulgently. Then he looked at me, still smiling, "Shure, Father dear, I had no intention of going again!" Then he said, as if to himself, "God bless Father Sheehan!" Pat's words were echoed strongly in my heart; for every one that met Father Sheehan would feel like wishing him the very best they could, and what is better than the blessing of God?

Just about this time I received from my mother a birthday present, which had been delayed along the way. It was a large volume entitled *Canon Sheehan of Doneraile*, by Father Heuser. I had long enjoyed the works of the gentle Canon, and I had always felt that I owed a lot to this seer and prophet. I had long wanted to read the life of one who had made many such unerring prophesies as the following some twenty years before the signing of the Armistice:

> Meanwhile, the new Paganism, called modern
> civilization, is working out its own destruction and

solving its own problems. There are subterranean mutterings of a future upheaval that will change the map of the world as effectually as did an irruption of Vandals or Visigoths. In the self-degradation of women; in the angry disputes between Labor and Capital; in the dreams of Socialists, and the sanguinary ambitions of Nihilists; in the attitude of the great Powers to each other, snarling and afraid to bite; in the irreverence and flippancy of the age manifested towards the most sacred and solemn subjects, in the destructive attempts of philosophers, in the elimination of the supernatural, in the concentration of all human thought upon the fleeting concerns of this life, and the covert, yet hardly concealed, denial of a life to come; in the rage for wealth, in the almost insane dread of poverty—and all these evil things permeating and penetrating into every class—there is visible to the most ordinary mortal a disintegration of society that can only eventuate in such ruin as have made Babylon and Nineveh almost historical myths, and has made a proverb and by-word even of Imperial Rome. Where is the remedy? Clearly, Christianity; and still more clearly the only Christianity that is possible and can bear the solvent influence of the new civilization. Nothing but the poverty of Christ, manifested in the self-abandonment of our religious communities; the awful purity of Christ, continued in a celibate priesthood and the white sanctity of our nuns; the self-denial and immolation of Christ, shown again wherever the sacrificial instinct is manifested in our martyrs and missionaries; the love of Christ, as exhibited in our charge of the orphaned, the abandoned, the profligate, the diseased, the leprous and insane—can lead back the vast masses of erring humanity to the condition not only of stability, but of the fruition of perfect peace. For what is the great political maxim of government but the greatest good to the greatest number—in other words, the voluntary sacrifice of the individual for the welfare of the Commonwealth? And where is that seen but in the ranks of the obscure and hidden, the unknown and despised (unknown and despised by themselves above all) members of the Catholic church.

I took the book down to the convent to show it to Father Sheehan. To my question if he had ever met Canon Sheehan, looking at me in that quizzical half smiling way that one regards a questioner when the information to be given far exceeds that asked, he said, "Yes, I have met him. I knew him, and he was my cousin."

LXI ⁓ Écoivres

This chapter marks a subtle yet significant turning point in The Red Vineyard. Murdoch's brigade is moved to a new location six kilometres from Arras, "The City of the Dead," to a place called Écoivres. While moving separately to the new location, both Murdoch and his batman, George, endure heavy shelling. Murdoch relates his experience. Suddenly, "shell after shell came screaming through the air.… I felt sick, dazed, and frightened, and whenever others crouched I did also, but we reached the little town in safety." George was not so lucky. The group he had been a part of lost both men and horses. As Murdoch relates, "there was in George's eyes that hurt, dazed look that I was to see so often in the eyes of men when the shells screamed by and took toll of their companions." It is worth noting at this point that George had already been diagnosed with shell shock and had become a batman in order to minimize his exposure to shelling. Before long, Murdoch too would share the fullness of George's experience. Statistically, in the Great War more Canadian soldiers died of shelling than of any other single cause. – RH

April was passing quickly. Very early in the morning, from the old trees about the convent, one heard the sweet, clear call of many birds; the leaves were unfolding; the fresh, revivifying odours of new grass and early spring flowers were in the air. All around us were signs of destruction by the ingenuity of man; yet nature was steadfastly following her laws, restoring, expanding, and quickening to new life—and cheering wonderfully many tired and war-weary men. On all sides Fritz was making advances, but we were holding him at Arras. I made frequent visits to this City of the Dead, and every time I passed through its gates—Arras is a walled city—an appalling sense of loneliness gripped me. Only seventy people of the thirty thousand inhabitants remained; and to see, now and then, a solitary civilian moving along the street, or about some shattered dwelling place, only emphasized the awful stillness. I visited the ruins of the great cathedral and saw the statue of Our Lady standing unscathed in her little side chapel. I walked through the corridors of the shattered seminary, where for many years young Frenchmen had walked silently, listening to the voice of the Spirit of God, forming them for the work of the holy ministry. The young men who should now be here were in the trenches, clad in the light-blue uniform of the soldiers of France.

Not far from the seminary, in the basement of their shattered convent, lived two Poor Clare nuns who had remained to adore our Divine Lord on the altar. I do not know how it had been arranged, but there was Perpetual Adoration of the Blessed Sacrament in that poor cellar. Perhaps it was for this reason that the Canadians held Arras. It was to these holy women of France that Father Sheehan made many visits, carrying pieces of meat, rolls of bread, etc. The quartermaster of the unit from which he drew rations was an Irishman, and many of the lads gladly stinted themselves so that he could lay by a little food for the Poor Clare Sisters at Arras.

Then, one day just after lunch, orders came to move. We were not going very far away—only to the little village of Écoivres at the base of Mont-Saint-Éloi, about five or six kilometres distant. I stayed with Father Sheehan for tea, and at four o'clock left alone for Écoivres. I had never been there before, but Father Sheehan had given me minute directions, and I knew I would have no difficulty finding the large château of the village. I had not gone more than a mile on my way when I noticed shells dropping into many of the little villages that lay scattered over the green countryside before me. I must pass through two of these villages before arriving at my destination. I suspected some big attack on the part of the Germans, as it was their invariable custom to shell heavily the back areas in order to prevent us from bringing up fresh troops. As I was revolving in my mind how pleasant it was going to be for me to run the gauntlet of fire, I heard the terrifying shriek of a shell, and as I turned, was just in time to see a great black shell burst only a few feet behind me. A group of men had been standing on the roadside, but not one was hit. I stood for a few moments dazed by the suddenness of it all, my ears ringing from the terrible explosion, while teams drawing general service wagons galloped noisily by and men ran like startled hares toward points of safety. Presently I continued my walk, every nerve tense, expecting another shell-burst. None came, however.

I passed through the two villages and no shell dropped near me till I came to the outskirts of Écoivres, then shell after shell came screaming through the air, exploding in the high bank that sloped up from the roadside. A few soldiers coming behind me on bicycles dismounted and crouched low as each one tore its way across our road. I felt sick, dazed, and frightened, and whenever the others crouched, I did also; but we reached the little town in safety. I passed the church, which was untouched, though many stone buildings about it were almost completely demolished. Then I came into the court before the château, where a great number of soldiers were quartered.

It was an old château, the ancestral home of a long line of French counts, which had been commandeered early in the war. The present owner, however, still had a room or two allotted to him. I went up an old winding stairway and walked from the landing along the hall till I came to a great wide room where a number of officers of different battalions of my brigade stood talking in little groups. They greeted me with true military friendliness, but I could see that they were restless and ill at ease. Fritz had struck again and broken the British line, taking many prisoners and great quantities of supplies. And as the officers talked, shells screamed into the village.

Just before dinner George came to the mess and his face lighted up when he saw me. He had come before me by a different route, and some of his companions—although none of our own brigade—had been killed, together with a number of horses. There was in George's eye that hurt, dazed look that I was to see so often in the eyes of men when the shells screamed by and took toll of their companions. George told me I was to be billeted in a large room with a number of other officers. While he was speaking, however, the billeting officer joined us to say that he had a fine billet for me; it was a little hut outside in the grounds. It had been reserved for the colonel, but as he wished to remain in the château, the billeting officer, remembering that I preferred, when possible, to have a billet alone, so that the men might the more easily come to see me, had given me the little hut.

After dinner, which was late that evening, I went down through the château grounds, crossed a bridge over a small river that ran through them, and followed the road until I came to a little burlap hut, built on the riverbank under the willow trees, that had just hung out their fresh green draperies. And as I stood surveying my billet, I became aware that the shelling had ceased; the stars were coming out; just the faintest rustle sounded among the treetops; there was a very pleasant tinkle and gurgle from the running water; from all around the wide green grounds came the low murmur of talking from groups of soldiers bivouacked here and there under the trees. George came up presently with four or five letters and a box of caramels that had come with the Canadian mail. It was one of those strange interludes that came fairly often during the campaign, when one actually forgot for a little while war and its gruesomeness.

In the morning, after a very pleasant night's sleep by the softly running waters, I went down to the parish church to say Mass. The curé was a large man and very kind; evidently the billeting officer had tried to place me with him, for he took great pains to explain to me that his house was extremely small and already it was full on account of the presence of some of his relations who had been evacuated from the Arras area.

I told the curé how pleasantly I was situated, and that the softly running water had sent me to sleep. He smiled, helped me to put on my vestments, and then served my Mass. After Mass, as I made my thanksgiving before the altar, I noticed on the Gospel side a large alcove. In it were five or six prie-dieux, and a communion rail ran the width of it. It was somewhat similar to a box in a theatre. On the wall in the alcove opposite to where I knelt was a large copper slab bearing the inscription:

To the Memory of
M. Edward Mary Alexander
Viscount of Brandt of Caolmetz
Died in his castle of Écoivres
the 9th October, 1894
R.I.P.

I concluded that this was the part of the church where the people of the château came to assist at Mass in the old days before France printed on her coins "Liberty, Equality, and Fraternity." I saw the present owner of the estate a few days later, and I wondered if he sat in the alcove to assist at Mass on Sundays. He was a tall, heavily built man in old rough clothes and looked more like a labourer one would see sitting idly about the docks. He had a large, heavy red face and a thick black moustache. When I saw him first he stood facing a pointed bayonet—though he kept at least three feet from the point—and an angry sentry at the entrance to the château was telling him in English that he could not enter. The owner of the château, still more angry than the guard, shouted in French that he would enter; that these were his grounds, though his manner of putting in practice his words resembled more the advancing of a horse on a treadmill. I was about to offer my services as interpreter and general peacemaker when an officer approached the angry guard and told him that it was the owner of the château whom he was keeping from entering. The guard sprang to attention, and as the angry owner entered his grounds looked after him sheepishly. "Well, Holy Moses!" he exclaimed.

LXII ∼ Écurie Wood

Although the brigade moved to a new location at Écurie Wood, Murdoch's exposure to shelling intensified rather than lessened. It was at this point that he began to carry the Sacrament (the consecrated breads) in his pocket. He relates that under close shelling he "would sit or kneel before the Blessed Sacrament, trembling, expecting each moment to be my last." One morning he was awakened from a deep sleep as "a shell came shrieking through the air," followed by a deafening explosion "just thirteen steps" beyond his little hut. He lay waiting for the next round, which, thankfully, did not come. All four battalions of his brigade suffered casualties, but the 14th Battalion lost the most. On April 19, its headquarters were struck, killing the second-in-command and another major as well as wounding the colonel and several others. Indeed, in the period of April 15 to 19 the brigade lost five killed and fourteen wounded. This does not count those wounded who died once removed from the front—and this was the casualty rate when the brigade was out of the trenches! Although not recorded in his military file, for he was not hospitalized, it was at this time that Murdoch contracted the "flu." His retrospective comment about the "charity of the army" provides insight into a seldom mentioned aspect of army life and helps explain the extraordinary esprit de corps of Canada's Great War troops. – RH

I had expected to stay at Écoivres for Sunday, and I had arranged with the curé for the soldiers' Mass, but on Saturday orders came for us to move to Écurie Wood. It was not very far away, about three miles. My billet here was a corrugated iron hut, barricaded without on all sides with sandbags piled about three feet high and two wide. There was no floor other than the natural earth. The seat of a general service wagon that very likely had succumbed to Fritz's shelling had been converted into a very serviceable chair; on a high bedding of mud and rocks was placed horizontally an empty five-gallon gasoline tin, from which pointed heavenwards, through the low roof, some homemade stovepipe. There was no door on this improvised stove. When I entered the hut, a fire of charcoal and small pieces of wood glowed in the opening of the tin, which the chair faced. There was no church near us, but there was a large moving picture hut just about two hundred yards away where Mass was said on Sundays; and only fifty yards from this was a small square tent, with the words "Catholic Chapel" painted in black on it, where a priest was on duty every evening to hear confessions. As there was no church near where the Blessed Sacrament was reserved, I now began to carry Our Lord with me. On Monday I consecrated about two hundred particles in my small military ciborium, and always, day and night, in the pocket of my tunic was the little ciborium where Jesus dwelt. And in the evenings, I used to go down to the chapel tent, place the ciborium on a corporal [a white linen cloth] spread out on the rough board table, and, saying a short prayer, sit on an empty box to hear the confessions of the men who came. We were in a very exposed territory and shells were continuously dropping into our area. Sometimes the shells would come so near us that I would sit on my box, or kneel before the Blessed Sacrament, trembling, expecting each moment to be my last.

A great number of men were assembling in the Écurie Wood area, and I began to meet many old friends. Some of the lads who had come overseas with me were in battalions quartered nearby; and just over the hill, in the military cemetery of Roclincourt, Lt. Lawlor, one of my Catholic officers and a very gallant soldier, slept softly under his white cross.

The work at Écurie Wood was very consoling: wonderful things happened in that little white chapel tent. One night a great giant of a man stepped in, and without any introduction said, simply, "Father, I want to be christened." I could not help laughing, for in my mind always associated with the word "christen" were thoughts of tiny, white-clad, helpless babies being carried to the baptismal font. But the big giant did not laugh. It was a very serious matter for him. I asked him to which religion he belonged. He said he belonged to none but that his people had been Presbyterians. I commenced instructions and in a short time I had the great pleasure of baptizing him in the little tent.

Sometimes men would come back to the sacraments after years of absence, and it was wonderful to watch the effects of Divine Grace in their souls. Often they would come back to the tent to have a chat and to speak of some fellow with whom they were trying to share their own great happiness. Frequently a returned prodigal would say to me: "Now, Father, I have a lad outside who hasn't been to his duties for many years. I got him to come down tonight. I'm just telling you this, Father, for he's got the 'wind up' pretty bad, but I know you'll take him easy, Father." Then perhaps a big, slow moving, puzzled figure would step into the tent, looking around mystified, not knowing what to do next. Then I would beckon him to come and kneel down, and then—I would "take him easy."

One night, when I was sitting on my box, a large one placed near me, against which the men might kneel when telling their little story, a man came rushing in and knelt so suddenly that he knocked over the larger box and then fell on it as it reached the ground. I stood up quickly, taking off my purple stole as I did so, and as the poor fellow got slowly up I said, "What's the matter? What's the matter?" He looked at me in a dazed sort of way, and then over his shoulder toward the open flap of the tent. "I'm willing to go, Father," he said. "I think you're a little too eager to go," I said. "There's no need, you know, to knock over that box. I put that there for men to kneel against." "Well," he replied, "I'm willing to go, but I want a little time to get ready. It's a long time since I was here before, and I need a little time to overhaul my mind." I could not help laughing, though I felt there was something wrong somewhere. "Well," I said, "what made you come in if you were not prepared?" Again he looked over his shoulder, and as he did the truth began to dawn upon me. "Father," he said, "I was pushed in." "Kneel down," I said, "and take all the time you need, and when you are ready just call me. I am going outside for a while."

I went out and in a few minutes three figures came noiselessly over to where I was standing. "Is he going to go, Father?" one of them asked. "He is," I replied, "but he needs a little time to prepare. Why did you send—I should say push—him in before he was ready to go?" They then told me that it was fifteen years since the man had been to confession and that he had been bragging about not having been there for that length of time. One of the number had told him three days before to prepare, and on account of this they had thought him ready to go.

I think, on the whole, these lay apostles did excellent work; still, now and then, there was an example of perhaps too great zeal. Father Miles Tompkins relates a story which perhaps showed a little overzeal. He was walking with Father McGillvary one day up and down before a little church of a village where troops were quartered when he noticed three khaki-clad figures coming toward them. His first thought was that some poor fellow had imbibed too freely of "vin blink"—the soldiers' name for the white wine—and that two charitable comrades were escorting him to his billet. When, however, the soldiers drew nearer, he saw that the man was not intoxicated, though somewhat indignant at being hustled so unceremoniously by two comrades who did not bear the insignia of military police. When they were within speaking distance, Father Tompkins asked one of the escorts what was the matter. "Father," they said, as they looked at their struggling victim, "this fellow wants to go to confession." "Well," said Father Tompkins, "he does not look very much as if he wanted to go!"

LXIII ～ The Different Dispensers

The Thirteenth and Fifteenth Battalions were at Anzin, a small village about three kilometres distant from Écurie Wood. There was a little brick church here with a great hole through the base of its tower. I used to go down there on my bicycle early Sunday mornings and hear confessions while Father Pickett, of the First Divisional Artillery, said Mass for my lads. Then I would ride back to Écurie Wood and say Mass at half past ten for the Fourteenth and Sixteenth. There were now three other priests quartered at Écurie Wood, and these would hear confessions during my Mass. In the evenings the priests would assemble in my hut—for, it seemed, I had the best billet in the area—and talk over many things. It was not often so many chaplains were together, and I, for one, enjoyed these pleasant evenings in the little hut before the blazing fire. It was a very dangerous area, however; shells were dropping all over the camp, and there was great loss of life. One morning on awakening from a very sound sleep, a shell came shrieking through the air, then the deafening explosion as it struck just outside my hut. I waited, scarcely breathing, for the next, but no more came. When I was dressed, I stepped off the distance from my hut to where the shell had struck. It was just thirteen steps. They were beginning to come very near!

Those gatherings of chaplains in my corrugated iron hut there on the Western Front were unique. I often used to think of it in the evenings as we talked, or when some chaplain read excerpts from a Canadian paper that had come from home. It was this—that while we talked away so casually about the ordinary daily affairs of the world, in the pocket of everyone present dwelt humbly Our Eucharistic Lord in his little home, the ciborium.

One afternoon while I was sitting in my hut, alternately reading my book and looking into the fire, a knock sounded on the door and a young officer walked in, smiling broadly. He was a lieutenant in the artillery. I had known him when he was a little boy and I was in senior philosophy at college. I had not seen him for ten years till I met him at the front. After we had talked for a while, he asked me if he could go to confession.

I put on my purple stole and sat down on the large general service wagon seat, while he knelt down on the earth floor—over which at times I saw worms moving—and he began his little tale. Often, in our old college days, when I was walking slowly on the track of the athletic field, he had come running up quickly behind me, given me a punch on the back, and then had skipped ahead of me, smiling pleasantly as he waited for me to catch up to him. Now he knelt humbly on the earth and confessed his sins, and I, with all the powers of the priesthood, absolved him! It was with great joy in my heart that I arranged my little portable altar on a box, spread out the clean white corporal and gave him Holy Communion. After I had closed the altar and the young lieutenant had finished his thanksgiving, we sat on the seat. He was the first to speak. "Father," he said, "these are strange times we are living in." I agreed with him, and among other things thought of the shell that had dropped just thirteen steps from where we sat; but he was not thinking of shells. "Three weeks ago," he said, "I was in Rome on leave, and on Easter Sunday all the Catholic officers in the city had permission to assist at Mass in the Sistine Chapel and receive Holy Communion from the hand of Pope Benedict XV, amidst great splendour and solemnity. Today, kneeling on the earth, I received Our Lord in this little corrugated iron hut on the Western Front!"

I did not speak for awhile; some strange emotion held me silent as I visualized the two scenes. Easter in Rome, in one of the most beautiful chapels in the world, the Pope in the richest vestments, assisted by many priests, giving Holy Communion. Then, a small dark hut, with not even a window in it, and no covering over the clay roof, the priest in a wrinkled khaki uniform and heavy trench boots, his only vestment a small white stole worn over his tunic—yet, in each case Jesus had come to the young officer!

LXIV ⟲ Incapacitated

The work at Écurie Wood was most consoling, but the shelling was incessant, and we were having many funerals in the military cemetery down the hill at Roclincourt. The Fourteenth Battalion suffered most. Early one morning a shell burst in the headquarters hut, wounding the colonel, killing the second-in-command and the adjutant, and disabling other officers and privates. The whole camp was under observation, and Fritz was doing deadly work.

One Sunday morning, as I prepared for the Holy Sacrifice, I seemed to feel much better than I had felt for some time, and as I preached, the words came quickly and without any great effort.

I wondered why I should feel so well. But after Mass, as I walked back to my hut after having seen so many of those wonderful lads receive Holy Communion, I raised my hand to my forehead; it was very warm and the day was cool—in fact, a fine mist of rain was falling. I now began to feel slightly dizzy and more inclined to rest on my camp bed than to drink my cup of tea. George came in, looked at me once, placed the cup of tea beside me on the seat, looked at me again, and then told me I didn't look very well. I told him I did not feel very well. Both agreed that I would be better in bed, so I went. The corporal of the stretcher-bearers came in, shook his little thermometer, looked at it, shook it again, then told me to open my mouth. He placed it under my tongue. Then, while I looked at the ceiling of the hut, he waited. "One hundred and two," said the corporal. "Is that high?" I asked, for I could not remember ever having my temperature taken before.

"High enough," he said. Then he told me I had a malady that was becoming very prevalent in the army. He did not know what to call it. Later, it was called the "flu."

I remained in bed for nearly a week, and it was one of the finest weeks I spent in the army; so many officers and men came into the little hut to see me. I was just beginning to understand the charity of the army.

Just as I was getting about again, the Fifty-first Division of Scotch Highlanders came into our area. This was the division that had met almost every advance of the enemy, so that even the Germans themselves could not but admire them. A sergeant in one of the battalions of the division possessed a paper for which he had refused six pounds: for the paper had been dropped into their lines from a German airplane, and this is what was written on it: "Good old Fifty-first still sticking it! Cheerio!"

LXV ❦ Anzin and Monchy Breton

In early May, the 3rd Brigade was on the move, first to Anzin and then back to a rest area far from the trenches. Although his four battalions were billeted in different villages, which necessitated much travelling on his bicycle, Murdoch enjoyed this time. Amazingly, he even relates the content of a sermon he preached at this period. Far from a jingoistic war rant, his talk contrasted the beauty of God's nature with the devastated countryside they had inhabited in recent months—lands "marred by the ingenuity of man." Murdoch admits that many in his audience may have similarly marred their souls to the point that they felt isolated from God and ashamed among their friends. He, however, assured them that "God was ready to receive them,…to cleanse them and make their souls beautiful again." The reaction to this sermon "was one of the strangest and sweetest experiences I had in the war." – RH

The Fifty-first "took over" from us and we went to Anzin. Here it was much quieter, and the battalion prepared to rest. I took charge of the village church, for I was the only chaplain in the area. The first day, I swept it out and dusted the altar and sanctuary-rail. The next morning, I said Mass, and after Mass a little sanctuary lamp twinkled softly before the altar. The Guest had come!

There was a beautiful statue of Our Lady in the church, and as it was her month, I decorated it as well as I could. A long walk by the Scarpe River, which flowed its narrow though very pretty way through Anzin, brought me to the grounds of what had once been a very fine country residence, now terribly battered from shellfire. The road that led to it sloped up from the river, and as I walked along it this beautiful May day, from the dark recesses of the trees came the repeated solitary call of the cuckoo. I stopped to listen. The whole countryside seemed very quiet and peaceful, save for the faint rumble, from far away, of our guns.

Though the grounds were pitted in different places with old shell holes, many flowers grew in the garden. I picked some white lilacs, although the season for these was now growing late, and a large bunch of Parma violets. It was very quiet and still there in the old French garden, but I could hear German shells whining through the air and dropping in a little village not very far away. Somewhere along the line battles were being fought, and I supposed the British were losing ground and that many men were being taken prisoners. Up to this time we Canadians had not lost any men as prisoners and had given no ground except a mile in depth near Neuville-Vitasse when we found ourselves placed in a very dangerous position by the general retreat of British troops, which in some places was more than twenty miles in depth.

Toward the end of May good news came to us. We were going back to rest. And it was to be a long rest, among green fields, far from the sound of the guns and the sights of the battlefield.

It was Saturday when we arrived in our rest billets after a long march through a peaceful countryside. My battalions were scattered in four different villages, and I was very busy Saturday afternoon arranging for Masses. Up to this time our rest billets had been always in mining towns or districts, but now we had come to one of the most beautiful countrysides I had ever seen. Open, unfenced farmlands stretched before us, while here and there clumps of ancient wide-spreading trees, almost hiding from view the little white-walled, red-roofed houses beneath them, rose as dark-green islands in a light-green sea. The memory of that Saturday afternoon is very vivid with me yet. It had been a warm day, and the long, dusty march had been most fatiguing. I was finding some difficulty in arranging hours for Masses, and toward three o'clock I dismounted from my bicycle, sat by the roadside, and wiped my forehead. Everything was intensely quiet; a Sabbath-day stillness was over all the land. It seemed more like a beautiful dream than a reality. For months I had been in the gruesome atmosphere of war, gazing on broken villages, torn roads, and ruined farmlands, walking always in danger and "in the shadow of death" through a country utterly desolate and foully marred by the ingenuity of men. Now my eye was being filled with the beauty of all things around me, of the wonderful things of God.

I picked a wildflower of a variety that grew in profusion along the roadside. It was about one-third the size of a morning glory and somewhat similar in shape. It was white and so delicate that it seemed almost transparent. As I gazed on its wonderful formation, my mind dwelt on God and all the beautiful things He had created; then my thoughts were of the soul and then of my men. Presently the plan of my sermon for the following day was mentally outlined. It was twelve o'clock Saturday night when I finished my work.

LXVI ∽ A New Sheep

I awoke the next morning to the sweet sounds of singing birds, to the glorious view of fresh green fields and peaceful lanes. I rode about three miles on my bicycle to a hamlet called Bailleul-aux-Cornailles where I said Mass at nine o'clock for the Thirteenth Battalion, which was quartered here, and a great number of the French civilian population. The curé of the parish was a soldier in the French army and was on duty in a large military hospital at St. Paul, about fifteen miles away. I made arrangements to be at the parish church certain evenings in the week for confessions. After this Mass I rode four miles further to Ostreville, where I said Mass for the Fourteenth, which was quartered here. The men were all there when I arrived. I found them sitting in the cemetery under century-old trees or along the low stone fence. I preached the same sermon that I had preached for the Thirteenth and it made a remarkable impression upon them. First I spoke to them briefly of the awful scenes we had been witnessing for some time; then I dwelt on the wonderful beauty and peace all around us. God had made the whole world beautiful; we had seen how foully men had marred it. But God's masterpiece of beauty was our own soul, and each one of us knew just how much we had marred that beauty. Then I told those lads that perhaps there were some amongst us who had stained greatly their immortal souls, who had done things for which certain of their friends might despise them, might turn them down. But God, in His infinite love, would not turn them down. God was ready to receive them, to blot out all their iniquities, to cleanse them, to make their souls beautiful again. As I continued, I saw a wonderful sight. I saw tears in the eyes of big, strong men, I saw them bowing their heads as they reached for their khaki handkerchiefs. It was one of the strangest and sweetest experiences I had in the war.

After Mass, when I had got just beyond the village, I dismounted, sat on the side of the road, and began to eat the luncheon I had brought—some sandwiches of cheese and jam and a water bottle full of cocoa. Rye was growing all about me, and it was yet dark green in colour. After I had finished my luncheon, I stood up to measure it and found that it was almost as tall as I. It must have been at least five feet in height. Two or three weeks later I walked along a path through a field of rye, which was so high that I could see only the stalks on either side of me and the heads just above me.

On Monday I learned that we were out for a long rest. Our program included drilling in the mornings and games in the afternoon. From the nature of the drilling, it was clear to all of us that we were training for an attack on Fritz. Part of the morning the men followed the tanks that clanked their ungainly way through beautiful fields of rye and wheat. We did not know till August why they were so ruthlessly destroyed.

One evening while I was sitting in the very small room that was my billet, a stout, red-faced soldier in a rather soiled uniform came in to see me. He saluted and I waited for him to state his business. "Father," he said, "I should like to become a Catholic." "Going to be married?" I questioned. An amused smile stole quietly over his face as he replied: "No, Father. I am already married and have five children." Then it was my turn to smile. I had judged him to be about twenty-two or twenty-three, but now I noticed that his hair was turning grey about the temples. I asked him to sit down, which he did, after removing his military cap. Then I saw that he was quite bald. We commenced instructions, and as the days went by I found him very quick to understand the different things I explained. Now and then he would ask such intelligent questions that I would start involuntarily. At last, I asked him what he did in civil life. "I am a solicitor, Father," he said quietly. I was very much surprised. It had never occurred to me that the soldier sitting before me in his greasy uniform was a lawyer. On June 7, in the little church of Monchy Breton, I baptized him and received him into the church.

LXVII ∿ Notre-Dame d'Ardennes

The soldiers greatly enjoyed the rest in this lovely district. It was very pleasant to bicycle through the country lanes to quaint churches where Catholic lads waited in the evening to go to confession. When I heard confessions for the Thirteenth at Bailleul-aux-Cornailles, I often stopped in the presbytery for tea. The mother and father of the curé lived there. Perhaps I should not say tea, for it was always milk and bread and honey that the kind old people gave me. They had their own apiary in the beautiful garden. The priest's old father was very interesting, and I enjoyed greatly the stories he told me while he sipped his wine and I drank my milk from the large white cup. He had lived in Arras before the war and was eager to hear what I had to tell him of my experiences there. I recall how anxiously he inquired about the church of Notre-Dame d'Ardennes, whether it had been struck.[42] I did not know all the churches of Arras by name, but I was very sorry to say that I thought nearly every one had been struck by the Germans. I could recall but one, which I had passed frequently on my way to the railway station (Gare du Nord), that had not been struck. I went on to describe it—a large red-brick building. "That's it! That's it!" he cried. "It's the

Church of Notre-Dame d'Ardennes." The old man's eyes brightened as he spoke. "Well," I said, "if that is the Church of Notre-Dame d'Ardennes, you need not worry, for it is still standing intact."

The old lady, who sat near me, her hand near enough to the jug of milk to replenish my cup almost as fast as I made room in it for more milk, exchanged looks with her husband, and although neither spoke for a while, there was such significance in their glances that I felt eager to hear the history of Notre-Dame d'Ardennes. I did not have to wait long, for presently the old man began to speak. As I listened, I held the palm of my hand spread wide over the top of my cup, for there was still plenty of milk left, and the kind old mother of the priest was beaming with hospitality; but I felt I could not drink all the milk in the jug!

During the fourth century—to be exact, in the year 371—there had been a severe famine in Arras. The people, being very pious, had recourse to prayer and in answer to their supplications manna fell from heaven. "The sacred Manna," as it was called, was gathered by the people and for a long time some of it was kept and venerated by the people of Notre-Dame d'Ardennes. Then there was "the holy candle," kept in the Church of Notre-Dame d'Ardennes. During a severe epidemic in the year 1105, this wax candle had been sent from heaven to Bishop Lambert. After it had burned for some time, the plague stopped. I had seen many strange things on the Western Front, so that I wondered not that Notre-Dame d'Ardennes was unscathed.

During those beautiful June days, from after Mass till three o'clock P.M., I had not much to do. I usually read books or wrote a little, while I sat under the tall trees in the open field behind the house where I was billeted. One afternoon while I was reading under the trees, a young officer in the tartan of the Sixteenth came up to see me. He was a fine-looking young fellow and had but lately returned to the battalion after a long absence. He was very downhearted and, although not a Catholic, had come to have a talk with me. (Non-Catholics often came to have a talk with me.) He was a captain and had come back expecting to hold his old position in the battalion. But, at times, promotion is rapid in the army and he found that men who were his subordinates when he went away were now of equal or superior rank. His position was now held by one who had come through many conflicts. There was no work for him to do. He felt a stranger among these new officers. He was returning to the officers' reserve.

I listened quietly till he had told me all his troubles. Sometimes it is a relief to have someone listen when one's heart is weighed down, but I am afraid I did not say very much that could help him. Had I possessed the gift of foresight, I could have told this anxious young officer that before three months the officers' ranks would be so thinned that orders would come to him to report for duty immediately at the front. But I did not know then that about the end of September I was to meet him again, coming up a shell-swept road in a terribly devastated countryside, with the eager smile of a boy on his fine young face.

Just beyond where I was billeted stood a large wooden structure that was being used by the YMCA as a moving picture theatre. In the army the name given to these places of amusement was "cinema." During the day the concert party of the Sixteenth was practicing a play, entitled *A Little Bit of Shamrock*, one of the chief characters of which was a priest. George had spoken to me of the play, for he had seen one or two practices. Now, I had seen a play staged by this very cast some time before in which was portrayed a minister, a most effeminate character, whose chief mission, it seemed, was to display a very great ignorance of life in general. The amusement for the audience was furnished by him as often as he was shocked or scandalized. The actor who had taken the part of the minister was now to take the part of the priest.

I went to the director of the company, who was an officer from the Second Division, and told him quietly that I had seen the play his company had put on before, and that I had not admired his clergyman, though I thought the actor had done excellent work. I hoped the character of the priest in the forthcoming play would not be like that. The director looked at me, and I liked the bright smile that spread over his pleasant face. "Don't worry, Padre," he said. "I think you will like Father O'Flynn. I have a lot of friends who are priests. I like them. I always like to talk to priests of your church, Padre. They are—they are—oh,—so *human*, Padre." And then he smiled a guileless smile, so that I understood that by "human" the young officer had meant something complimentary. Many days were to pass before I should see the play.

LXVIII ❧ The Procession

The following story of Murdoch's participation in a Corpus Christi procession in June of 1918 is one of the most foreign incidents in the entire work. At another level, however, it is a most revealing moment. The Feast of Corpus Christi (the Body of Christ) is a Roman Catholic religious observance wherein the consecrated host is publicly paraded and adored. Due to the unavailability of the local priest, Murdoch was asked to participate. He was honoured. A fellow non-Catholic officer, amazed at the elaborate preparations, wondered how Murdoch would know what to do "among these strange people." Murdoch replied that while the people were strange, "the religion was not." This incident reveals the built-in advantage Catholic chaplains had over all varieties of Protestant chaplains serving in France. While France was foreign territory in one sense, in another it was familiar territory, for its people shared the same expression of the Christian religion—they were Roman Catholics. As we have already seen, Murdoch had the added advantage of being able to speak the language. The other less obvious implication is that as a Catholic, Murdoch belonged to an institution that transcended national boundaries. A Canadian Presbyterian minister, for example, was limited in being a cleric of a single and limited Protestant denomination. Murdoch, by contrast, while in the Canadian Army was at the same time an internationally recognized priest of a transnational institution— the worldwide Roman Catholic Church. – RH

Sunday within the octave of Corpus Christi was a beautiful day. Just before I began Mass for the Thirteenth at Bailleul-aux-Cornailles, the father of M. le Curé came in to see me. The usual great procession of the Blessed Sacrament had been planned, but word had come from the parish priest that he could not be present for Mass and that very likely he would not be able to reach the church in time for the procession, which was to start at half past three in the afternoon. If M. le Curé could not come, would M. L'Aumonier [the chaplain] have the goodness, if it would not inconvenience him too much, to carry le Bon Dieu in the procession?

I assured the good people that I would be only too pleased to have the great honour of carrying the Blessed Sacrament in their procession. They promised to send a messenger to let me know whether or not the curé would come for the procession, as they would have definite word by twelve o'clock. At one o'clock, while I was taking lunch, a messenger arrived from Bailleul-aux-Cornailles saying that M. le Curé could not come for the procession and that the whole parish respectfully requested me to carry the Blessed Sacrament.

When I reached the village for a second time that day, I found all along the way evidences of great preparations. On each side of the road approaching the church, for a long distance, at intervals of about twenty feet, saplings of different trees had been placed so that they appeared to be growing there. Little girls, robed in white, were flitting along the road, some carrying banners, others holding decorated baskets of cut flowers. From one side of the road a narrow lane, marched darkly by old trees, led to a brightly decorated altar under a large Calvary. Just opposite the orderly room of the Thirteenth, where the road turned down to the village church, a high green arch had been erected, and on either side appeared in silver letters the words "Panis Angelicus." Alongside the arch was built another repository. While I was admiring this, for there was yet much time, the adjutant of the Thirteenth came down from the orderly room and asked me the meaning of all the great preparations.

When I explained as briefly as possible what was going to take place, he seemed surprised that I was going to take part in the procession. He wondered how it happened that I should know what to do among these strange people. The people were strange, but the religion was not. At half past three, sharp, the procession left the church. It was led by a white-surpliced, red-cinctured sanctuary boy, carrying the processional cross. Behind him walked about a dozen confreres similarly clad; then came the young boys of the parish, with white ribbons on their arms. A lad perhaps eleven years of age followed, clad in the skins of animals and carrying a small cross on which were the words "Ecce Agnus Dei." The little girls, in snow-white dresses, came next, and a few feet behind the column walked a young girl of perhaps fifteen or sixteen, wearing a long cream-coloured dress with white, gold-bordered wings coming out from her shoulders; a band of gold encircled her head, to which was attached a gold star, which shone above her forehead; her right hand was raised and the index finger pointed always toward the sky. Then came four young girls in white carrying on a pedestal the statue of

Our Lady, and four others, bearing on high the statue of the Sacred Heart. The women of the parish, most of them wearing a kind of light-blue badge, were next, followed by the men of the parish, with here and there the blue uniform of a French soldier home on leave. A few khaki-clad lads also walked, but I think they were strangers. (I wondered where my lads of the Thirteenth were.) Then came the choir of middle-aged men singing hymns that today were being sung over all the world: "Lauda Sion Salvatoris," "Pange Lingua," and "Panis Angelicus." Behind these walked six little girls strewing flowers in the way and two sanctuary boys swinging censers. Lastly came four old men, no caps on their venerable heads, bearing on high the white and gold canopy over Jesus Host in the great gold monstrance, carried by a Canadian priest in the beautiful Benediction vestments.

The varicoloured procession went slowly down the village street, banners carried aloft and the beautiful old Eucharistic hymns sounding on the summer air, while very old people and others who for one reason or another could not take part in the procession knelt reverently in the dust on the roadside, as Jesus passed. Then something happened that had never before happened in that little village during a procession of the Blessed Sacrament. Lining each side of the road for quite a distance were men of the Thirteenth Battalion, Catholic and Protestant, and as the procession moved slowly along in all the sweet simplicity of the deep faith of these French peasants, the soldiers stood reverently to attention. I felt proud of these lads. We had met together in many strange places; but I am sure I shall never forget those gay, lighthearted lads standing so quietly and reverently as we passed—Jesus and I!

LXIX ⁓ On Leave

After almost a year in France, Murdoch was finally going on two weeks' leave. Although entitled to leave every six months, he had declined his earlier entitlement. He was now finally off to England. As with all other soldiers proceeding on leave, he relates the long, slow, overnight train ride to the French coast crammed into a boxcar with other soldiers. Once in London, he stayed at the St. Michael's Club, a posh London hotel reserved for priests. He also relates his trip to Bramshott to visit his friend Fr. Knox. While at Fr. Knox's, he received an invitation to stay at the home of the authors Agnes and Egerton Castle, who would later encourage him to write.[43] The most telling chapter of his leave, however, was his return to Parkminster, the monastery of his previous year's retreat. He went seeking peace and quiet; what he found was that such things were now elusive to him. He could "not settle down to the deep quiet of the monastery." Why? "The year at the front had done its work too well." What it had done was not good for his mind or his soul. "I now experienced the effects of that tension which all who have taken part in the World War know so well. A strange restlessness possessed me." Very uncharacteristically for a priest ending a retreat, he confessed that he "felt a distinct relief when my time was up." Murdoch was beginning to exhibit signs of shell shock, what has come to be known as PTSD. What lay in store for him in the next few months would certainly exacerbate his mental state. – RH

I had now been in France about one year and had had no "leave." During this period of the war officers were entitled to leave every six months. I had not applied when the first six months were up, as I was too busy at the time. Now I had applied and daily I was awaiting my warrant. The Sunday following the procession, I had just returned home after Mass when a runner from headquarters arrived to tell me that my warrant had come from brigade headquarters and that if I would call at the battalion orderly room and sign the necessary papers, I could procure it.

I left a little place called Tinques at five o'clock, and although the distance was only fifty miles, it was six o'clock the following morning when we arrived at Boulogne. The "Pullman" was of the side-door variety; sometimes it held eight horses and at other times forty men. It seemed to me, as we sat so closely packed on the floor of the car, as if there were more than forty of us. I sat the whole night long with my chin almost resting on my knees. It would not do to stand, for the space thus made would be quickly filled, so that it would be almost impossible to sit down again. Although many miles away from the sound of the guns and cheered, furthermore, by the thought of fourteen days' leave, I have always felt that that night-ride was one of the hardest of the war, for sitting in that cramped position became actually painful. I longed to stretch my limbs, but this was impossible. It was cold in the car, for the doors were kept open so that we could have air. It is almost incredible how that boxcar bumped us about. But even through these hardships we were compelled to laugh from time to time at some witty joke or at some incident that was funny, though not meant to be so. Once quite an altercation arose between an officer and a private; the officer was accusing the soldier of actually putting his feet in the officer's face. The soldier thus accused was protesting in a very high-pitched voice: "They ain't my feet! They ain't my feet!" Everybody was laughing. Then came the gruff voice of the officer, demanding: "Well, whose feet are they?" But nobody seemed to know whose feet they were.

LXX ~ St. Michael's Club

S t. Michael's Club, 38 Grosvenor Gardens, London, was an ideal hostel for priests, as it was open only to men in Holy Orders. Before the war it had been the city residence of Lady Lovat. But shortly after the commencement of hostilities it had been rented from her by the Duchess of Norfolk and very kindly given over as a club for priests. Though there were many chaplains in the building when I arrived, I was lucky enough to secure an airy room. I actually felt like a boy as I took off my haversack and flung it on the bed, after the hall porter had left the room. It seemed so good to think that for fourteen days the danger of being shot or blown up by shell was very remote. Then there were many friends and brother priests in the house, and outside the door was London, and in London there were lots of bookshops, and to a booklover this meant bliss. The cathedral was but ten minutes' walk from the club, but we had our own little chapel in the building, and the chaplains had the privilege of saying Mass there.

In the smoking room, which was on the ground floor, there were many large and deep-cushioned armchairs that were very comfortable. There was a big open fireplace, and whenever the weather was damp or gloomy outside in the London streets a bright fire burned in it; one could count on there being a fire very often. Sometimes in the evenings it would be very quiet in the great wide room, as the priests sat around reading the evening papers, the only sounds being the occasional crackle of a newspaper as it was turned and the purring of the fire. From outside could be heard faintly the dull roar of the city, made up of a medley of sounds: the rumbling of great elephantine buses that bumped along the streets; the whir of hundreds of taxis spinning along over the pavement; the rattle of wagons and squeaking of innumerable horns. Now and then the house would shake very slightly, though perceptibly, as far below the basement the cars of the underground railway whizzed through the tubes.

I stayed at the club for four or five days and enjoyed very much the time spent there. Bishop Fallon, a Canadian prelate, whose diocese was London, Ontario, was staying at the club. He had but recently returned from a visit to the Canadian soldiers at the front and was soon to go to Rome. I met there, also, the chaplain general to the New York state forces, Monsignor James N. Connolly. He was a most lovable man, and I enjoyed talking to him in the evening. He was vicar-general to the Catholic chaplain-bishop. He gave me his address, Hotel Castiglione, Paris, and told me to call on him if I ever visited that city.

Staying at the club were Irish, English, Scotch, American, Australian, New Zealand, and Canadian priests. And of all the chaplains, I found the Americans the finest. They were lovable, friendly, broad-minded men; one needed only to be in the room a few seconds till he was on speaking terms with the American priest. There was a certain friendliness about him that was irresistible. "I'm Father Whalen, from Dubuque, Father," or, "I'm Father Joyce, from naval headquarters in London, Father," or, "I'm Father Waring from New York City, Father" would greet you on meeting for the first time one of these priests. Whereas an English priest would look at you coldly and perhaps say in a chilly voice, "Good evening, Father." Father Knox came up from Bramshott and invited me down. He said he had a surprise for me. I wondered what it was. Shortly after seeing Father Knox I received an invitation to spend a few days at Anthony Place, Hindhead, Surrey, the country home of Agnes and Egerton Castle, co-authors of many books. Hindhead was only about three miles from Bramshott. I had visited Anthony Place while there. I promised Father Knox to visit Bramshott from Hindhead.

LXXI ∼ Parkminster Again

Father Knox returned to Bramshott the following morning, and in the afternoon, I left for Parkminster. The life at the front had been one of such excitement and turmoil and frequent changes that I longed for quiet and peace. The very day I left for Parkminster, Bishop Fallon and party left by auto for Oxford University. They had invited me to accompany them, but I had already made arrangements to revisit Parkminster and did not wish to change my program. I shall always feel sorry, however, not only that I missed seeing Oxford University, but also that I lost the opportunity of meeting a number of priests whose names were then famous in the literary world, among them Fathers Martindale, Plater, and Ricaby.

It was a beautiful afternoon when I walked up the winding drive that led to the gates of the monastery. This time I was greeted as an old friend. But the aged monk who had been Retreat Master on my former visit did not appear this time. He had been succeeded by an alert young English priest who, I think, had but lately come to the monastery. I missed greatly the dear old priest with whom I had made my former retreat.

This time I did not settle down to the deep quiet of the monastery. The year at the front had done its work too well, and I now experienced the effects of that tension which all who have taken part in the World War know so well. A strange restlessness possessed me, and I felt a distinct relief when my time was up. But a little surprise was awaiting me.

I was told, when about to leave, that the prior wished to see me, and so I waited in the parlour till he came. He was a very tall man, and I think had he followed the routine of life that ordinary mortals follow he would have been fat. But now he was slight. He was from France but had been at Parkminster a number of years. He enquired about my work, and I related some of my military experiences. He took a great interest in all I told him and agreed with me that the war, terrible as it was, was bringing many souls back to God. When I told him of the procession of the Blessed Sacrament at Bailleul-aux-Cornailles, his eyes opened wide and he looked at me strangely, so that for a second or two I became just a little perturbed. "Where," he asked quickly, "did this procession take place?" as if he felt he had not heard aright. "At Bailleul-aux-Cornailles," I repeated. Then he sat back in his chair and the tense look went out of his face and he regarded me smilingly. "Why," he said, "that is my own parish. It was there I was born!" It was now my turn to be surprised, and I am afraid I did not pay very much attention to his words as he continued speaking. I just sat there quietly wondering at the strange things that take place up and down the ways of the world.

LXXII ∾ Another Surprise

F rom Parkminster I went to Hindhead, and I was delighted
with the cordial reception given me by Mr. and Mrs. and Miss
Castle. Their home, almost hidden from the road, looked
down into a valley and then away across a moor that stretched up
and over a long, high hill. I was not the only guest in the house.
There was a private chapel upstairs, and they had been given the
rare privilege of having the Blessed Sacrament reserved in the little
tabernacle. Here I said Mass each morning for the household, and
nearly all went to Holy Communion.

The following morning, I went up to Bramshott to see Father
Knox. He had now a beautiful chapel built near the CWL [Catholic
Women's League] hut under the patronage of St. Peter and St. Paul,
so now the Catholics were no longer obliged to use the garrison
church hut. After I had talked with him for a while, he told me to
go alone to the hospital, which was just a few hundred feet away.
Somebody wished to see me in Ward 18, bed 20. "You will see what
you will see," said Father Knox enigmatically, as he followed me to
the door.

This is what I saw after I had entered Ward 18 and had walked
a few steps down the aisle. A young fellow was sitting up in bed 20,
his finger marking the place in a little black book with red edges, his
eyes smiling a friendly greeting. But who was he? I approached still
nearer. Then I recognized him. It was the Spanish lad who had come
to Father Knox's room about one year and a half before to tell him
that he had lost the faith and was no longer a Catholic. He seemed
glad to see me and held my hand after he had shaken it. I also was
very pleased to see him, for the strained look that I had noticed
when I first met him had gone from his eyes, and instead there was
a look of real joy there. The little book he held in his hand was *The
Imitation of Christ.* "It is all right! It is all right!" he kept repeating,
as he smiled up into my face. "I have gone to communion. I have
made peace. I am very glad." I, too, was very glad. I had thought

of him often and had asked other priests to bring him back. And here he was now, safe in his Father's house! The strayed sheep had come back into the fold. Not for a long time had I felt so happy! I remember now, as I returned to Anthony Place that day, while walking along a secluded part of the way, twirling my cane around my fingers as the drum major does at the head of a procession.

LXXIII ⌖ Back to the Battalion

Upon his return from leave, Murdoch found a large pile of correspondence awaiting him. This would have included letters from his parents, but also letters from relatives (wives and mothers) of deceased soldiers to whom he had, in his capacity as chaplain, written. This was one of the crucial services provided by the chaplains— information concerning the circumstances of a soldier's death. The government sent a stark, terse telegram; chaplains and nurses sent a personal letter. Murdoch quotes at length the letter from Captain E. W. Waud's widow thanking him for his detailed and consoling correspondence. Murdoch also relates his most unsettling task of having to inform a serving soldier of his mother's death back home. In this instance the soldier was an American serving in the Canadian Army. It is worth noting that Murdoch goes out of his way to draw attention to the wartime plight of mothers and wives throughout the conflict. Juxtaposed next to the marching bands, fluttering flags, and boisterous send-offs were the silent, empty rooms and the long vigils awaiting news. He ends, "And I thought how many women there must be over the world bearing great sorrows, but the eyes of the world were not focused on these." Note that Murdoch's comment embraces not only Canadian and Allied mothers and wives, but the enemies' as well—his perspective deliberately transcends both national boundaries and warring sides. - RH

The men were never told on coming back from leave where they might find their battalion, and when the troops were on the move, often a soldier was put to very great inconvenience trying to reach his unit. I, however, was in great good luck, for just at the base of Mont-Saint-Éloi, while the train stopped, I noticed some of the soldiers of the Sixteenth standing nearby. I called one of them and asked the whereabouts of the battalion. "Just over here in Écoivres, sir," he said. I stepped out of the train and in twenty minutes was sitting in the transport mess talking of my leave.

I had found my friends in England somewhat downhearted, which was but natural considering the great losses the British army had sustained during the recent German advances. On all sides one heard only gloomy forebodings as to future attacks. But back again among the gruesome scenes of devastation and ruin, I was struck more than ever by the buoyancy and lightheartedness of the troops. Here were no gloomy forebodings, but on all sides were friendly faces, and the air was merry with sounds of whistling, singing, bugle calls, practicing bands, and good-natured banter. Of one thing I felt sure—old "Major Gloom" did not belong to the Third Canadian Brigade!

After I had talked awhile with the quartermaster and transport officer, my mail was brought in. It was very large, the accumulation of two weeks. It was a long while before I had finished reading all the letters. The transport officer had gone outside, but the quartermaster was in the room adjoining the mess, from which came now and then little explosions of partly suppressed laughter. And whilst I read my letters, I wondered what was the cause of the mirth. In a little while the quartermaster came out of the room and stopped in passing to ask me if I had ever read *Seventeen* by Booth Tarkington.[44] Indeed, I had, and I wondered no longer why sounds of laughter had drifted out to me.

Among my letters were a few edged in black. One of these, heavily crossed by a blue pencil, was registered, and when I opened it a ten-dollar bill dropped to the table. I had been accustomed to receiving many letters edged in black, answers to those I had written to next of kin at home, telling them of the death of dear ones and how they had been prepared to meet God. It was not often, however, that they came registered. But as I read the letter, I forgot altogether that a ten-dollar bill had dropped from it and was now lying on the table.

The letter was from the wife of Captain Waud, the young officer who had fallen at the head of his men—he who had knelt so reverently with them to receive Holy Communion that day in New Plymouth Cave. It was not only a beautiful letter, with a deep note of Catholic faith sounding throughout it, but it told me something of the young officer that I had not known. He had not always been a Catholic. I learned from the letter that he had been wounded previously. "You know, he did not have to go back to France," wrote Mrs. Waud, "but duty called, so I let him go with as brave a heart as I could and brought my little son home. I had prayed so that my husband would be spared to me, but indeed God knows best and He is helping me now. Everything of that last day is comforting and very beautiful. And although the heartache and longing will not leave, I feel that I have a great deal to be thankful for. I am enclosing a little offering for whatever lies near your heart. It is little and I wish it were more. I thank you for all you have done for my husband, and indeed I will pray for your lads. Trusting that you will remember me, and that God will give me the grace to do my duty as worthily as my husband did his, I am, gratefully yours, Ruth Waud."

For a long time, I sat there thinking of the letter I held in my hand and then of other letters that had come to me from time to time. And I thought how many women there must be over the world bearing great sorrows, but the eyes of the world were not focused on these! They were on the battalions that had marched away to the war while flags fluttered, and bands played, and people cheered. They watched the papers for accounts of great deeds of arms. But whenever I read such letters, my thoughts would go back to the roads over which the soldiers had marched so bravely away, and I would see figures leaning over gates, white handkerchiefs held to eyes that had strained down the white dusty road over which their soldier sons or husbands had marched away. They would go back into silent rooms where so many little things would remind them of their men. Then, as the days would pass, to many would come words to chill the heart and make homes desolate: "Killed in Action." Whenever I wrote to these poor mothers or wives, I would see a great lonely hill, on which stood a cross whereon was nailed a scourged, thorn-crowned Figure whose eyes rested with great pity on one who stood below—the Mater Dolorosa. It was on her feast, the Feast of the Seven Dolors, that the bishop had decided I should go to the war, and perhaps it was she who helped me to write the letters of sympathy that brought comfort to so many sorrowful hearts. With the ten-dollar bill I bought comforts for the men.

LXXIV ∾ No Man's Land Again

I was billeted in a little hut with the billeting officer. It was a very tiny hut, with two berths in it, one above the other. As I was on leave when the battalion came to Écoivres, no provision had been made for me, so I was obliged to share the billeting officer's hut, which he so kindly offered. He was a genial companion, but he used to sit up very late at night puzzling over a chessboard. He was playing a game of chess with a partner who was actually residing in England, and every night, after great puzzling over the board, he was obliged to write the result of his efforts to his partner in England. One evening—I suppose it was his partner's turn to play and it was for this reason that his chessboard was idle—he took his Bible from his table and said, naively, "Now, Padre, I won't try to change your views, and you won't try to change mine, but just take your Bible, and I will read certain passages from mine, and you will read the same passages from yours." I could not help smiling, as I reached for my Bible, at the thought of the billeting officer not wishing to change my views, for these words had just come to my mind: "Upon this rock I will build My Church."

I can't recall the texts he picked out and asked me to read from my Bible, but I remember that each one seemed contrary to the teachings of the Catholic Church on the subject treated. As everyone familiar with the Douai-Rheims version of the Bible knows, there are little notes on texts that might be disputed, giving the true meaning and also reference to other texts that would prove the teaching. Glancing at the footnote, I would give the true interpretation and then refer the amateur exegete to the other texts. In a little while he closed his Bible. "Why, Padre," he exclaimed, "you know the whole Bible by heart!" "Well," I said modestly, as I suppressed a desire to smile, "I don't think I know it by heart, but you know, it is my business to teach the truths that are in it"—but I did not mention the footnotes!

The following morning the billeting officer came hurriedly into the room. "Padre," he said, "we are leaving here tomorrow night for the trenches. We're taking over the line in front of Monchy."

For just a second or two a peculiar numbness seemed to spread through every nerve in my body: it was nothing new, however, for years before, when a boy at the public school, after the teacher had opened the drawer in her desk and removed a black, snake-like piece of leather, and had said quietly, "Bennie Murdoch, come up here," this strange numbness had come over me together with a slight contraction of the muscles of the throat. But it quickly passed, and after I had swallowed once or twice to make sure of my throat, I said the obvious thing: "Well, that means another move!"

Going into the trenches was not the only hard piece of work I had to do. A very difficult task was before me, though I did not know it till I went up to the mess for lunch. Three or four letters were lying near my plate. One envelope was much larger than the others and bore in the upper left-hand corner the words "Assembly Chamber, State of New York, Albany" and beneath, was the address of Joseph V. McKee, 890 East 176th St., New York City, the brother of one of my "Canadians" who was an American by birth and had lived all his life in the United States. There were many such in the Third Brigade—Private McKee was in the Fifteenth Battalion. I knew him well, and he was one of my best Catholics. I opened the letter and began to read it, and as I did I felt that I was turning sick. The letter contained a request that I please notify Private McKee that his mother had departed this life.

After lunch I left on foot for Anzin, for I had learned that the Fifteenth Battalion was quartered there. It was a distance of only three miles, yet it was one of the hardest journeys I ever made in France. Life at the front was very hard for these lads, but it was always brightened by the hope of finally seeing the dear ones at home.

It had not been very long before that Private McKee had spoken to me of his mother. One of the loveliest things in this world is the love of a good man for his mother. Every step was bringing me nearer the lad, and I so dreaded the thought of telling him! My head began to pain, and I went back in memory to the first time I was called on to break sorrowful news. I had been a priest just a little over a year when one night the telephone bell rang, and a trembling voice told me one of my men had been killed by a falling log. There were fifteen men in the small railway station where the voice was coming from: they were only about two hundred yards from the house where lived the widow of the man that was killed, and I was six miles away. Yet not one would break the terrible news. I was implored to come.

I shall never forget that night. A full moon was throwing its light over all the white land, darkened here and there by a clump of green, white-patched trees, but the thought of what I had to do had numbed me to all sense of beauty. And as I drove along, even the horse seemed to feel what terrible work had to be done, for once he actually stopped in the road and I had difficulty in starting him; yet I could see no reason for his having stopped.

As I walked along, dreading all the time what was before me, I noticed that the soldiers who were quartered along the road wore the purple patch of the Fifth Division. They were artillerymen. Then a sign on a door of a shell-torn house told me that an RC chaplain dwelt within. I inferred that it was Father MacPherson, the Fifth Divisional Artillery chaplain, one of the holiest priests in France; often I had seen him kneeling down in a dugout or some poor billet reading his breviary. I knocked on the door and was shown up to Father MacPherson's room, and the sight of his pleasant, kindly face did me good. I told him of the task I had to perform. He spoke sympathetically and invited me to call in on my return and have tea with him.

After leaving Father MacPherson, the thought of what I had to do did not weigh so heavily. Perhaps it was that the prayers of the good priest I had just left followed me. They told me at the Fifteenth Battalion orderly room that Private McKee was quarantined—the "flu" was now becoming quite prevalent among the men. I found him sitting in a bell tent, one of a group pitched in a large garden of a château. I called him, and when he came, we walked up and down a long garden path under the trees while I broke as gently as I could the terrible news I had for him. He took it well—took it bravely and quietly like the good soldier he was, with great submission to the holy will of God, like the good Catholic his dear mother had brought him up to be. I talked with him a little while, and when I left I asked Our Lady of the Seven Dolors to stay with the lad and to comfort him.

LXXV ⁓ No Man's Land

In late July 1918 Murdoch underwent another intense period of shelling—this time while underground in a captured German dugout. Awakened from a deep sleep by a German box barrage, he awoke "trembling violently...not sure whether through cold or fear." Once he moved about a little and spoke with his fellow officers, his trembling ceased. They then passively waited for the German assault, which, if it came, meant almost certain death by explosives tossed down the dugout shaft. Thankfully, the assault never materialized. As a counterpoint to this very dramatic event and illustrative of the alternating terror and mundaneness of war, Murdoch next relates watching a local French woman make bread. By this device of literary juxtaposition, Murdoch imitates in print how his war experience was a roller coaster of both terror and trivia. – RH

The following day we took over the line just before Monchy. The quartermaster, transport officer, and I had a nice little mess at Berneville, near Arras. I was billeted with the curé of Berneville, and he proved a friendly old man. His old sister was housekeeper for him. She was very kind, and George received many cups of hot coffee.

It did not happen very often that battalion headquarters were in the front-line trench, yet it so happened when we were at Monchy. Indeed, the first night, on going up to the trenches, I actually walked through No Man's Land in order to reach headquarters' dugout. It was a part of the line that we had retaken from the Germans, and for this reason the opening of the shaft leading down to the dugout faced the German front instead of our own back area.

The second night I spent in the line at Monchy I was awakened suddenly by a terrific bombardment by the Germans. The dugout was shaking from the concussion of the shells bursting on the ground above us. I had been sleeping fully dressed and with my trench coat on, for although it was July it was very cold underground. My bed was a berth of meshed wire stretched between rough scantling—nothing else, not even a blanket; my pillow was my haversack. When I awoke I was trembling violently, I was not sure whether through cold or fear. Yet after I stood up and walked up and down a little while talking to the officers, I ceased to tremble.

The Germans were putting on a box barrage, that is, they were bombarding us in such a way that the shells were dropping behind us and to our left and right, so that we could not retreat and no troops could come to our aid. The only way open to approach us was from the German trenches opposite, by way of No Man's Land. This was the way the Germans would be coming presently, either to order us up or to throw bombs or tubes of amenol down to blow us into minutest fragments.[45] We talked quietly as we waited there at bay, but we were all a little nervous. I shall never forget those minutes we spent there, caught like rats in a trap.

We waited and waited; the very atmosphere of the dugout seemed heavy and sickening. Then suddenly the bombarding ceased. Surely, Fritz had not changed his mind; it was always under cover of his own artillery fire that he made his advances or raids. We became a little cheerful. Finally, after half an hour of quiet we concluded that for some unknown reason Fritz had decided not to come. Then, our hearts filled with relief, we sat about the candle-lit dugout chatting like happy boys on their way home for vacation.

The following morning, with God's beautiful sunlight over all the land, I stepped out into No Man's Land with Colonel Peck and we took a little walk. Beautiful red flowers resembling in size and shape the sweet pea, only they were short-stemmed and in clusters, grew near an old pile of stones. It was the first time I had ever seen flowers growing in No Man's Land, and I began to pick a few. The colonel, however, told me to hurry. Indeed, it was no place to loiter, for although No Man's Land was very wide here, one could see the parapets of the German trenches.

LXXVI ∼ Cambligneul

Here we came for a week's rest after our turn in the line. We little knew then what strenuous days were before us, nor what terrible toll was to be taken of our ranks before we would rest again. It was a very pretty countryside, though not so open as the area we had occupied in June. It was now the end of July, and although my troops were scattered over very wide areas, I managed to do good work with the Thirteenth and Fourteenth. Indeed, one evening I found 125 lads of the Fourteenth waiting for me in a quaint little church at a place called Chelers, or Villers-Châtel. This was indeed extraordinary for an evening during the week, when there was no hint of our soon leaving for the front line. The Fifteenth and Sixteenth had not been having a very good chance of late to go to confession. Whenever the four battalions were separated, I always gave the Thirteenth and Fourteenth the preference for Masses, as there were more Catholics in either one of these than in the Fifteenth and Sixteenth together. These two latter battalions were often obliged to attend the village Mass said by the curé of the parish in which they happened to be.

August came, and the rich promise that was over all the land in June was now being fulfilled: great brown stacks of hay, like dark hillocks, stood over all the green land, and here and there were large golden patches of rye, weighted and bent low with the full kernels, so that now they were not much higher than my waist. In fields and gardens were low bivouacs, about three feet in height, where soldiers slept at night.

Cambligneul was a very small village and had no resident priest but was served from Camblain-l'Abbé, which was only about a mile and a half distant. I was billeted in a farmhouse not far from the church. The old lady of the house resembled very much the wife of the captain in "The Katzenjammer Kids."[46]

One rainy afternoon the old lady made bread, and as I had never seen bread made in France, I was very interested in the process. It was a different one than that employed in country houses at home. The old lady mixed the dough in a large trough-like affair that resembled a half-barrel that had been cut horizontally on a wood-horse. Into this was poured a great quantity of flour and water, which the capable arms of "mamma Katzenjammer" worked quickly into dough. When it was kneaded sufficiently, an iron door was opened in a large brick oven, and from it a few embers were quickly drawn. This part of the process surprised me very much as I did not know that a wood fire had actually been made in the oven. Then the old lady took a long-handled, flat wooden shovel that stood near the kneaded dough, which had not been set to rise but had been placed on paper in flat wicker baskets. She picked up each basket and upset the dough on the shovel; each basket contained just enough dough to cover the shovel and still be about two inches in thickness. The shovel was pushed far into the oven and then with a quick jerk by the experienced hands of old Madame, was drawn out empty. When all the dough in the baskets had been put in the oven, the door was closed, and if I remember rightly, it was two hours before the oven was opened again. It was George who came to tell me that Madame was going to open the oven. I went out just in time to see the old lady pull to the front of the oven by means of a long-handled hook the great flat loaves of dark-brown bread. There were fifteen loaves in all, about one foot and a half in diameter and two inches deep. It was very good bread, as I discovered when I tasted some the following day.

Before the following Sunday, orders came to march. First we went to Berneville, and on Saturday, after I had arranged for church service for Sunday, we were moved to Lattre-Saint-Quentin. The other battalions were quartered in the same area. It was late

Saturday night when I finished organizing for Sunday, but the services were not to be. More marching orders came. We were to leave in the morning at five o'clock for Avesnes-le-Comte, where we were to entrain, destination not given. The hour had struck; big things were before us.

LXXVII ⁓ A New Front

Although impossible to know at the time, "big things" were indeed afoot! The great Canadian victory at Amiens was about to occur. This surprise attack launched the famous One Hundred Days Offensive that would culminate in the armistice of November 11, 1918. The battle and its location were a tightly kept secret. Murdoch soon learned that the entire 3rd Brigade was on the move. As the journey took days, Murdoch sought to minister to his scattered battalions as they travelled. His attempts, however, only brought him confusion, indecision, near panic, and a head-first spill off his bicycle. That his reaction was more intense than might otherwise have been expected may well be a reflection of his altered mental state. It is interesting to note that as the suspense mounts, Murdoch references the comic strip The Katzenjammer Kids as well the popular song "Roses are Blooming in Picardy," thereby easing the narrative tension. Eventually, the 3rd Brigade arrived at their destination of Boves, just outside Amiens. Murdoch could now minister to his men. Everyone knew that a major battle lay ahead. As Murdoch notes, the troops could always tell "by the quantities of strawberry jam they received two or three days preceding action." Murdoch heard confessions non-stop for five hours the evening of August 5. Although most satisfied with his work, afterward he was exhausted. Murdoch had fasted all day and had not slept much over the preceding days. He records swaying as he walked. Seeing this, his batman, George, fed him and put him to bed. Murdoch slept for ten and a half hours straight. He woke on August 7; the battle of Amiens would begin before dawn the following morning. – RH

It was half past three Sunday morning when I awoke. I dressed quickly, went down to the little church, and said Mass. When I left the church, the road was filled with soldiers moving in different directions, carrying mess tins of steaming porridge, across the top of which was placed some bread and butter with a strip of fried bacon; in the other hand was the cover of the mess tin filled with hot tea. They were all joking and in excellent spirits, yet before the following Sunday...

We entrained between eight and nine o'clock, and all day long there was great speculation as to our destination. Some thought that the division was returning to the Ypres salient; others guessed that we were on our way up to the North Sea coast. Later in the day it was rumoured that we were going to Étaples, where there was to be more drilling. For awhile it seemed that we were returning to the area about Étaples. But toward evening we knew the truth; we were coming into the area on the Somme.

It was late in the evening when we detrained, and to this day I do not know the name of the place. We took supper and then began to march. We crossed the Somme River and then in the darkness went through what seemed to be a very pretty country, one more wooded than I had yet seen in France. And as we went on and on under ancient, wide-spreading trees, I began to wish it had been daylight, for surely it must have been some famous forest of France. There had either been come confusion of orders or else our guides did not know the way, for we spent the whole night marching over dark roads, through quiet villages and dense forests. One little scene stands out in my memory quiet vividly. We had been marching for a long time when the order came ringing through the darkness: "Fall out!" The men fell out and immediately began to sit around on the damp earth; a fine mist of rain had been falling for some time. Permission was given to smoke, and presently hundreds of tiny red circles glowed in the darkness of the forest. "Where are we now?" someone asked. Of course he was bombarded with replies, but none of them proved correct; indeed, many went very wide of the mark as they meant to do, for they were names of Canadian towns or counties.

Presently I noticed the white circle of light from a flashlamp move over a field map spread out on the ground, and in the relative silence that had now ensued I listened intently, as the low murmur of the voices of the officers regarding the map came to my ears. They mentioned the name of some place, but I did not catch it; then one officer spoke louder, so that I heard it quite distinctly: "It's Picardy we are now in, Picardy." He stopped speaking, and from the opposite side of the glade came the sound of a murmured conversation. It ceased, and in the silence a wonderful clear voice began to sing softly, yet not so low but that all could hear, the song "Roses are Blooming in Picardy." I had never heard the song before. It seemed fitting for that young soldier to be singing there in the damp forest while his companions listened and joined in the chorus. I suppose for many of those brave young lads who sang, the words had a special significance. We kept marching slowly and resting; five o'clock showed on our wristwatches. Then we came to our halting-place.

It was a strange little village to which we came. Perhaps I should not say that it was "strange," for it was built like all other farming villages of France, but the people were strange: they had never seen Canadian soldiers before, and only rarely since the beginning of the war had they seen the soldiers of their own country. All the people turned out to see us as if a circus had come to town. The soldiers were treated with very much more consideration than they had been accustomed to, and the prices in the village stores were extremely low.

I slept a few hours and then took my bicycle and went out to try to find the Fifteenth Battalion. I could get no information from the orderly room. Everything was being done with the utmost secrecy; we might move at any time. But George, ever-faithful George, told me he had seen the Fifteenth transport officer going to a little village said to be only three miles distant. I started but found progress very difficult once I had left the village. The gentle mist of rain that had been falling through the night had increased toward morning and caused the wet, oily clay to adhere to the tires of my bicycle; sometimes the wheels skidded, and sometimes I was obliged to dismount and remove the clay that clung so tenaciously to the fork above the front wheel. Once I saw a number of the Thirteenth going toward a village on my right. After I had passed them I became worried. I was not sure of finding the Fifteenth, but I felt that I could reach the billets of the Thirteenth by following the lads I had just seen. I continued a little farther on my way, still thinking of the

Thirteenth. I dismounted, turned, and began to ride in the direction the Thirteenth soldiers had gone. I had not gone far, however, when I began to think that after all the Fifteenth had much greater need of my services than the Thirteenth; for all I knew then, we might be in the line that very night. I stopped again in the road and stood by my bicycle. Never in my life had I felt such indecision, but it was serious work I had to do—perhaps by tomorrow many of the lads would be killed. And here was I standing in the road almost in a panic—doing nothing!

I now began to pray to the Little Flower. I had never prayed to her before; the Blessed Virgin had always looked after all my wants. I remounted and presently I was going down a long hill very swiftly, finding great difficulty in managing my wheel. Just when I was halfway down I met a runner of the Sixteenth. He had passed me before I could stop, so I turned my head a little to call to him. The next thing I knew I had shot completely over my machine and was on my hands and knees on the road, a severe pain in one of my knees. The runner turned quickly, a look of concern in his eyes; but I had twisted my face into a smile and his face brightened. He pointed out a clump of trees on the opposite hill and told me I would find the Fifteenth there. I did and gave some of them Communion.

LXXVIII ⁓ Boves

I returned to the Sixteenth and succeeded in giving Holy Communion to a few soldiers, among whom was the solicitor whom I had baptized at Monchy Breton. But I was by no means pleased with my day's work, for I had not gotten all the Catholics in each battalion. At six o'clock we left this area, and toward morning, after marching continuously, were met by a long line of buses that brought us through the city of Amiens to within three or four miles of Boves. We marched for nearly two hours and about ten o'clock came into the city of Boves, from which all the inhabitants had gone. I was very tired and hungry, but I had not broken my fast, for I wished to say Mass, if I could find time, in order that I might offer it for the success of my work among the soldiers. I easily found the church of Boves, and just as I entered, met a chaplain of the French Army coming out. I saluted and told him who I was. He was a friendly priest and had one of the kindest faces I have ever seen. We talked for a little while, then, as there was no parish priest at Boves, he came back to the sacristy to show me where to find things. Then he served my Mass.

I had lunch in the mess of the French chaplain, after which I went out into the highways and byways seeking my men. I had excellent news. The whole Third Brigade was billeted in the city. This was the first time since March 28 that I could remember having all my units together. Not content with announcing confessions at the orderly rooms of the different battalions, fearing there might be some miscarriage of orders and that some of the men might not be notified, I went all over the city visiting them. It had not been very long since the majority had gone to confession, yet I wished to give everyone an opportunity. I had learned at brigade headquarters that the battalions would not go into the trenches till ten o'clock that night.

At five o'clock, when I entered the church of Boves, I was somewhat nervous. At Mass that morning I had forgotten to look in the ciborium to see how many consecrated Hosts there were. I went straight to the altar, opened the tabernacle door, took out the ciborium, and opened it. As I feared, there would not be enough Particles for one-tenth the number I expected! I closed the door softly, saying a little prayer as I did so, and walked back to the confessional in the rear of the church, for the men were beginning to arrive. I had not reached the confessional when I noticed the French chaplain coming into the church. I went to him quietly and made known to him what I had learned from my visit to the tabernacle. He was sympathetic and immediately began to think what we could do. First, he thought of saying Mass, although it was then five o'clock in the afternoon and he had broken his fast;

it seemed, however, to each of us that he would be quite justified in so doing. Then suddenly he remembered a convent chapel, about seven kilometres distant, where he felt sure there would be a ciborium with a sufficient number of consecrated Hosts. He said he would go on horseback. Seldom have I felt more grateful than I did to him that night. I began to hear confessions, and the lads came in great numbers. Soon the light became dim in the great church, and lads who had come first began to be a little restless: they wondered why I did not give them Holy Communion.

It was now becoming so dark that I could just distinguish the crowds of kneeling soldiers. I was hearing confessions very quickly. Once a fellow knocked on the confessional door and told me he hoped I would soon give Communion, as he had some things to do before going into the line. He had now been waiting a long time, he said. I asked him if he could wait a few minutes longer, as time was so precious and such crowds of men were coming that I did not wish to leave my confessional for a minute. I was praying between the drawing of slides for the appearance of the French chaplain. No soldier had yet left the church, yet I feared they might. Then away up in the sanctuary I noticed a little flame flash out in the darkness and then move quickly to one side of the tabernacle, where it touched the responsive wick of a candle and another gleam of light shot up, then, on the other side of the tabernacle, the other candle flashed. As I heard the slow moving of many feet towards the altar-rail, I thanked God.

For a long while the priest, after placing two lighted candles on the sanctuary railing, moved up and down between them dispensing the Bread of the Strong to those Canadian soldiers. When all who were ready had received, he put the ciborium in the tabernacle and knelt to pray till I had prepared more lads for him. I did not move from my confessional till after ten o'clock, and it was after this hour before I left, for still men came. They were now coming fully equipped for battle, hoping to catch up with their companions, who must have already left. When the last man had been shriven, the chaplain came down to have a little talk with me. I was almost overcome as I thanked him for what he had done, for I was now beginning to be very tired. "Well," he said, with a beaming face, "are you happy? Are you happy?" "Happy?" I repeated. "Indeed, I am, for wonderful things have been done tonight for God!"

As I walked down to my billet that night I was swaying, as I went, from sheer exhaustion; I tried to recall when it was that I had a night's sleep. It seemed months, yet it was but a few days. My billet was upstairs in a house that had not been struck by enemy fire. George met me at the door and told me to go to my room, that he would bring my dinner. I stumbled upstairs, for I was weak with hunger and fatigue. I sat in a chair and was almost falling asleep when George came in with a large granite plate filled with roast beef, mashed potatoes, and green peas. He had kept it hot for me. I picked up the knife and fork and they seemed heavy. George began to arrange my bed. New strength came as I ate the excellent food— we were always well fed before a battle; in fact, the men could always foretell a battle by the quantities of strawberry jam they received two or three days preceding action. I had not finished the meat and vegetables when the cook himself came up with some strawberry jam, little cakes, and a huge granite mug of hot cocoa. When I had finished the cocoa, I can just remember George saying, "Hadn't you better take off your boots, sir?" And the next thing I knew it was broad daylight, and as I looked at my wristwatch, the hands pointed to half past ten A.M. I had slept about ten and one-half hours.

I had learned the preceding night that the battle would not begin till very early in the morning of August 8. It had taken, I supposed, the whole night for the troops to assemble. Very likely they would sleep or rest today. There was no need for me to go up till evening. I looked about the room. The dinner dishes had been removed and so had my boots, but with the exception of boots and leggings I was completely dressed. It did not take me very long to put on my boots and shave, yet it was twelve o'clock when I came out of the church of Boves after I had said Mass. That evening, August 7, I went up to Gentelles Wood.

LXXIX ⁓ The Battle of Amiens

Murdoch devotes a disproportionate amount of space in The Red Vineyard to describing the events of the last hundred days of the Great War. Comprising just over three months of his thirty-one months of service, he devotes fully 20 percent of The Red Vineyard to this one-hundred-day period. The reasons for this are clear—it was by far the most intense period of the war for the Canadian Corps, the 3rd Brigade, and personally for Murdoch as a chaplain. Fully 30 percent of the total casualties suffered by the Canadian Corps through the entire war were sustained in this short period.[47] Victories were won and great progress was made in driving back the German forces but at a very high cost in wounded and dead Canadians. Furthermore, as opposed to earlier in the conflict, when chaplains were ordered to remain in the rear areas, by this stage of the war chaplains went forward with the attacking forces. Murdoch was found forward, working with the field ambulances under steady shellfire, caring for the wounded, and ministering to the dying. Given the fluid nature of open warfare, he even found himself exposed and under direct enemy fire.

The first battle of what became the One Hundred Days Offensive began on August 8 with a massive artillery barrage at 4:20 A.M. Shortly after, the wounded began streaming in to the field ambulance to which Murdoch was attached. His work was "among the wounded, hearing confessions, giving Holy Communion, anointing those mortally wounded, and taking messages for dear ones at home." Despite the language barrier, his task included ministering to dying German Catholics, many of whom he absolved and anointed and to whom he administered Holy Communion. After describing his work among the German wounded, he summarizes the result: "Many lads were ushered up to the gates of heaven that day." The next day, Murdoch and his batman, George, moved forward, following the attacking troops. The signs of advance were everywhere: "broken war-wagons of every description, dead Germans and dead Canadians, deep shell holes, shattered buildings, and always in the air with the dust that rose from the busy road were the odours of gas and sulphur." The Canadians would fight in the Amiens region for three weeks. In *this new "open warfare," there were no trench systems in which to shelter, so while out of action, the men were hidden in apple orchards and any location that would afford screening from searching German bombers. Nonetheless "most every evening we were bombed." – RH*

I t was a wonderful sight that met the eye as George and I left Boves that evening and turned our steps toward the battleground. The artillery had assembled, and on all sides were great guns in cuttings of embankments or hidden in woods or camouflaged in the open. At times the roads were blocked with the heavy lines of traffic, but as we drew nearer the line, the movement was not so great; yet coming through fields and woods were the huge, clanking tanks. There must have been at least one hundred of them careening along up hill and down dale. Nothing seemed to be able to stop their unwieldy bulk. I learned afterwards that great bombing planes had swooped low over Fritz's trenches, making a great noise so as to deaden the sounds of the assembling tanks.

I did not sleep at all that night. Indeed, very few slept, for during the night the troops were taking their place for the assault, and it was not till 2:10 A.M. that the assembly was complete. At 4:10 A.M., August 8, a terrific crash of heavy and light guns broke the silence of the dawn on a twenty-mile front. I had never before been in a great battle and was not prepared for action on such a stupendous scale. The earth seemed to be rocking. The full-leaved treetops of Gentelles Wood behind us twisted and broke, as shells from our back areas shrieked their way toward Fritz's line. I stood for awhile waiting for Fritz's "comeback," but the Germans had been so completely surprised by the unexpected bombardment that their artillery gave but a very faint-hearted reply. On seeing this we felt that victory was assured. I did not have long to watch the tide of battle, for presently a long line of stretcher-bearers, their burdens raised shoulder-high, told me my work was to begin.

All day long I walked up and down among the wounded, hearing confessions, giving Holy Communion, anointing those mortally wounded, and taking messages for dear ones at home. Among the dying were many Germans, and a number of these were Catholics. I knew only one sentence in German—"Sind sie Katholisch?" "Are you a Catholic?"—but it was sufficient, for I understood when the reply was "Yes," or "No." When a German would say he was a Catholic, I would put on my stole, open my little ciborium, hold up the Sacred Host, and then I would look at him. Always his two hands would fold, and I would wait kneeling by his side till he had finished his act of contrition; then I would give him Holy Communion. It was a beautiful sight to see the tears of gratitude come into the eyes of those dying Germans after they had received their Lord; and after I had anointed them, invariably they reached out and gripped my hand before passing out. Many lads were ushered up to the gates of heaven that day.

The following morning, George and I went up to Caix. My own brigade was now out of the fight for a while, but I was following with the Second Field Ambulance. For a long time we waited on the side of the road, as the place we intended to hold for an advanced dressing station had not yet been taken. About 1:10 P.M., I stood on a hill and watched the men of the First Brigade come up into action. An Irish chaplain whom I had once met at St. Michael's Club was riding behind them. He told me that he had just given them a general absolution. All that afternoon, and late into the evening, I worked with the Second Field Ambulance. A great number of wounded passed through. Once some enemy airplanes swooped low and dropped bombs amongst us, but they failed to kill anyone. We were now in open warfare, and for the first time I saw the cavalry in action. They came cantering across an open field, their spears, held at their sides, pointing heavenwards; ribbons fluttered from the long handles, and the burnished points flashed in the sunlight.

That evening I was relieved by Father Locharay, and I found a small dugout where I got a few hours of sleep.

LXXX ❧ At the Wayside

Early in the morning George and I left to find the Sixteenth, which had passed through in the evening. We anticipated some trouble, for to find one's battalion after an attack is not the easiest thing in the world. However, we saw the Sixteenth Battalion water cart in the great procession that filled the road before us, so, keeping our eyes on it, we slipped in behind a transport wagon and followed along on the right side of the road. We went slowly, and at times halted for five and sometimes ten minutes. Now and again some of the horses in the procession, as we passed dead horses on the side of the road, would begin side-stepping in their fear, and this would interfere somewhat with the progress of the line.

We had been walking with many halts for over an hour, and I remember how surprised I was that our soldiers had advanced so far. All the marks of the advance were along the way: broken war-wagons of every description, dead Germans and dead Canadians, deep shell holes, shattered buildings, and always in the air mingled with the dust that rose from the busy road were the odours of gas and sulphur. We had been walking on the right of the procession, and to this day I cannot say why I decided to change my place. For no reason that I can remember, I stepped in front of a team of mules hitched to a general service wagon and crossed to the left of the road. Then I noticed two soldiers approaching carrying a wounded comrade on a stretcher. I am certain that if I had not crossed to the left of the road, I would not have noticed them. Just as the lads came alongside me, they halted and I heard one say, "He ain't dead yet." Then gently they lowered their burden to the road in order to take a short rest.

I stepped over to the wounded lad and a glance told me that he had not much longer to live. I knelt quickly on one knee and pulled out the little round identification disc attached to the string around his neck. I looked at it and saw the letters "RC." I remember throwing off my shrapnel helmet ("tin lid," the lads called it) and it rattled on the hard road, though the noise was deadened by the rumble of passing traffic. Then I spoke to the lad, telling him I was a Catholic priest. Finding him conscious, I told him to make a good act of contrition for all the sins of his past life and that I would give him absolution. Then, as the great procession went lumbering by, I pronounced the words of absolution and anointed him there on the roadside. In a little while he passed away peacefully.

I copied from the little leather disc his name, number, and battalion: Private W. J. Daze, No. 788567, Third Canadian Infantry Battalion. A few days later I got his mother's address from the Third Battalion orderly room and wrote her, telling how grace had come to the lad.

LXXXI ⁓ In An Apple Orchard

We remained on the Amiens front nearly three weeks, and we were lucky enough not to have much rain, for we were in trenches where there were no dugouts. The transport mess was in an apple orchard, one of the great old orchards of Picardy where in days before the war, happy peasants picked the apples to make the golden cider.

There were many troops quartered in this orchard, as the trees offered shade and screened us fairly well from the ever-baleful eye of enemy airplanes. Yet almost every evening we were bombed. We would hear the signal of his approach long before the whir of his motor became audible. We would be sitting in groups, sometimes around little fires of wood or charcoal, talking in low voices, when suddenly there would come three shrill blows of a whistle, the kind used by referees of football matches. Instantly water would be poured on fires, or a few shovelfuls of earth would be thrown over the bright embers, and then a hurrying and scurrying to trenches; the sounds of laughter and pleasant talk would die away with the hissing of the expiring fires. Then profound silence, save for the champing of horses tethered at one end of the orchard under the trees. Presently from far up in the sky, coming nearer and nearer, would sound that peculiar err-rum, err-rum, err-rum, which left no uncertainty in our minds as to whose airplanes were approaching.

Sometimes they would go far beyond us and we would hear the terrific crash and explosion as their bombs dropped in our back areas; sometimes they would drop near our own lines, and we would lie there waiting. From a certain point in the orchard, we had a very good view of many of our observation balloons, far in our rear. I remember one day, while a group of us were sitting talking, suddenly hearing from high in the air, near one of our balloons the quick rat-tat-tat of machine-gun fire. Immediately all eyes were raised in time to see a German airplane swoop down from a bank of clouds perilously near our observation balloon. The enemy was firing from his machine gun, for every three or four seconds we could see the flash of phosphorous as the tracer bullet sped through the sky. If one of those touched the great silk bag of gas—it did, and almost simultaneously there was a burst of dark-red flame, fringed with black, waving out from the balloon. There was a cry of consternation from many voices in the orchard as two figures were seen to jump from the aerial car of the balloon. We held our breath. Then with a spring, one after the other, the white parachutes opened, and we breathed a sigh of great relief as they came gracefully to the earth.

Our observation balloons must have been doing excellent work, for after this Fritz was very busy bringing them down. One afternoon the same airplane actually brought down, one after the other, five balloons. Then, as it started on its return flight, it seemed to be flying very low. Immediately every machine gun in the area began firing on him. There must have been thousands of bullets soaring toward the speeding 'plane; but it is very difficult to judge, from the ground, distances in the air.

Suddenly the machine stopped in its course and came spiralling slowly downwards. A great cheer burst from hundreds of throats, and simultaneously the machine guns ceased to fire. There was complete silence in the camp as we watched the falling airplane. But we had reckoned without our host, for suddenly it ceased to fall, then like a lark shot gracefully up, up, till it reached a safe distance. Then with admirable audacity it looped the loop and finally winged its way toward home. What did we do, gentle reader? For a few seconds, overcome with amazement, we stood there gazing skywards, then from all over the area there were sounds of clapping hands as we good-humouredly applauded "Old Fritz."

LXXXII ⌒ A Strange Interruption

*The new reality of open warfare meant the necessity of accommodating established practices to vastly altered circumstances. Far from the familiar trench systems and a static no man's land, adaptations were required. To cite an example, Murdoch relates celebrating Mass while standing in a hole dug into the bottom of a shallow makeshift trench with only a burlap bag stretched across the trench top as a roof. He also relates, almost as a contest, an encounter with the legendary Anglican chaplain Canon Scott. After Canon Scott had addressed the draft of seventy men new to the front, only about six followed him for Anglican Holy Communion. Murdoch then addressed the remaining troops, and all thirteen of the Catholics present followed him for confession and Communion. Although Murdoch does not indicate how many of the remaining fifty-one were Anglicans, and perhaps he assumed (incorrectly) that all Protestants would accept Anglican ministry, his assertion nonetheless holds true—Catholic troops clearly did love and follow their priest. – **RH***

Every morning I said Mass in the part of the trench where I slept, which was covered overhead with a piece of camouflaged burlap, spread across pieces of scantling. The trench was so low that I was obliged to dig a hole in the ground, so that I could stand upright at my little portable altar. One morning while I was saying Mass, a little fox terrier, belonging to George and the transport cook, began walking on the burlap above my head. As the burlap was taut, the small paws made a kind of drumming sound above me. Both George and the cook, although they were non-Catholics, wished to show every respect to the chaplain; knowing I was saying Mass, they began to call off the dog. The little fellow, however, was stubborn and wished to remain on the burlap. I think that the cook and George then got sticks and tried to poke him off, for I could hear him dancing up and down as the points of the sticks tapped the burlap roof. It was a long time before he was captured, and it was at the cost of so much extra noise that I think it would have been better had they left him to follow his own inclinations— but the lads' intentions were good.

New drafts now began coming to the battalions to reinforce the ranks, broken in the Battle of Amiens. One afternoon the adjutant told me that a draft of seventy men had come and that they were going into the front line that night. The senior chaplain of the division, Canon Scott, an Anglican clergyman, was going to address them first, after which, he said, if I wished I might say a few words to them. I went to the orderly room, where I learned that thirteen out of the seventy soldiers were Catholics. I waited a long time that evening for the Canon to finish. When, at last, he had ceased speaking and had invited those who wished to attend the Communion service to step over to the side of the lines, I spoke to the men. My talk did not take very long. I first asked the Catholics to fall out. Immediately, from different sections in the ranks, thirteen men stepped out before me. I told them that as they were going into the front line and did not know what might be before them, perhaps they would wish to go to Holy Communion. I told all who wished to do so, to follow me down into the trench where I would hear their confessions and give them Holy Communion, I turned and proceeded toward the trench. Thirteen men followed me.

That night, after I had wrapped myself in the blankets of my bedroll, a lieutenant, a middle-aged man who was sharing part of the trench with me, came down to retire for the evening. As he lay smoking a last pipe before drawing the curtains of sleep, I was surprised to hear him give utterance to this monologue: "Self esteem! Self-esteem! Too much self-esteem. That's what's the matter!" I wondered to whom he referred, and after waiting a few seconds to see if he had any more to say, I asked him if he were speaking to me. "No, no, Padre," he exclaimed. "I'm thinking of those fellows this evening. Did you see them when Canon Scott invited them out to the communion? Only about half a dozen went, out of all the crowd. Self-esteem, self-esteem—that's it!" "Well," I replied, "I didn't notice. I asked my men—I had only thirteen in the draft—if they wished to go to the sacraments of their church, and immediately the thirteen followed me down to the trench." He looked at me keenly and there was not the slightest rancour in his voice as he spoke again: "That's it, Padre! That's it! Of course your men would go! That's to be expected." A kind of musing note came into his voice, as he continued: "What is the secret? What is the secret? They don't fear you. Indeed, they love you."

I told him as clearly as I could the secret, and as he continued smoking quietly, I felt how truly he had spoken of our Catholic lads. How they loved the priest, how on battlefield or muddy trench their eyes lighted with love as the priest drew near. No wonder thirteen men followed me down to the trench: they knew what I could do for them. They knew in a few minutes they would be friends with Christ, that He would visit them, abide in their souls. They were so absorbed in the sublimity of what was to take place that no thought of what others might say flashed across their minds. There was no human respect there.[48]

LXXXIII ∾ Boves Again

The first Sunday on the Amiens front we had no church parade. But the second Sunday we managed to have one for the lads out of the trenches. We had Mass on a wooded hill that had been heavily shelled during the week by the Germans, though they left us quiet on Sunday.

There was a huge, crippled tank on the hill, and workmen were busy repairing it. I found a rough table placed against the tank, and on the table a portable altar already set up for Mass; grouped about this were some men from other brigades and a few of my own men, with a draft that had come for the Thirteenth. Father MacDonnell had just finished Mass. He and Father Fallon heard confessions and the workmen repaired the tank, while I offered up the Holy Sacrifice for the men.

The following Friday evening, after a long, weary march, we came back into Boves. It was a different looking city from the one we had entered almost three weeks before. On the outskirts, high on a hill, dozens of great marquee tents rose in the darkening twilight, and from a large flagstaff waved, on a white background, the red cross: it was one of our Canadian clearing stations that had moved up. We came around a turn in the road and there, standing in a group, were the nurses, orderlies, and many patients from the tents on the hill. They cheered and cheered as the lads marched by and the nurses fluttered their white handkerchiefs, while the band played a merry march. Down the street of the city the merry pipers piped our way, while house after house opened its doors wide and the good French people who had returned, whole families of them, came out and cheered us as we passed up the street. I had a fine billet in the classroom of a school just next door to the church; yet it seemed somewhat stuffy and closed in after having lived for almost three weeks in an apple orchard.

The following morning, after I came in from Mass, I noticed the cook standing on the outer sill of the window, looking closely at the grapevines that grew up the sides of the building; many bunches of white grapes grew among the thick green leaves. A few minutes later, as I sat down to breakfast, George walked in with a great cluster, almost as large as a pineapple, on a dish and placed them near my plate.

All day long I was hoping to have the opportunity of having my men to confession before leaving Boves, for it was being rumoured about the city that we were on our way back to the Arras front where we were to take part in other big battles. I could not learn from headquarters at what time we were to leave, but I surmised it would be early Sunday morning. I was praying the Blessed Virgin to let me have the men, but at seven o'clock P.M. it seemed certain that we were to move early in the morning. At eight o'clock, the quartermaster came to me, saying, "The move's off, Padre. We don't leave here till tomorrow evening."

I called George, and soon he and I were out organizing a church parade of all the troops in the city. I called at the CCS on the hill, thinking there might be a chaplain there who could help me with confessions. I learned that there was a Catholic chaplain attached to the unit but that at present he was absent on leave.

I heard confessions for about an hour before Mass, but as the time for Mass drew near it became evident that I would not be able to hear one-quarter of the great throng of khaki-clad lads that filled the church; all the pews were filled and many were standing. When the hour for Mass had come, even the large sanctuary was filled with soldiers, some of them wearing the blue uniform of France.

I was just about to leave the confessional to say Mass when I heard someone knocking on the door. I looked up quickly: there stood Father MacDonnell in his Scottish uniform. I was so overjoyed that I stepped out quickly and cried, "The Blessed Virgin sent you here!" He looked at me with his shrewd, kind eyes, and there was not the shadow of a smile in them as he said, "Never mind, now, who sent me here. What can I do for you?" I asked him which he preferred, to say Mass or to hear confessions. He said he had already said Mass and had taken his breakfast. So I asked him if he would kindly hear confessions.

I walked up the aisle toward the altar, past row and row of those great-hearted Catholic lads, and as I went I thanked the Blessed

Virgin for what she had done. But it was a little too early: she had not yet finished answering my prayers, for just as I entered the sanctuary, I noticed one of the French soldiers sitting on a bench reading his breviary. I touched him on the shoulder and asked him if he were a priest. He was. Then I asked him if he would hear the French confessions, for more than half the men of the Fourteenth Battalion were French. He closed his breviary, after he had marked the place with a coloured ribbon. Then he bowed and said he would.

About two years after the Armistice had been signed, I was travelling in New Brunswick when a young man came down the car to shake hands with me. He had been one of the officers of the Fourteenth Battalion assisting at Mass in the church at Boves that Sunday. After we had talked a little while, he remarked, "Father, I have often thought of that Sunday at Boves. It seemed to me a beautiful thing to see officers of high rank going over and kneeling down at the feet of one clad in the uniform of a French private of the ranks to have their sins absolved."

Just before Mass I announced that during the celebration of the Holy Sacrifice Father MacDonnell would hear confessions in English while the French Father would hear the French confessions, and that after Mass, if there were still some who had not gone to confession, the two priests would continue to hear and I would help them. I added that confessions would be heard and Communion given again that afternoon. I said my Mass slowly and preached about twenty minutes. During my sermon I saw something that gratified me very much. Among the officers of one of the battalions was one whom I had never seen at the sacraments. I had approached him some time before and had met with the greatest rebuff I had ever received from a Catholic: he told me quite gruffly that he had no time for that kind of thing. His words had actually struck me dumb for a few seconds, so that I walked away from him without saying anything further. But as I preached that Sunday at Boves, looking out over that sea of reverent faces, I saw the officer stand up and walk reverently to the confessional, and when I gave Holy Communion I saw him at the rails.

As I write these words there stands on the little table before me a tiny plaster statue of the Immaculate Conception. Since I began writing this story it has been always present on the table. It was given to me by a soldier of the Fourteenth Battalion just after the Battle of Amiens. Cut into the base of the statue is the one word "Boves," and the dents made by the letters are filled with the red clay of France. I will keep this statue always, for it brings back memories of a town where great things were done for God among my Canadian soldiers, and of her who brought these things about.

That evening, as I entered the classroom that was my billet, two figures looked up quickly: one was George, who had a right to be there; the other was one of the assistants in the veterinary section. There was a very strong odour of iodoform in the room. On a bench between the two soldiers was my washbasin filled with some solution, and the little dog, who had broken his paw, was having it washed in the solution. I said nothing. I was not even cross, for I knew how difficult it was to procure a vessel in which to wash dogs' broken paws.

LXXXIV ◷ The Battle of Arras

Although significant advances had been made on the Amiens front, progress gradually slowed. As a consequence, the Canadians were withdrawn, briefly rested, reinforced, and then moved to a new area to renew the attack. At Arras, the Canadians were to attack the Drocourt-Quéant Line. Although reputed to be impregnable, for the Germans had carefully constructed it over several years, the Canadians struck on September 1. Murdoch relates the intensity of those days. He tells of sharing a two-foot-square hole with the doctor of the First Field Ambulance before the battle as it rained both water and German shells. He recounts being caught in a German "creeping barrage" a few days earlier in which, out of fourteen men, he, George, and two privates were the only ones not killed or wounded. He recalls seeing friends come in wounded and of burying several acquaintances, including his old bunk-mate "Wild Bill" along with dozens of others. In one day alone, Murdoch and an unnamed Anglican chaplain buried 125 Canadians in a new burial ground they called "Dominion Cemetery." Finally, he tells of being bombed nightly by German planes with nothing for cover but his bivouac sheet. One wave of planes would be followed by another. He relates, "often I have gripped the grass beside me with both hands, as I lay there waiting to be blown into a thousand fragments." – RH

Our journey was uneventful, save that we were derailed at St. Paul; no one, however, was killed. All along our journey we spoke of the Battle of Amiens, "the greatest isolated victory to the credit of Canadian arms." It had taken but five days to free Amiens and its railway. The allied troops engaged in the battle were one American division, five Australian divisions, four Canadian divisions, and four English divisions. There were also four hundred tanks and three British cavalry divisions. These troops had met and routed twenty German divisions and taken twenty-two thousand prisoners and over four hundred guns. The line was advanced twelve miles from points held at the hour of attack on August 8. Of these totals the Canadians claimed ten thousand prisoners, nearly one hundred and seventy guns, one thousand machine guns, over one hundred trench mortars, and great quantities of other materials. They had freed over sixty miles of territory. They had been the apex of the wedge that attacked. It was, indeed, a great victory!

Later I read in Hindenburg's account of the war, entitled *Out of My Life* (Harper & Brothers, New York), the following:

> I had no illusions about the political effects of our defeat on August 8th. Our battles from July 15th to August 4th could be regarded, both abroad and at home, as the consequence of an unsuccessful but bold stroke, such as may happen in any war. On the other hand, the failure of August 8th was revealed to all eyes as the consequences of an open weakness. To fail in an attack was a very different matter from being vanquished on the defense. The amount of booty which our enemy could publish to the world, spoke a clear language. Both the public at home and

our allies could only listen in great anxiety. All the more urgent was it that we should keep our presence of mind and face the situation without illusions, but also without exaggerated pessimism. "The military situation had certainly become serious. Of course the position on the part of our front which had been attacked could be restored, the lost war material made good, and fresh reserves brought up. But all this did not exhaust the effects of our defeat. We could only expect that, encouraged by his great victory, our enemy would now open similar attacks at other points." (Vol. II, pp. 217 and 218)

This is just what we did. On August 26 the Second Canadian Division had opened the Battle of Arras, and as we hastened toward them, were in the thick of the fight. We detrained at Aubigny and were taken from there to Arras in buses. During the night of August 28 we moved up from the ruins of Arras to relieve the Second Division. We had been waiting in reserve at Arras. Already the Second Division had been gaining victories. Before September 1 we had gained a minor engagement or two. On the morning of September 1 I received word that we were preparing for a great attack; we were to break the Drocourt-Quéant Line. The line had been accounted impregnable, for the whole system was the result of years of patient toil on the part of the Germans. In the attack, the Canadian Corps was to be the battering ram of the advance.

The night of September 1 was very dark, and rain fell as the men assembled for the attack. Zero hour was to be five A.M. Captain O'Shea, one of the Medical Officers of the First Field Ambulance, with whom I was going to work the following day, found a square hole in the ground about two feet deep, and he and I rolled ourselves in our blankets and tried to sleep. The Germans were shelling this area very hard, and shells were dropping all about us and the rain upon us. Every little while I could hear the doctor, who was a very devout Catholic, give voice to the following soliloquy: "Think of a priest lying out in the mud a night like this! What awful times we are living in! I wonder what his people at home would say if they could see him now. A priest sleeping in a mud-hole!" Then, perhaps a shell would drop very near us, and I could hear him say, optimistically, "Well, the worst we can expect is to be buried alive!" I could not help laughing as the doctor continued. Everything seemed so strange to him, for he had but lately come to the front. And I had now been long enough in the army to take things as they came.

At five o'clock A.M., the earth began to thunder and rock as the terrible barrage began that was to sound the death-knell of the Drocourt-Quéant Line. We watched the men advance, then we were busy with the wounded. A great number passed through our hands, including some Irish lads from the Naval Division on our right. It took but an hour or two for the Canadians to break the Drocourt-Quéant Line, which had been considered impregnable. Passing through the trenches and over the battlefield that day, I marvelled at the system of deep trenches from which led great dugouts lighted with electricity. We encountered many wounded Germans lying in shell holes and dispatched German prisoners to bring them to the Field Ambulance that had now been established near Cagnicourt.

We had not been shelled very much that day, but two or three days before, in one of the minor engagements, the shelling had been terrific. George and I had run the gauntlet of shellfire known as a "creeping barrage." Wall after wall of bursting shells had swept over us, killing nearly all our companions. George and two privates and I were the only ones out of fourteen who were not casualties.

Toward evening, as I was anointing some German wounded, one of our prisoners, an officer, stepped over and began to speak to the lad to whom I was administering. The officer told me in French that he would interpret, as he was a Catholic. I asked him to try to dispose the dying soldier for absolution. He did, and then helped me while I anointed the lad. When I was through, I thanked the officer for his aid and remarked that he seemed well grounded in his religion. He smiled a little at this, as he said, "I should be, for I am an ordained deacon." I was still talking to this young ecclesiastic when I heard a friendly call from a stretcher, and, looking in that direction, I saw it was Lt. Maxwell-Scott—he who had first served my Mass at Fosse-dix. It seemed years ago. He was wounded, though not seriously.

The following day I waited, with an Anglican chaplain from the Third Brigade, till all the dead were brought in from the battlefield. Among the officers of the Sixteenth were two or three of my dear friends. One was the gentle officer who had slept in my billet at

Carency, months before—the one who had been called "Wild Bill";
even in death there was a gentle expression on his kind face. We
buried 125 that day and called the place "Dominion Cemetery."

> Few and short were the prayers we said,
> And we spoke not a word of sorrow,
> But we steadfastly gazed on the face of the dead
> And bitterly thought of the morrow.[49]

We remained in this area till September 4, and each night we
were bombed almost continuously. It was terrible and there were
many casualties. One could scarcely count the airplanes. We could
hear them coming from a great distance and each moment drawing
nearer and nearer. We would lie on the ground unprotected—
nothing between us and the airplanes but the thin sheets of our
bivouacs. When they would arrive over our camping ground, great
lights resembling arc light would drop slowly down, lighting up the
entire area. Then would come in quick succession the awful crash of
bursting bombs. Often I have gripped the grass beside me with both
hands, as I lay there waiting to be blown into a thousand fragments.
Then, one fleet of 'planes having exhausted its supply of bombs,
there would be relative silence till the next was heard approaching.
During the interim, slowly, silently, and anxiously, our searchlights
swept the sky, the great long shafts of light crossing and recrossing
each other.

LXXXV ⁓ Berneville Again

*After breaking the Drocourt-Quéant Line, the Canadians were
withdrawn from the battle front for much needed rest and many
desperately needed reinforcements. Casualties had been very high.
As well as rest at Berneville, the troops began training for a renewed*

attack. Murdoch's recent battle experiences, however, had not left him unscathed. He remarks that "the awful strain of battle was beginning to affect us all."

During this time, Murdoch had a heavy task to perform. He had to write to the families of the soldiers who had been killed. He gives both an example of the letters he penned as well as return replies from grateful mothers and wives. The replies came from across Canada, the United States, England, and Ireland. He notes receiving letters of reply from grateful non-Catholics as well.

Even in the autumn of 1918, all was not death and grief. Murdoch relates his anxiety as well as his joy and satisfaction over a play the 16th Battalion's concert troupe was performing. Murdoch's mind was filled with forebodings, for an earlier production had portrayed a Presbyterian minister in an unfavourable light. The new play was said to depict a typical Catholic priest back home! In the end, the actual portrayal of the priest was tactful, humorous, and respectful. Murdoch was much relieved and pleased. – RH

"When they had a day or two of good sleep, regular meals and rest, they seemed quickly to forget all they had suffered, even their mental torture. Of course, for this purpose the rest had to be real rest, undisturbed by enemy shells and bombs, and, if possible, somewhere where the thunder of the guns could not be heard."

I quote these words from the second volume of *Out of My Life* by Von Hindenburg, for they apply to all soldiers. The Germans had retreated to the opposite bank of the Canal du Nord, where they were prepared to defend themselves stoutly. To carry a position like the Canal du Nord, careful plans must first be made. Our troops were tired, and they needed a rest; therefore, on being relieved we came out to the areas about Arras, and the Sixteenth came to Berneville.

"The operations which broke the Drocourt-Quéant Line closed with the departure of the victors. These men had accomplished great deeds. They had won a great moral victory, which had far-reaching effects. They had conquered a trench system of which the world had spoken with bated breath in one triumphant rush. Many material things had passed from the enemy's possession into theirs. Among these should be numbered eight thousand prisoners, sixty-five guns, and four hundred and seventy-five machine guns. Their line was only seven miles from Cambrai." (From *The Canadians in France*, by Captain Harwood Steel, Copp Clark Co.)

The above quotation was written of us. So we came out to Berneville to rest. Those days of September were very pleasant at Berneville. Roses still bloomed in the garden of the old curé, with whom I was again billeted; grapes were plentiful all over the countryside. They grew in the garden of the old house where we had our mess, and often they were served at our meals. Every morning when I came back from breakfast to my billet, I found on the table a large yellow, red-cheeked pear. These little acts of kindness of the old curé's sister used to affect me almost to tears. I think the awful strain of battle was beginning to affect us all. I said Mass every morning in the church and a young fellow from the Fifteenth—which was also quartered in Berneville—used to serve it. Every morning he went to Holy Communion.

The old sister of the curé seemed very much interested in the young man, for she also attended my Mass and received Holy Communion daily. She used to talk to me about him and say he must be a brother from some religious community. So one morning I asked the lad his name. He was James Diamond, and his home was in Philadelphia—another of my Canadian lads who hailed from the United States. He was not a member of any religious community though he had two brothers who were priests. I told the old lady this, and although she was somewhat disappointed to learn that the young man was not religious, still she was delighted to know that he had two brothers who were priests.

I visited my battalions every day and we had confessions every evening. The men came in great numbers. Although we were in rest, the lads knew by the training they were undergoing that another attack was imminent.

During the day I often walked up and down the old rose garden of the curé. It was a beautiful old garden with high stone walls, against which pear trees and peach trees had been trained to grow so that the branches spread out against the wall. There were roses here of almost every variety. Often, as I walked up and down the paths of the garden reading my breviary, I stopped and gazed for a long time on the wonderful beauty before me. Soon we would be into the war again!

LXXXVI ⁓ Letters of Sympathy

During these days of rest, I devoted a large portion of every morning to writing letters of sympathy to relatives of those who had fallen in the recent attacks. I had many of these letters to write, and I always went to work with a heavy heart; but it was always very consoling to receive the wonderful replies that came. I quote from a few that I managed to keep, although the reader will learn later that I lost nearly all my possessions before the end of the campaign.

This one comes from Morningside Avenue, New York:

> Reverend dear Father:
> Your comforting letter has just been received. Father, words would be useless to try to express what relief and consolation your message brought, for naturally my heart ached, wondering whether my poor son had an opportunity to offer up his repentance before God took him. The cross is indeed a heavy one to bear, but with the knowledge contained in your letter and the fact that his sacrifice was made for so glorious a cause, I shall reconcile myself to the will of Almighty God, and pray for the repose of his soul. My daily prayers shall indeed be offered for you, Father, who brought such happiness to my heart, and for your many soldier boys.
> Very sincerely yours.

The next is from Frontenac Street, Montreal:

Reverend and dear Father:
Words fail to convey how soothing was the intelligence that previous to his last attack my son had had the happiness of receiving our dear Lord, and that after he had paid the "Supreme Sacrifice" he had one of God's representatives near him. In life he was devoted to religion, in death he must assuredly be happy with God. But to us who are left it has been a crushing blow, and especially to me, his mother, to whom a kinder and more dutiful son never was given. Our Lady of Sorrows is certainly the one to turn to in this hour of trial, for she likewise gave up her son. So, like her, I shall endeavour to carry my cross, but I fear it shall not be carried so well. And now, dear Father, allow me to extend to you my most sincere thanks. You will always be remembered in the prayers of his sorrowing mother.

The next is from Grimsary, England:

Dear Father Murdoch:
I should feel I was neglecting a great duty if I did not write a line to thank you for your kindness in informing us of my dear brother's death, RIP. It was indeed a great consolation to know that he received Holy Communion before going into battle, also to know that he was buried in a cemetery. We shall be ever grateful to you for your kindness and for your prayers. With every best wish for your safety, I am, Yours sincerely.

The next is from Gilford PO, Co. Down, Ireland:

Dear Rev. Father:

It is with a sad heart I write to thank you for your consoling letter to my mother concerning the death of my poor brother. Your letter gives us all strength to bear our heavy burden of sorrow. It is hard to think that he has really gone from us. But God's will be done! We all lift our hearts in thanksgiving to know that he was prepared to die. He was a good boy, and his youngest sister will miss him. My mother is in great sorrow at the loss of her only son. She has had great trouble, as my father died when we were very young. But God will give her strength to bear and persevere until we shall all meet never to part.

Dear Rev. Father, I will close this letter now and I wish you to know that all of us will never forget you in our prayers. And I earnestly implore of God to reward you for all you have done for my poor brother and for us, and that our Most Holy Mother will intercede for your safety through this suffering you are enduring. I am going to confession and Communion Sunday for your intentions. Always remember that there are three hearts raised to God night and morning imploring His blessings and mercy for you. Thanking you again, Father, I wish to remain your grateful friend who will never forget you.

This one from a non-Catholic:

Rev. B. J. Murdoch,

Dear Sir:

I received your very kind letter today. Thank you so much for writing. Although I am not of the Catholic faith, I know just how much he would value your services before going into battle. God sends us a cross to bear, no matter what faith we own. I will remember you and the other soldiers who are fighting, in my prayers, just the same. I will write and tell his father of your kindness, and ask him to thank you. I forgot to say that I belong to the Church of England, but that does not make any difference, for God hears all prayers. I shall pray for you and your boys and teach our little girl to do the same. Kindly pardon any mistakes and believe me to remain very grateful to you for your sympathy. Yours sincerely.

These are but samples of letters from different countries that I received during the campaign. The people seemed most grateful to me for writing. True, the censor prevented me from saying much that I should like to have said, but always I was free to write what I had done for the lads in my ministry. Sometimes I have written many letters at a time, and for this reason the message sent was brief. I shall try to give the reader a sample of the simple letter that evoked such grateful replies:

Dear Mrs. ____
   No doubt you have already received from the War Office the sad news of your son's death. I am writing these words to let you know that just before the battle of ___, I gave all the soldiers of his unit Holy Communion in a little shell-torn church on the Western Front.
   If I had anointed him I would add this, and if it were I who had laid him to rest I would say: I buried him in a peaceful military cemetery behind the lines, far from the sound of the guns. This knowledge should give you some consolation in carrying the heavy cross that God has sent you to bear. I shall remember your son's soul in the Holy Sacrifice of the Mass, and I shall ask Our Lady of Sorrows to pray for you that you may be comforted. Asking you to pray for my lads and for me, I am,
      Yours sincerely in Christ,
      B. J. Murdoch, RC Chaplain 16th Can.

LXXXVII ❦ A Little Bit of Shamrock

lthough I had many letters to write, this did not keep me from having a little enjoyment. We had not been very long in rest billets when it was announced that the Sixteenth Canadian Battalion concert party was to put on soon the play entitled *A Little Bit of Shamrock*. This was the play the soldiers were practising while we were at Monchy Breton, and because of the fact that one of the characters was a priest, I was very anxious to see the play.

The concert party was to be with us three nights, so I hoped to be able to attend at least one performance. The company had been playing for the large base-hospitals while we were taking part in the recent heavy fighting. I had met a Presbyterian chaplain in Arras who told me that he had seen the play and that it was one of the finest in France. They had been furnished with hundreds of dollars' worth of scenery and costumes. So we looked forward with pleasure to seeing it. I noticed as I worked among the men that the rest was doing them very much good. The village streets used to ring with laughter and merry jokes, especially in the evening. It was wonderful how much like boys those soldiers would become, given a few days' rest.

I remember one day, while sitting in the mess waiting for lunch to be served, listening to an animated conversation going on among a group of soldiers, of which George was the dominating spirit. George held in his hand a pair of German field glasses, which evidently he wished to barter for something some other soldier had. The other soldier thought George had placed a too high valuation on the glasses, and their voices fell and rose in debate. Finally, all the voices were silent; then the voice of George sounded clear and distinct, as he said impressively, "Gentlemen, I tell you, these glasses are so powerful that they will bring a church, miles distant, so near that you can actually hear the church bells ringing in the tower!"

Although a few derisive groans greeted this statement, the great bursts of merry laughter that accompanied them did my heart good and showed me how lighthearted were the troops. A day or two following the episode of the field glasses, I was again sitting in the mess waiting for lunch to be served. The transport officer and quartermaster were with me. Suddenly the lieutenant who had been billeting officer when we were at Écoivres walked in and sat down. He had a little business with the quartermaster, and as he stated it his eyes turned toward the table, which was set for lunch, and rested longingly on a dish of cold bread pudding with raisins in it. The pudding was cut in pieces resembling in size and shape an ordinary helping of Washington pie; there were three slices in all. Now, I never liked bread pudding, not even in wartime; neither did the other two officers of the mess. So when the billeting officer made known to us his weakness for bread pudding, we gave him a most pressing invitation to have a piece. He took one piece, and as he ate it with great relish we could not help smiling. He stopped for a second or two and looked around on us. "My," he said, "I like this! Our cook never thinks of giving us anything like this." Then he continued earnestly to devote his attention to the pudding. We offered him another piece, and with boyish delight he accepted it. When he had finished this, I offered him the remaining slice. The other two officers were now laughing. "Ah, Padre!" he said reproachfully, but his eye wavered and his hand without any apparent reluctance reached out and took the third piece. He stayed for a little while longer, and I wondered if he could be quite well after eating so great a quantity of such soggy food. I began, indeed, to feel a slight twinge of conscience. Perhaps I should not have offered him that last thick slice of heavy bread pudding. He was now quiet, and for a second or two a faraway look came into his eyes. Then, suddenly, he seemed to recollect something. He stood up quickly. "Well," he said, "I think it is about time for me to be going home to lunch." "Will he be all right?" I asked the other officers, as he disappeared on his way. "Sure," they both said, and then the quartermaster continued: "Why Padre, that's just a little hors d'oeuvre for him, just a little appetizer, just enough to convince him that it's time to take a little substantial food." Then, as we lunched, they told me such wonderful stories of this officer's capacity for food that I laughed and laughed all through the meal.

I could not attend the play till the third evening; George, who had gone both nights, seemed very anxious that I should see it. I had tea with the concert party the afternoon of the third day, and in the evening, I went to the play and was given a very good seat.

I shall never forget that play given by those splendid boys on the Western Front. Even as I write these words the tears come to my eyes as they did that night, but they are tears of joy. It was a wonderful play—wonderful in its presentation, wonderful, especially, in its beautiful interpretation of the character of the Catholic priest—bubbling with gaiety and gladness and spotless humour. I was transported with joy and amazement.

The curtain rose, disclosing the library of an Irish priest's house, through the open window of which came in excellent harmony the sound of male voices singing:

"Och, Father O'Flynn, you've a wonderful way wid you.
All ould sinners are wishful to pray wid you,
And the young children are wild for to play wid you,
You've such a way wid you, Father avick!
Still for all you've so gentle a soul,
Gad, you've your flock in the grandest control:
Checking the crazy ones, coaxing unaisy ones,
Lifting the lazy ones on with the stick.
Here's a health for you, Father O'Flynn,
Sláinte and sláinte and sláinte agin,
Pow'rfulest preacher and tindirest teacher
And kindliest creature in ould Donegal."

As the last sounds of the chorus died away, a young Irish girl, attired in typical colleen fashion, and a boy of about nineteen or twenty, in knee-breeches, entered. The colleen was a perfect impersonation. The young man, who carried a gun and an empty game-bag, had returned from the chase. He was telling Molly how many birds he had seen and how many he might have shot had it not been for—etc., etc. The more voluble Shaun became, the more Molly shrugged her shoulders. It seemed Shaun had often hunted before and had often come "very near hitting a bird." Just as good-natured Shaun was becoming more eloquent and Molly more disdainful, a stately old figure in cassock and cincture walked slowly into the room, carrying his breviary and biretta. There was a look of benign interest on his face as he regarded Shaun and Molly. The two greeted the priest warmly, in true Irish fashion; yet the three actors were non-Catholics.

I am certain I did not follow the plot of the play. I was too delighted with Father O'Flynn. He was the ideal priest, genial, kind, grave. He possessed all those lovable qualities that we Catholics always associate with the priesthood. I was really delighted with the impersonation of the character. Where had he, the actor, acquired his wonderful knowledge of the priesthood? If it had been a play that the lads had procured already written, I would not have been so surprised, but they themselves had composed it. There was one scene that was almost uncanny in its faithful reproduction of one of the little dialogues that take place often in the office of a country parish priest. Old Mrs. Nolan—off the stage "she" was Private M. Dawes, No. 1 Platoon, Sixteenth Battalion, and in civil life an actor who had taken parts with the great Du Maurier[50]—had come to call on Father O'Flynn concerning her husband, who was not working and who for reasons known only to himself had no inclination to work. She spoke quietly at first, but gradually, animated by righteous indignation, a certain piquancy and forcefulness coloured her words. She had just begun rightly to denounce "himself" when Father O'Flynn, with a gentle raising of one hand from his knee, where it had rested palm downwards, said softly, "There, now, Mrs. Nolan! There, now! Don't mind, it will be all right! It will be all right. In a little while Timmy'll be at work again."

Then Mrs. Nolan, somewhat mollified, would concede, "Yis, Father! Yis, Father! Perhaps you're right, Father. Indade, he's not so bad; if he would stay away from that Dinny O'Shea, he might be better. And look, Father, dear, I wouldn't be mindin' what that Liz of his would ever be saying. Look here, Father, if she'd stay at home and look after her man and not go galavantin' over the parish! Look here, Father, she's one of the worst— " Then with a gentle smile Father O'Flynn would again quiet the indignant Mrs. Nolan. But she was irrepressible. And as she continued her rapid-fire talk, the house roared with laughter, so that we forgot that we were in a building on the Western Front into which at any minute a long-distance shell might fall, killing and wounding half the people there. We forgot this completely as we continued to enjoy one of the finest plays ever staged on the Western Front.

As I looked on, laughing heartily, another emotion began to manifest itself; gradually, as I listened to the dialogue, the whole setting before me took on a certain familiarity: it was a priest's room, my own language was being spoken, a scene was being enacted with which every priest is familiar. I felt as if I saw my Catholic people at home; then a kind of mist seemed to pass over me, and my eyes filled up—yes, gentle reader, I was lonesome!

The old curé and his sister had waited up for me, to hear about the play. I had told them before leaving that I was going to see a non-Catholic take the part of a Catholic priest, and they had been very interested. They were like two children in their delight when I came bursting in on them with the news of the play. They rejoiced with me when I told them how splendidly the part of Father O'Flynn had been taken by one of the lads. The old lady seemed the more enthusiastic of the two, until I told the story of Mrs. Nolan, then the curé broke into rippling laughter, but Madame just smiled quietly. We talked for a long time that evening, for the three of us were very pleased. I had told them before going that I had my fears lest the actor assigned the part of the priest should not interpret it according to the best traditions of the priesthood. But now they were quite relieved and very joyful when I told them that the play would be shown wherever there were Canadian soldiers in France.

LXXXVIII ∾ Left Behind

I was well satisfied with my work among the soldiers during these evenings, and we were all benefiting very much by our rest. But we did not know just how soon we would be going into action. One evening toward seven o'clock, on coming back to Berneville after having attended a meeting at corps headquarters, I found men of the Fourth Division walking up and down the street. I was somewhat surprised at this, for when I had left in the morning the village had been occupied only by First Division troops. Now I saw no men of the Third Brigade. I stopped the first soldier I met and asked him where was the Sixteenth. He told me he did not know, that the Sixteenth had "pulled out" about four o'clock and that another battalion had "taken over" these lines.

I went up quickly to the place our mess had been, only to find other officers occupying it. They were just about to sit down to dinner and invited me to remain, but I was too eager to have news of my troops. This was the first time they had ever stolen a march on me. I opened the gate of the old curé's garden, hoping to see George standing in the twilight somewhere among the roses; but there was no khaki-clad figure there. In fact, there was no one in the garden; everything was very quiet. Knocking on the door that led to the office and dining room combined, I advanced into the lamp-lit room to find the curé and his sister just about to sit down to their evening meal. They welcomed me warmly. It was good to see the kindly, beaming faces of my old friends; and as my eyes wandered from them to the table, I saw that places had been set for three.

"Come," said the old priest as he motioned me to the seat beside him. "Come, you are just in time, for we were about to begin, fearing you would not arrive." I sat down quickly, for I did not wish to delay any longer these good people. The memory of that evening is still very vivid; the low, lamp-lit room with its quaint engravings on the wall, the old-fashioned furniture, the spotless white linen cloth, heavy silver, and thick china, with blue scrollwork bordering of old châteaux and rustic-bridged streams. A large roll of coarse though wholesome brown bread, such as I had seen old "Mamma Katzenjammer" make some time before, was on a plate in the middle of the table, and beside this was a black-handled bread knife; a huge bottle of golden cider stood near the bread. Opposite me was a wooden bowl of salad and a large wooden fork and spoon.

Madame brought from the kitchen a small brown earthenware casserole and placed it before M. le Curé. The removal of the cover disclosed three plump little pigeons. Simultaneously M. le Curé and Madame looked at me. "In your honour," said the priest as both bowed, jokingly. I remembered how, when a boy, I had shot a few pigeons, which when cooked I was unable to eat because they were so tough. But the pigeons of old Madame were not tough. Indeed, I had never eaten any meat more tender. They had been pot-roasted. It was one of the pleasantest evenings I had ever spent in rest billets. As we sat at table they told me that the battalion had left for the front at four o'clock. George had packed my bedroll and had placed it and my portable altar on the general service wagon, leaving my haversack with articles I would need for the night. He had left word that we would not be going into action for a day or two and that I would be quite safe in staying that night in Berneville.

As we sat talking in the quiet lamp-lit room, and I realized all that was before me, I could not help thinking how pleasant it would be to live on in this peaceful old house, far from the horrors of war, and preach to the quiet peasants, and teach them the ways of God. But quickly I put this thought from my mind. The Master for whom I laboured had sterner work for me to do. And tomorrow morning early I must leave, to go once more into The Red Vineyard.

LXXXIX ❧ With the Fourteenth

On September 23, Murdoch's brigade was on the move again. Upon arriving at their destination, Murdoch learned of two disappointments. First, his batman, George, informed him that a fire had destroyed Murdoch's blankets, cloak, overcoat, and other personal items. Thankfully, his portable altar had escaped. A few days later, new orders and a new bicycle arrived for Murdoch from headquarters. The orders were a shock. Murdoch was to leave his beloved 16th Battalion to be attached to the 14th Battalion. That evening, he said goodbye to his officer friends and to his ever faithful and reliable batman, George. While Murdoch was to enjoy the services of another batman at the 14th Battalion, all that is said of that individual is that he was an Englishman; Murdoch never mentions his name. Clearly the new batman was no George! – RH

Early the following morning after Mass I said *"au revoir"* to the old priest and his sister, who walked down to the gate to see me off. On the way, fearing it might be evening before I would find my battalion, I bought an ordinary three-ounce tin of sardines and paid sixty-five cents for it; but I never ate it. I had the great good fortune to meet a lorry, going toward the front, which brought me to within a few hundred yards of the Sixteenth Battalion, which was camped in a wide green valley. I was fortunate in finding my unit, but soon I was to learn of what was the first of a series of misfortunes.

George met me as I came along and there was a look in his face that I had never seen there before. "I'm sorry, sir, but I have bad news for you," he said. "Your bedroll and all your belongings have been burned." Poor George turned his face away. It really hurt him to have to tell anything so unpleasant. "My portable altar, too, George?" I questioned, as fear tugged at my heart. George turned toward me, his face brightening. "No, sir. We saved that. Everything in the little church is all right." George always called the altar the "little church." Then he went on to tell me that a fire had broken out, during the night, in the corrugated iron hut where I was to have slept and that when it was discovered it was too late to save two bedrolls; he had managed, however, to bring out one bedroll and my portable altar. It was now late in September and the evenings were becoming quite cold. I would miss my blankets, cloak, and overcoat very much, all of which, together with many other articles, had been burned. I still had my trench coat, which I was wearing at the time. "Well, George," I said finally, "it could have been a great deal worse. I am very thankful that I did not lose my trench coat."

A few evenings later, while I was standing outside my hut examining a new bicycle that had come to me from headquarters, a runner came up and passed me a DRLS letter. As I read it, I felt my hand tremble. I was to report immediately to the Fourteenth Battalion, where I was now attached for quarters and rations; Captain the Rev. G. Colthurst was to exchange places with me.[51] He was a Church of England chaplain. That evening I left, my heart filled with regrets; but a soldier must obey. I said goodbye to George, although I hoped to see him often. He thanked me for the way I had treated him, though I had only given him the consideration which as a thorough gentleman he deserved. I thanked him in return for all he had done for me. Twice, if not oftener, during the recent heavy fighting he had come through a terrific barrage of shellfire and gas to guide me to the transport mess. He had actually risked his life where he was not bound to do so.

The second-in-command of the Fourteenth, Major Price, welcomed me cordially to the battalion. The colonel was then absent. Major Price, though a very kind man with a most gentle disposition, held one of the finest records in the army, rising from a private in the ranks to be colonel of the battalion. The officers of the Fourteenth were a fine lot of men, yet they never filled the place in my affections that the officers of the Sixteenth had won.

XC ∾ Telegraph Hill

The following Sunday I said Mass on Telegraph Hill. It was a very high elevation and on all sides we could see, far below, the great green valley. I counted as many as six light railway trains steaming their way from different points toward the front. I think we were then about seven or eight miles from the Canal du Nord, where the next big battle was to take place. Some of the men came early, and I stood talking to them till all the soldiers, excepting the Thirteenth Battalion, had come up. Thinking that there must be some mistake in orders and that they had failed to receive notice of church service, I began to say Mass. I had a large crowd of lads and they were formed up very near the altar; some stood almost touching the altar in order to keep the wind from extinguishing my candles. Nearly all my men had received the sacraments while in rest, so I gave a general absolution today, then all went to Holy Communion.

Just as I had given the last men Holy Communion, the Thirteenth came up, their pipe band playing merrily. There was nothing left for me to do but say another Mass for them. It was very gratifying to notice, as I turned to make an announcement before beginning the second Mass, that many of the men who had received Holy Communion at the first Mass still remained kneeling on the ground as they made their thanksgiving.

During the second Mass a number of German airplanes tried to fly near us, but from down in the valley our anti-aircraft guns barked and shells shrieked upwards, bursting near the 'planes. All the men of the Thirteenth, after a general absolution, went to Holy Communion. I came down from Telegraph Hill that morning feeling that my men were now ready, spiritually, for battle.

XCI ∽ Canal Du Nord

The Battle for Canal du Nord was the third and final in the series of massive engagements fought by the Canadian Corps in the early autumn of 1918. Again, the Canadian Corps carried a very heavily fortified and defended position, but at great cost. Murdoch was in the midst of this battle. His narrative communicates something of the intensity of the experience. Waiting for the barrage to lift, he first worked with the regimental doctor and then went forward with the field ambulance looking for the wounded. While under almost constant shellfire, the field ambulance orderlies discovered great numbers of wounded and attended to them. Murdoch both assisted the medical staff with the wounded and ministered to the dying. It was, quite literally, bloody work. As the day grew warmer, he removed his trench coat; when he returned for it, the coat was gone. He had now lost all means of staying warm in the chill September nights. – RH

On the night of September 26 we moved up to the trenches just before the Canal du Nord. It was a rainy night and quite dark. We marched a long time, for our guides had lost their way. Finally, as we approached the trenches, Verey lights hissed a trail of light through the sky, and as they broke to descend, we stood very still. Every little while orders came for us to fall on our faces, and we lay motionless on the ground, listening to that strange, sweeping sound of machine-gun bullets as they tore their way through the air just above us.

Before we entered the trenches, we had supposed all the Germans to be on the opposite bank of Canal du Nord. But we were not in the trenches very long till we learned that there were machine-gun outposts on our own side. Indeed, not forty-eight yards from where we stood was a machine-gun nest. Every time a flashlight would show, or someone would speak above a whisper, there would be a rat-tat-tat from almost beside us, and then a pattering of machine-gun bullets. I listened to the grim preparations that were being made to surround the nest just as soon as our barrage would open up.

At 5:20 A.M., two thundering crashes from an eighteen-pound gun broke the stillness, then the whole barrage opened up, the like of which had never before been heard on the Western Front. I quote below from *The Canadians in France*.

> Never had the world known anything to compare with the strength and majesty of that terrible artillery fire. It was as if the pillars of the earth had fallen and God had struck the Germans in his anger. The gloom behind the advancing troops was blazing with fire, and the gloom in front. The night overhead shrieked and moaned and howled with the passing of the shells, hurrying—hurrying—hurrying to keep their appointment with death. The German machine-gunners in the Canal and immediately behind it were blown to pieces and the German guns were throttled with their answers to their lips.

We stood in the trenches listening to the terrible roaring and crashing of the guns. When we spoke we were obliged to yell in order to make ourselves heard. It was still quite dark, yet all about us were sharp yellow flashes of light from our guns. In a little while the men were ready to start over the Canal. The officer in command looked at me. "Coming, Padre?" he asked. I smiled. I was not free to go then. I must stay with the doctor, to attend the wounded that would be brought in by the stretcher-bearers. Later I was to go with the field ambulance.

Shortly after daylight I was moving along the Canal looking for the Second Field Ambulance, with which I was to follow, when I saw coming up through a shower of shell explosions the young officer who had come to see me at Monchy Breton. He was looking for the Sixteenth Battalion. He was no longer downhearted. The light of battle was in his clear blue eye. He shook hands with me and smiled a bright, fearless smile as the shells dropped about us. He told me he had been sent up to the battalion, which was sadly in need of officers. As he spoke, all about us were dead men and horses.

I found the field ambulance at crossroads near Inchy, and I worked with them till noon. It was terrible work, performed under great difficulties, as all morning long a constant rain of enemy shells poured over the roads. A great number of wounded passed through. As the morning advanced, the day became very warm. I took off my trench coat and began to carry it on my arm. I remember laying it down on the side of the road as I went to minister to a wounded lad. When I had finished my work and had wiped the blood from my hands on the thick grass alongside of the road, I turned to pick up my trench coat. It was no longer where I had put it. I looked everywhere but I could not find it. It was a very serviceable coat, lined with oiled silk and rubber and impervious to rain and wind. Now I had no coat whatsoever. My overcoat and cloak had been burned, and now my trench coat was gone! I often smile when I recall that morning. I worried more at the time over the loss of what was in the pockets than I did over the loss of the coat itself. In one pocket was the tin of sardines that I had bought a few days before. I had not yet broken my fast and I did not know when I might do so. In the other pocket was a "Baby Ben" alarm clock: it was very useful sometimes when I wanted to sleep between attacks. I never found the coat. I think some stretcher-bearers must have placed it on a wounded man thinking it had been left by some officer who had been wounded or killed.

It was now the twenty-seventh of September, and I was not fitted out very well to stand the rigours of a fall campaign. Just before I left the Sixteenth I had been given an old wagon cover, which George and I had converted into a bedroll, and I had been able to procure two army blankets; but now I had no overcoat. During a little lull in the afternoon, I made my way to headquarters of the Fourteenth, which was in a dugout that the Germans had left them. There I had some food, after which I made my way back to the field ambulance.

That night I slept on the opposite side of the Canal du Nord. We had gained another great victory and had captured one of the strongest positions that the enemy still held. Nearly five thousand prisoners had been taken and about one hundred field guns, together with a great number of machine guns and large quantities of stores. For several days one battle followed another; at almost every hour of the day some brigade of the Canadian Corps was attacking. I followed with the field ambulance, and I was kept very busy.

XCII ⸎ The Most Terrible Day

The Canadian attack did not slacken but pushed forward toward the outskirts of the city of Cambrai. Here Murdoch would experience his most terrible day. Seeking the First Field Ambulance in a village, Murdoch had to run a gauntlet of German shellfire. As he states, "My will said, Go! Yet every nerve in my body seemed to rebel; my feet were as heavy as lead." Then he adds tellingly, "I felt that that hurt, dazed look, which I had seen so often in the eyes of the men, was in my own eyes." Soon, however, he found what he was looking for—the Red Cross flag of the field ambulance. It was located in the cellar of a small house. Three doctors were frantically working on the steady inflow of wounded. Showered by shells and poison gas, Murdoch worked there non-stop for two days. Although his brigade was out of the line, Murdoch could not retire, for Fr. O'Reilly, the RC chaplain of the 2nd Brigade (the men now engaged), had been wounded.

The next night, Murdoch learned that his brigade was scheduled to soon go into battle a few kilometres away. He left and found the field ambulance servicing their wounded. The position was at an exposed crossroads, and German planes strafed the wounded indiscriminately—riddling a man just before Murdoch anointed him. When the wounded ceased flowing in, Murdoch went forward seeking his brigade. He ended up in an open field, completely exposed and under direct enemy fire while ministering to a dying stretcher-bearer. "Those were the most terrible minutes of my life. I knew the enemy could see me and was firing at me." Once finished, he played dead and eventually crawled off the field alive. Exhausted, hungry, and "utterly dispirited" he finally found refuge and food in a cellar that served as the temporary headquarters of the 15th Battalion. – RH

On Sunday I could not have a church parade, but I said Mass in a bell tent near the Canal du Nord. That morning I joined the First Field Ambulance in a little village not very far from Cambrai. I think the name of the village was Raillencourt. As I approached its outskirts, I saw that it was under fire. Shell after shell was whistling over from the enemy lines, bursting in black clouds of smoke and yellow clouds of gas that mingled with red clouds of dust rising from the ruined brick buildings. No traffic was coming along the road. I must walk alone into the village. My will said, Go! yet every nerve in my body seemed to rebel; my feet were heavy as lead, and it seemed an effort for me to lift them from the ground. I was now very tired from the work of the past week. Almost sick with fear, I continued to advance. It was a strange experience; my feet kept going heavily forwards while the rest of me seemed to be trying to hold them back. I felt that that hurt, dazed look, which I had seen so often in the eyes of the men, was in my own eyes.

I remember going down the little street of the village bewildered and almost stupefied while shells crashed into buildings and the sickening fumes of gas poisoned the air. Then, suddenly, I saw what I was in search of—a little red cross on a white background, floating from a window of a small house. I entered the yard; a ruined field kitchen lay in a lake of porridge, and nearby, where they had carried him to die, was the cook.

I found the cellar filled with wounded men with whom the doctors were very busy. My old friend Captain O'Shea was here and two other Catholic doctors. I stayed in the cellar two days. Those were horrible hours. I could not be relieved, as Father O'Reilly of the Second Brigade had been wounded a day or two before I came to the cellar. It was his troops who were now in action. My own were back in reserve. While I worked, Canon Scott, an Anglican chaplain who had been in the war since the beginning, was brought in wounded.

It was a miracle that we were not struck. At different times during the day the Germans shelled the little house heavily; many shells dropped in the garden just outside the windows of the cellar. The nauseating fumes from the gas shells penetrated into the cellar, and often we worked with our gas masks on.

At two o'clock Tuesday morning word came that my brigade was going over the top near Haynecourt. As soon as it was daylight, I left to join my troops. I found the Second or Third Field Ambulance, which was clearing that day at a crossroad near Cambrai. I could see the city from where we worked. I was very busy all day. At times the German airplanes swooped low over us and swept our wounded with their machine guns. One poor fellow near me was riddled with bullets, and I had just time enough to prepare him for death. Toward three o'clock I felt something was wrong. Wounded from the Fourteenth and Sixteenth were no longer coming in. The men of the Fifteenth were in reserve just behind where I worked. Seeing this, I started forward. The shellfire was intense, but I prayed the Blessed Virgin to see me through. I met a soldier from the Sixteenth who showed me where the soldiers were, but he advised me not to go any farther. I'm afraid I was too worried about my men at the moment to heed advice of this kind.

I found a number of them in a cutting of a railway, together with a lot of other troops. The battle was not going well; many members of the Fourteenth, cut off, had been taken prisoners. The young officer did not know where the rest were. I stayed with them, crouching in little holes in the side of the sunken road, and read my breviary while the clay scattered by bursting shells fell on its open pages. Presently, I joined a party of stretcher-bearers going out upon the field. The shelling was terrible as we passed down the cutting of the railroad. I was now getting among machine-gunners of the Third Division who had their guns set up in the side of the cutting. The stretcher-bearers had no sooner reached the field than the Germans, seeing them, commenced firing with small shells at point-blank range over open sights.

Three of the stretcher-bearers went down, two of them mortally wounded. I ran quickly to them and began to anoint one of them. The other bearers ran to points of safety, and I was alone on the field. Those were the most terrible minutes of my life. I knew the enemy could see me and was firing at me, for shells were crashing all about me. Terrified, I crouched flat on my stomach until I finished anointing the lad, who passed away before I had done my work. Then I rolled over and lay still, as if I were dead; a little later, I crawled from shell hole to shell hole, off the field. When the roll was called that night seventy-one men out of six hundred answered. We had lost many [as] prisoners.

I could not find my battalion to march out with them. I had not eaten any food all day, and it was now six o'clock. I had gone through the most terrible day of my life, and I was utterly dispirited.

I had never before felt so strangely. Of course, we had had many engagements during the past week, and constantly I had been looking on men mangled and broken and torn; and besides, I had eaten scarcely anything. I seemed to be moving in a world that was all upset; somehow, suddenly, everything had gone wrong with the Allies! I bumped along till finally I came to the dugout that had been occupied by the Medical Officer of the Fourteenth. He had gone, but he had left behind a white bag, resembling in size and shape an ordinary pillowslip, half-filled with sugar. I thought of taking it along with me, but I left it. As I moved on dazedly, suddenly I remembered I had seen the Fifteenth back in reserve. I had come through them in the morning on my way up to the Fourteenth. I would go to them and ask for something to eat. How I missed George! George would have had a breakfast for me in the morning and would have found me in the evening.

Headquarters of the Fifteenth were in a cellar, and a kind-hearted kilted laddie guided me to the door. I was greeted very kindly, and in a little while the waiter placed on the table some white bread and margarine and a plate of cold beef. "I'm sorry," said Major Girvan, OC, of the Fifteenth Battalion, "that we have no sugar, Padre." I then remembered the bag of sugar I had seen in the Medical Officer's hut. If I had only brought it, I could have given it to the Fifteenth Battalion! I did not mind the lack of sugar in the tea. And I was not bothered that most of the smoke from the improvised fireplace was floating out over the cellar instead of rising through the chimney. But I began to feel my spirits revive with the kindly talk of the officers. They seemed pleased that I had dropped in on them. The Fifteenth was the one battalion of the brigade that had no chaplain. They used to say jokingly that they were so good that they did not need a chaplain. I related my experiences of the day to the officers. They were sympathetic, for they had had many similar ones. I stayed with them for an hour or two till the Twenty-sixth Battalion came to relieve them. The officer who took over from us was an old friend, and one of the very best Catholics of the old One Hundred and Thirty-Second Battalion. I was delighted to see Captain Barry, and we talked for a long time in the cellar.

XCIII ⁓ In Reserve

Murdoch's frazzled mental state is indicated by this next chapter. Although moved to the rear, the 14th Battalion was still within German artillery range. Surrounded by ammunition trains that were being hit and exploding, Murdoch says "the shelling was terrible; beyond description." Despite shells landing just outside his tent, he was so tired that he decided simply to stay put. He did awake the next morning and said Mass, the first time in five days. He comments, "no words can express the consolation it gave me." The battalion remained at this most inhospitable site for one more day and then finally marched farther to the rear for true rest! – RH

During the night we marched back to Inchy. Very early in the morning I found the transport of the Fourteenth and, later in the day, the remnants of the battalion. They were in reserve, some miles from the firing line, yet in a very hard-shelled area; to make matters worse, we were in an ammunition dump, one of the largest I had ever seen. It was a very poor place to bring men to rest after battle!

There was a little Catholic chapel-tent here, similar to the one we had had at Écurie Wood. In the afternoon I went up to this and found Father O'Sullivan of the First Divisional Engineers in charge. I slept in the chapel-tent that night. Just before I retired, a number of lads came in to see me. The last one was a runner from the Fourteenth. He had had a terrible time carrying messages to different companies of the battalion in the battle the previous day. He showed me his tunic, from which a bullet had torn a strip across the chest. He had only begun to speak of his narrow escape when he burst out crying and immediately left the tent.

Father O'Sullivan was sleeping down in the lines of the engineers. The shelling was terrible, beyond description. Not far away whole trainloads of munitions were being hit by German shells, and car after car was exploding with a deafening noise. A great many horses were being hit, for there were horse lines of the artillery nearby. Shell after shell was dropping around my tent, but I felt too tired to move. I remember my conscience bothering me a little as to whether I were justified in remaining in the tent when at any minute I might be blown up. After a little puzzling, I decided I was, and for this reason: perhaps, in looking for a place of safety, I might be struck by one of the shells. And at any minute Fritz might stop.

I said Mass the following morning, and no words can express the consolation it gave me. I had not said Mass for five days—not since the previous Sunday. We remained another night, but the shelling was so intense that it was no fit place for troops to rest in, so on Saturday afternoon we marched farther back. Many men who we thought had been taken prisoner found their way back to the battalion; they had become separated from their companies and had lain hidden in shell holes till they could come back in safety. We now numbered nearly three hundred, we did not present an unfavourable appearance as we marched along. The band at the head of the column played "The Great Little Army" and "Sons of the Brave" and many other old favourites; already the lads were becoming more cheerful.

XCIV ᕗ Frequent Moves

In early October 1918 the brigade is finally in a rear rest area, but Murdoch is ill at ease. He and a doctor are billeted in a German ammunition hut next to the battalion's spark-emitting cookhouse! On October 9, word is received that the Canadians have taken Cambrai—the battle that had commenced at Arras on August 26 has ended. In recognition of the accomplishment, the Canadians are reviewed by the Prince of Wales. As for the enemy, the Germans are forced to fall back. The battalion moves forward to a city called Somaine. The band plays and the grateful French citizens welcome the soldiers after four years of occupation. Billeted in Somaine for several weeks, Murdoch relates the deaths of malnourished citizens and the play of children who seemed "too tall for their years," due to having endured four long years of German occupation and the consequent undernourishment. – RH

It was afternoon when we came into our area, and it was Saturday. The doctor and I had been given a hut almost filled with German high explosives—barrels of cordite, rolls of gun cotton, and boxes of amenol were on all sides. There was just room for us to spread two bedrolls on the floor. Woe unto anyone who smoked in this powder magazine! The cookhouse was almost touching us, and sparks flew from the short stovepipe that pierced the low roof. If a spark or two should happen to fall on our little room! The doctor became uneasy, and hearing that a field ambulance was quartered a few hundred feet away, he left and found shelter with his brethren.

During the afternoon we received a draft of three hundred fresh men to reinforce our shattered ranks. I watched them as they stood to attention and were inspected by the colonel. Tomorrow I would have them at Mass, for it would be Sunday. Sunday morning the wind was blowing a rather stiff breeze, and as I was to say Mass out of doors, I knew it would be impossible to keep my candles lighted unless I should build a wind shield, or break-wind. Accordingly, at nine o'clock I called the Englishman who had been appointed to look after my wants, and we went up to the field and tried to build the wind shield. For nearly an hour we laboured unsuccessfully with the material we had at hand. I was quite discouraged when I heard the pipes of the Thirteenth Battalion coming up the road—and I had no place arranged to say Mass! I looked around, not knowing what to do next, and there, not more than a hundred yards away, stood the remnants of the corner walls of a house—exactly what I had been trying to build. The two walls were just about five feet high, and there was a trough about two feet high and three feet long built into the corner. Quickly the Englishman and I filled this with brick, and in five minutes my altar was fitted up and ready for Mass.

I had been told by the staff captain of the brigade to hurry, as the place where I was to say Mass was under German observation. I said Mass very quickly, dispensed with the sermon, and gave a general absolution to the men as they knelt on the green field among piles of shattered masonry. That evening we moved back to support trenches, and I was not sorry to leave my munition storeroom. The doctor and I were given a dugout to ourselves. As it was very cold, we made a little trench heater out of an old bean tin, cutting a number of holes in the sides of it and filling it with pieces of paraffin candles and torn shreds of burlap. When we set fire to this we had quite a brazier. Headquarters was some distance from our trench in a corrugated iron hut, and as Fritz was shelling a balloon headquarters not far away, we often had to run the gauntlet of shellfire. We remained here nearly a week, and it was relatively quiet. On October 9, when we went over to lunch, the colonel told us that the Canadians had taken Cambrai. The taking of Cambrai closed the battle of Arras-Cambrai, begun on August 26, after we had come back from Amiens. From this date the Canadian Corps had advanced twenty-three miles, fighting for every yard of ground and overcoming tremendous obstacles. We had taken over eighteen thousand prisoners, three hundred and seventy guns, and two thousand machine guns. We held the front line for a few days, then came out to reserve, where the Prince of Wales reviewed us.

XCV ~ Somaine

On October 17 word was brought that the Germans were falling back. The following day we crossed the Canal de la Sensée. Cyclists, cavalry, and motor machine guns were in immediate pursuit of the enemy. I shall never forget Saturday, October 19, on which day word was brought to us by runners that there was a thickly populated city not far away called Somaine, from which the enemy were marching out. In a little while we would be marching in.

It was evening when the draft I was accompanying marched into Somaine. The band was accompanying us. It had been silent for quite a while, as we did not know but that some lurking nest of machine-gunners might be near to fire on us. It was dark as we passed the first group of houses near the city. I suppose the soldiers were wondering why the band was silent, for it was our invariable custom to play when entering a town. Suddenly, from the rear of the ranks, a voice calls out in the darkness, "Give us the band!" And then, "Good old band!" says another voice above the swinging, grating sound of marching feet over muddy cobblestones. Then there is a great medley of calls, of which the motif is "Band! Band! Give us the band!" Usually when the lads voice their request for music, the band always plays. Tonight, however, the lads call longer than usual, and the young officer wrinkles his brow a little as he wonders if it would be wise to give the order. He begins to think that the responsibilities of a subordinate officer are great. Meanwhile, the lads keep calling for the band. Finally, the young officer decides to risk it and word goes relayed up to the bandmaster: "Let's have the band." The bandmaster turns slightly in the darkness and calls out, "Over There." The bandsmen swing their instruments into position, while insistent demands for the band still come shouted from the rear of the ranks. The lads do not yet know that orders to play have been given. The snare drums roll; the large drum booms three times, twice; there is a clash and a clang of cymbals. A cheer of satisfaction goes up from the marching lads. Then clearly in the darkness sound the inspiring notes of "Over There." As we march down the streets, doors fly open in the houses, and grateful French peasants, who have been prisoners of the Germans for the last four years, come running to the street: old men stand by the wayside and, holding their hats in their hands, bow their heads. Women pass waffles and cups of coffee to the men, and little children run up and down the pavement shouting and dancing in their glee. But no bells ring from towers. These have been taken long ago to be melted into bullets and made into shells.

We were billeted in very comfortable quarters in the town of Somaine. I called on the old curé and made arrangements for Mass for my lads the following morning. He asked me if I could say Mass at nine o'clock, as his Mass was to be at ten. This was done, and at ten o'clock I returned to the church to be present at the Mass of the parish. The church was crowded with people as the old priest, looking like the Curé of Ars, with his beautiful white hair hanging down to his shoulders, came to the altar.[52] He was naturally rather pale, but today his thin face was flushed and his clear blue eyes were lighted by excitement. I could not keep my eyes from the straight old figure that went so quickly up into the pulpit and faced his people.

"Gratias agamus Domino Deo nostro!"—"Let us give thanks to the Lord our God!" The words ring clearly out over the church. One wonders at the strength and clearness of the priest's voice. As he continues: "Thirty years ago, my dear friends, when I received the holy oils of priesthood those words of gratitude came to my mind. Five years ago, when I knelt at the feet of our Sovereign Pontiff to receive his blessing on the occasion of my silver jubilee of priesthood, again I said those words: 'Gratias agamus Domino Deo nostro'— 'Let us give thanks to the Lord our God'. But today as I stand at the altar of God, knowing that my people are free, knowing that after four years of continued intercession of the Sacred Heart of Jesus our prayer has been heard, my heart breaks forth in gratitude the like of which I have never before experienced. 'Gratias agamus Domino Deo nostro'—'Let us give thanks to the Lord our God'!"

Then the old priest continued his sermon, asking his people if they did not remember how he had told them never to give up; to keep on praying; that surely their prayers would be heard. Many eyes were wet when he finished his sermon. The following day, we pursued the enemy a few miles, for he was still retreating, but on Tuesday we were ordered back to rest. My brigade was in Fenain and Somaine, and I was billeted with the saintly old curé.

XCVI ∾ The End Draws Near

Every day for about a week, troops were almost continuously passing through Somaine and all the heavy guns were being brought up. Soon railway communications were established and some of the people of the city were making visits to Paris.

Every evening I used to sit with the curé in his little kitchen before the fire and tell him stories of the war. The old priest was kept very busy; his assistant, a young priest, had been taken, together with all the men of military age, by the Germans in their retreat. Almost every day I saw the hearse drawn up before his church, and I knew another funeral cortège was soon to pass along the way. He spoke to me one evening of the frequent deaths, and then added: "The people are dying of joy." True, the people had been so weakened through hunger that many were not able to stand the great joy of deliverance. It was pitiful to see the little boys and girls playing in the street. At first it seemed to me that they were all too tall for their years; then I knew it was that they were undernourished.

A touching incident occurred one day when I was called upon to bury a Catholic lad from one of the battalions of the Third Division, then fighting toward Valenciennes. As I read the prayers over him, a little French girl of about eight or nine years approached the grave, carrying in her hand an oblong box of Canadian biscuits. The little one was holding the box close to her side. I assumed that one of our lads had given it to her; they were forever doing such kind acts. Presently, she saw that it was one of her gallant liberators over whom I was saying the last prayers. Immediately she began to sob and the big tears ran down her cheeks. She actually shook in a paroxysm of grief. It was hard for the lads standing near, and for me, to go on with our work. Always during the war our hearts had been steeled, not knowing what was to come next. In a few minutes the mother came from somewhere behind us, took the child by the arm, and gently led her away.

We were in Somaine nearly three weeks and the men were greatly benefited by the rest. I recall a humorous incident that occurred during our stay there. One day the curé of Fenain, which was just five minutes' run on my bicycle from Somaine, invited me over to a disinterment that was to take place in his cemetery. Having seen enough of gruesome things, I politely declined to be present. Then as I saw the curé's face break into a smile, I felt there must be some joke, so I promised to attend. In my presence the casket was exhumed, and lo! gentle reader, there appeared beautiful vestments and precious altar-vessels, together with the municipal books and documents. Then the curé told me the story. The coffin had been filled with its strange contents and drawn solemnly in the hearse through the streets just as the Germans had taken over the town; and as the funeral procession moved through the street the Germans themselves had saluted through respect to the "dead"!

XCVII ∾ November Eleventh

Unexpectedly, November 11 brought the cessation of hostilities. Murdoch records neither wild celebration nor even joy. The typical reaction among the soldiers was quiet. Murdoch tellingly suggests that "the terrible experience of war had left us incapable of expressing emotion." All that remained was a "strange tension." He quotes, at length, a poem by the American Roselle M. Montgomery. It makes three main sobering points: first, that civilians at home can neither speak nor understand the language of those who were in no man's land; second, that the returned soldier "will never be as they were again"; and third, that the returned are in some sense fated to forever be citizens of no man's land and to walk among the living much as ghosts who haunt familiar pathways. By quoting this poem at length Murdoch clearly identifies with these sentiments. – RH

November came, and I helped the parish priest of Somaine to give Holy Communion to the vast crowds of his people who received on All Saints Day. In return, he helped me with the confessions of my men, for now nearly all the members of the Fourteenth Battalion and very many of the Thirteenth were French-speaking soldiers. I was beginning to feel that all were ready spiritually for more battles when November eleventh arrived, and we learned that hostilities had ceased.

If this were fiction, I might write a lengthy description of how the troops went wild with joy, etc., etc.; but as it is the truth, I am constrained to say we took it in a strangely quiet manner. We could only look at each other and say, "Well, it's over at last!" and we would add, "thank God!" Perhaps we were dazed by the good news. Perhaps it was that the terrible experience of war had left us incapable of expressing our emotion. Perhaps these verses from "The Citizen of No Man's Land," by Roselle Mercier Montgomery, express the strange tension that had come to us during the war:

Why is it that, although we settle down
And live the lives we lived, a strange unrest,
A something, haunts us as we work or play—
A restlessness too vague to be exprest?

Is it that we who, out there, walked with Death
And knew the fellowship of Fear and Pain,
Are citizens for aye of No Man's Land
And never shall be as we were again?

To those of us who played the game out there
And saw brave men who failed to win lose all
Where Fate was dealer, Life and Death the stake,
Shall other games forevermore seem small?

'Tis true that home is dear and love is sweet.
And pleasant are our friends to be among.
Yet, something lacks to us from No Man's Land—
Is it that no one here can speak our tongue?

We cannot tell them what befell us there,
For well we know they cannot understand;
So each sits quiet by his own hearth fire
And sees therein the sights of No Man's Land.

They feel our strangeness, too—those at one side
Who chatter of the things of every day;
They mark our silences, our strange reserve,
"Ah, he is changed!" they shake their heads and say.

They say the dead return not, but I think
We know, who have come back from No Man's Land,
How ghosts must feel, who walk familiar ways
And yet find no one there to understand!

XCVIII ᵔ Through Belgium

*Although the war was over, Murdoch's marching days were far from
ended. His brigade was to be part of the Occupation Force sent into
Germany. Their destination was to be the far side of the Rhine River
near Cologne. First, they marched out of France and into Belgium.
They passed near the site of the Battle of Waterloo and saw streams
of happy, returning Belgian refugees. Once they entered Germany
their reception was decidedly cooler but nonviolent and respectful.
The lands they crossed were Catholic territory, and Murdoch, as a
Catholic priest, was always made to feel welcome. On December 12
the Canadians, with fixed bayonets, victoriously marched across the
Rhine bridge at Cologne.*

*Murdoch's last Mass with his men was on Christmas Eve,
1918. His leave had come through. With difficulty, he acceded to
the German parish priest's request to administer Holy Communion
to Murdoch's Canadian soldiers. The transnational reality of the
Catholic faith and living out the "peace of the Christ-child" overcame
Murdoch's hesitancy and his desire to administer the Sacrament to
his men one last time. – RH*

The evening of the Armistice I was sitting with the old curé
of Somaine when the Englishman came up to tell me that
orders had come for the brigade to march in the morning.
We were to follow the retiring Germans, who had promised as one
of the conditions of the Armistice to withdraw to a certain number
of miles on the opposite side of the Rhine.

I looked at the old curé; I had just been telling him that I
expected a long rest now. And here we were to traverse all Belgium
on foot and continue through the Rhineland of Germany till we
reached the opposite bank of the Rhine!

At four o'clock in the morning, after I had received Holy
Communion from the hand of the saintly old curé—I did not have
time to say Mass—I left. It was a long march before us, yet we
did not foresee that it was going to be interesting. We reached the
border between France and Belgium before the end of the week. We
descended a long hill, the band at the head of the column playing the
"Marseillaise," while on both sides of the road from many windows

waved the tricolour of France. We then crossed a small bridge over a dyke, in the middle of which stood a pole about six feet high; at the top of the pole was a small metal signboard about a foot long and eight inches high, running parallel with the road. On the end nearest us was the one word "France," then a little line about one inch long, then the word "Belgique." So we stepped from France into Belgium, and the band, which was the first to cross the line, having ceased to play the "Marseillaise" began "La Brabaconne," the national anthem of the Belgians.

We spent our first Sunday in a little place called Quaregnon, where we witnessed a demonstration of the wonderful patriotism of the Belgians. The church was crowded and after Mass the curé, in stole and cope, intoned the "Te Deum." Instantly, all present took it up, and the great volume of sound filled the church as Belgian, Frenchman, and Canadian joined in the mighty hymn of thanksgiving. Then the little curé did something I had never seen done before: he turned toward the people and cried, "Long live Belgium, free and independent!" The people repeated his words. Then he cried, "Long live the Canadians, our liberators!" and as he passed to the sacristy, a full orchestra played "Le Sambre et Meuse," while a number of the congregation joined in this war-song of the French.

At one place where we stopped a tall, thin priest spoke to me of the summer when the Germans had passed through—it seemed so long ago now, that summer of 1914—when great trainloads of enemy soldiers passed his house daily. He recalled one train in particular: the cars were gaily decorated with flowers, bunting, and flags, and from the engine floated a big white pennant on which was printed: "William of Germany, Emperor of Europe." He recalled the endless battalions that passed along the highway, fully equipped from boot to helmet, marching in perfect order. Their horses, too, were in excellent condition. Their wagons were shining. Every little while a voice from the ranks would call out, "Nach Paris! Nach Paris!"—"On to Paris! On to Paris!" and little Belgian children, terrified, scurried to cellar or other hiding places. "Yesterday," continued the priest, "I saw the last of the German army pass through on their return march to Germany. They had scarcely any horses, and those that they had were exceedingly thin.

Men were hauling wagons and carts. Their uniforms were worn and soiled; in fact, many were nondescript. Yesterday many of the boys remembering the words the Germans had called out on their way, four years before, standing on pavement or in doorways called out: 'Nach Paris! Nach Paris!'—'On to Paris! On to Paris!'"

It was very pleasant marching off early every morning while the band played some old favourite that had cheered the weary men after a hard day on the battlefield. All along the way, for the first week or two, we were greeted by happy peasants, who had been refugees for years, returning to their own country. Nearly always they pulled handcarts piled high with bedding and gaily decorated with flags of the Allies. I remember once on the roadside we found that the railway track had been blown up, and a great length of rails, with the sleepers still attached, had been thrown completely over a two-storey building, like a wide, curving ladder.

I found the Belgian priests very hospitable and very much interested in conditions in America. They were filled with gratitude to the people of the United States. In many shop windows we saw a picture representing the ocean and Columbia passing bread across the waters to an emaciated woman sitting on the shore with two starving children near her. In the upper part of the picture were insets of President Wilson and Brand Whitlock, and underneath was written: "Grateful Belgium."

I was in a little town not far from Brussels the day the king came back. Most of the broken railways had not yet been repaired, and as the Germans had taken the horses away from the people, many walked from ten to twenty miles to see the king come back to his kingdom.

We marched by Waterloo and through an old monastery called Villers Abbey, built by St. Bernard. In one place where we halted overnight was a tiny three-nave church of grey granite, which had been built in the ninth century. Napoleon had stopped here once in passing and had given a crown of gold for one of the statues. It was the finest three-nave church in the world. It was pure Roman architecture. Gradually we were drawing nearer the German border.

XCIX ∽ Through the Rhineland

S hortly before we reached the frontier, one of the officers came into the mess and said to me, "It may be a little exciting crossing the line, Padre. I hear there are some revolutionists who are going to snipe at us." I did not care for this kind of excitement. I felt I had seen all I wanted of shooting for the rest of my life. There was no need to worry, however, for our march into Germany was a very peaceful one. But nobody cheered us; no flags waved; everything was silent in the land as our khaki swung through the winding road. We passed through a very hilly country, and we soon had evidence that it was a Catholic country, for all along our march were little wayside shrines.

Our first billet was a low, white farmhouse, very comfortably furnished. On the wall of our mess was an oleograph of the Holy Family; a similar copy had hung in my bedroom when I was a boy. Presently an old lady came in, looked at me, and said something. I replied in French, but she shook her head. I pointed to the oleograph and said, "Katholisch?" The old lady looked at me, beaming. I pointed to myself and said, "Katholisch" and then added, "Prester," as I thought this was the German word for priest. During my stay in that house, I was treated as the Catholic priest is always treated by the humble.

In one place a young woman, learning that I was a priest, came to me with her brother, who spoke excellent English; he had been a waiter in the Savoy Hotel, in London, previous to the war. The husband of the young woman had been killed in the war, and passing me her offering, she asked if I would say Mass for the repose of his soul the following morning in the village church. This I did, and while I said Mass the village choir sang two hymns. It was a low Mass I said, and in the colour of the day. I asked the young man the name of the hymns and he told me. I cannot recall the name of the first one, but I think the second was entitled "O Komm, O Komm, Emanuel." It must have been an Advent hymn, for I heard it almost every morning as I said Mass in those little churches of the Rhineland.

I have never seen such excellent Catholics: every morning the village church would be crowded as if it were Sunday. Sometimes I gave Communion to German people who came reverently to the rails. The time passed quickly and at last, on December 12, we arrived in the city of Cologne. The following morning we marched across the Rhine, while the band played the "Regimental March" and "The British Grenadier"; the men, with fixed bayonets, marched rigidly to attention. Some officers near me sang softly the words: "When we wind up the watch on the Rhine." We marched about twelve miles beyond the Rhine to a little place called Altenbruick. Here we halted. And it was here that I said goodbye to the battalion on Christmas Day.

We had Midnight Mass in the German church on the hill overlooking the village. Father Madden, who had returned to his battalion after being discharged from hospital, came to help me with confessions. My lads were scattered over different parishes, but I had arranged for church parades for all who could come. I heard confessions from seven P.M. till midnight, and as the clock struck the midnight hour, one of my lads from the Fourteenth began to sing that beautiful Christmas hymn that was being sung that night in French churches all over Canada, "Minuit, Chrétiens" ("O Holy Night"). Every Christmas, just at midnight, I had heard it sung in the basilica of old Quebec, where I had made my studies for the priesthood. And as the clear, strong voice sang those beautiful notes of [Adolphe] Adams's famous composition, memories of peace swept over my soul. I had seen horrible things, but now they were past and this was the night of the Christ Child, when the angels sang "peace on earth to men of good will."

I was fully vested and was about to proceed to the altar for the last time before these lads, when the German parish priest came in to the sacristy. He spoke quickly in French, telling me that at the Communion I need not descend to the rails, that he would give Communion to my men. For an instant I seemed dazed. I had brought the Bread of Life so often to many of those soldiers and officers who now waited for me to draw near to the altar of God. Very likely I should never have the opportunity of again ministering to them. But then I thought, this German priest wishes to give Communion to my lads. Centuries before, the angels had sung "Peace to men of good will." I must show good will. Yet how hard it was! Then, mastering a great reluctance, I said quietly, "Very well, Father, you will give Communion to my men."

So this is the last memory I hold of those wonderful soldier lads—the Midnight Mass at Altenbruick. The sound of the voice of the German priest, "Corpus Domini Nostri Jesu Christi," etc., as he dispensed the mysteries of God to my soldier lads! And, above all else, the presence in our midst of Jesus of Nazareth, the Saviour of the world—The Prince of Peace!

C ∾ L'Envoi

Murdoch concludes The Red Vineyard *at the moment he leaves his position as an active chaplain ministering to the troops in Germany. His is clearly a "war diary" devoted to recording his active service from sign-up to the end of his active ministry to his men. Murdoch did not return to the continent. He remained in England until his return to Canada in March of 1919.*

Murdoch closes his account as only a priest could. He provides the reader with a reflection. He ends with a highly emotive meditation on the relationship between a Catholic padre and his men. By highlighting themes of mutual respect and reciprocal prayer, and contrasting mortality to eternity, Murdoch ends his story with a multilayered reflection on the topic of "rest." – **RH**

It is all over now, yet often I think of those wonderful days; of long night marches; of long days of weary waiting; of quiet resting places, with their rows and rows of "little green tents" and small white crosses, landmarks of our warfare in France and Flanders. Sometimes I think of all those lads who answered so quickly the final roll call; and my thoughts go back to those nights in France where such great numbers knelt to ask pardon of God and to become fortified with the Bread of the Strong. Many of those lads I ushered up to the gates of heaven, which swung open to them so soon after they had left me. Now "they are numbered among the children of God and their lot is with the saints."

They do not forget me. Sometimes, when the force of circumstances presses greatly and the way along which I must walk seems exceptionally hard, I call on them to stand by. I ask them simply to remember Arras, Amiens, Cherisy Valley, Canal du Nord, and Cambrai—then I feel those lads are praying for me.

And sometimes "when thoughts of the last bitter hour come like a pall over my spirit," a thought most comforting comes to my mind.[53] I see in imagination the street of heaven and, coming marching toward me, great hosts, their faces lighted with the Vision of God. I see them turned toward me, as I have seen them so often on battlefield and in hospital ward. That look of loving trust is there—only so many times glorified! They look at me, who am a little dismayed, a little afraid. Then I hear their voices: "Come, Father, your billet is ready!"

Then I feel very confident, for I know that my warfare is over, that I am going back to rest—back to Eternal Rest.

The End

AFTERWORD

As we have seen, Murdoch ends *The Red Vineyard* in Germany with the local parish priest administering the sacrament to Murdoch's Canadian boys at a Christmas Eve Mass in 1918. The next day he left for two weeks' leave in England. Aware of his fragile mental state, authorities did not send him back to the continent. Murdoch appeared sufficiently fragile that his Roman Catholic superior in London penned three letters to various authorities highlighting Murdoch's tenuous mental state. Colonel Workman described Murdoch as "thoroughly played out and unable to work further" and stated that he "was suffering seriously from the results of his work in the field."[54] Between a trip to Bramshott Camp and resting in London, Murdoch was fortunate to wait only six weeks before boarding the *Belgic* for Halifax. There he boarded the Ocean Limited Express train and returned to Chatham. On his discharge medical examinations, both in England and again in Fredericton, Murdoch registered no complaints. He replied in the negative when asked whether or not he "ever suffered from…any affection" of the "nervous system" or "disturbance of mentality."[55] As was the case with many returned soldiers, Murdoch calculated that demobilization from the CEF would equate to leaving his wartime experiences behind. Regrettably, such was not to be the case.

Upon his return, Murdoch spent two months in Chatham and another two months substituting in Bathurst. Bishop Barry of Chatham was not unaware of Murdoch's condition. At the same time Murdoch had sailed for Halifax, Col. Workman had written Murdoch's bishop praising him as "an excellent priest" who is "quite worn out as a result of his strenuous work." Workman hoped that Bishop Barry would grant Murdoch "a little rest and every consideration at home in view of the exhausting and excellent work which he has done."[56] Gauging that four months was sufficient, Bishop Barry assigned Murdoch to a parish in Jacket River, halfway between Bathurst and Dalhousie. While actually not wanting to return to parish ministry, Murdoch nonetheless obeyed. He found the posting difficult. In his second autobiographical work, *Part Way Through*, he suggests that in order to accomplish all that was expected of him he would have to be a lawyer and a doctor as well as a priest.[57] He experienced trouble sleeping and went to see a physician. He could not seem to relax. After two years, his bishop posted him to a much smaller and quieter parish in Douglastown. There, with a map of France posted on the wall, he began, in earnest, to write *The Red Vineyard*.

Writing was both therapeutic and difficult, often extremely difficult. He relates that "sometimes the scenes described became so vivid that involuntarily I would stop writing. So great was my absorption that I would not advert to the fact that I was not working. For I was seeing again the miniature forests of little white crosses.... Again, I was following the slow-marching soldiers down the aisles as they carried shoulder high a fallen comrade.... Sometimes the tears dropping suddenly on the white paper would bring me back again to the dancing firelight in the warm little room at Douglastown."[58] Decades before the term was first entered in a dictionary, Benedict Joseph Murdoch describes his experience of "flashback."[59] Sadly, it would be many decades before flashbacks would become a recognized symptom of PTSD.[60] Murdoch was unable to complete *The Red Vineyard* that winter. In January of 1922, describing himself as "tense" and "greatly depressed," he checked into the local hospital. He would remain there for weeks. On January 29, his unwell father managed to come and visit him. He passed away while sitting in the chair in his son's room. The shock of this event further shook Murdoch's mental health. He could not attend his father's funeral.

He remained in hospital until a rest and recuperation trip to Florida was arranged for him. By the time he arrived at Montreal, on the first stage of his rail journey, he had been sleepless for days. He "felt numbed, helpless and with a strange undefined fear shadowing me."[61] He again checked himself into the hospital. Here he received specialized treatment—injections of strychnine. After several weeks' treatment, he was able to journey to Florida. Afterward, he returned to Douglastown and was able to complete *The Red Vineyard* on July 26, 1922.

Unfortunately for Murdoch, writing and publishing *The Red Vineyard* did not get the war out of his system. In 1924 he had to take a leave from ministry. He secluded himself in a vacant cabin at a lumber camp in the woods. The quiet and solitude helped. During this period he resumed writing. He crafted a few short stories, some of which would be published in two separate volumes later in the decade. He returned to ministry at Douglastown for seven more years until, in 1930, he again had to ask his bishop for a reprieve. He returned to the cabin, but this time for a full year. He found the experience most beneficial. When he returned to Chatham, his bishop placed him in a trial hospital chaplaincy for a year. This too proved problematic and Murdoch again sought release from his duties and a return to the woods. This time it was permanent; in 1932 he was granted permanent leave from regular ministry. He retreated to the North Brook lumber camp on the Bartibogue River, miles from the nearest house, road, or railroad. Apart from temporary employment as chaplain at a Sussex military camp from 1943 to 1945, Murdoch lived in the woods for the next fifteen years.[62] He celebrated Mass daily, wrote and published two more books, entertained occasional guests, and came out of seclusion to conduct various annual retreats. Due to the decay of the lumber camp site, in 1947 Murdoch moved out of the deep woods to an old house located at the nearest railroad line at Bartibogue Station. He lived there until the mid-1960s when advancing age and deteriorating health forced him to move into Mount Saint Joseph Nursing Home in Chatham. In 1971, Fr. Murdoch received the honour of being designated a Monsignor by Pope Paul VI. He died in his hometown of Chatham two years later on January 31, 1973.[63]

Works by Benedict Joseph Murdoch

The Red Vineyard (memoir), 1923
Sprigs (short stories), 1927
Souvenir (short stories), 1928
Alone With Thee (devotional), 1934
Part Way Through (memoir), 1946
Far Away Place (memoir), 1952
The Menders (novel), 1953
Fear Ye Not (devotional), 1961
Swing High (novel), 1963
The Murphy's Come In (novel), 1965
Facing into the Wind (novel), 1973

ACKNOWLEDGEMENTS

A work such as this is a collaborative effort. I wish to acknowledge the assistance and encouragement of Fr. Leon Creamer of Chatham, executor of Benedict Joseph Murdoch's estate, who granted me permission to republish the text of *The Red Vineyard*. Moreover, Fr. Creamer's extensive knowledge of Padre Murdoch's postwar life was essential to understanding Fr. Murdoch, the man. This is especially true given the great paucity of extant documentary evidence of Murdoch's postwar life. Leaving church-provided housing in 1932 and then living first at an abandoned logging camp and then in a rail siding shed, Murdoch was not in a position to retain many possessions. Of the few precious items he did have, including his wartime portable altar, most were looted by thieves and destroyed by vandals in the 1950s. In all probability, this included his wartime diary, which constituted the textual basis of *The Red Vineyard*.

I also wish to acknowledge the assistance of my friend Wilfred Allison. As in previous instances, his thorough proofreading of the text coupled with his insightful suggestions have undoubtedly improved the final draft of this work. In addition, the careful copy editing of Marianne Ward for Nimbus Publishing has added both clarity and polish to the completed manuscript. I owe a debt of gratitude to archivist and fellow scholar Glenn Wright. It was his insight, direction, and assistance that unlocked the elusive identity of Murdoch's batman, George.

Not only is effective historical research a collaborative activity, but it also requires time and resources. I would be remiss if I did not acknowledge the assistance of the Canon W. A. Morris scholarship. This funding has enabled me to continue my Great War research with particular emphasis on chaplains. This ongoing support and encouragement is most appreciated.

Finally, the insightfulness of Angela Mombourquette at Nimbus in recognizing the importance of a little-known Great War cleric from Chatham, New Brunswick, must be gratefully acknowledged. The persistent willingness of Nimbus to bring to light these hidden treasures of Maritime Canada's Great War heritage is indeed commendable.

ENDNOTES

1 Duff Crerar, *Padres in No Man's Land: Canadian Chaplains and the Great War* (Montreal & Kingston: McGill-Queen's University Press, 2014), 5.

2 *The Red Vineyard*, ch. LXXXIII. Hereafter referred to as *RV*.

3 B. J. Murdoch, *Part Way Through* (Toronto, Mission Press, 1946), 251–3. Hereafter referred to as *PWT*.

4 Leon Creamer, *Shepherd of the Woods: Father Benedict J. Murdoch* (Miramichi: Lightning Demand Press, 2011), 14.

5 Creamer, *Shepherd of the Woods*, 22–23.

6 *PWT*, 118.

7 Crerar, *Padres in No Man's Land*, 276, n. 127, and 301, n. 37.

8 Mark McGown, "Harvesting the 'red vineyard': Catholic religious culture in the Canadian Expeditionary Force, 1914–1919," *Historical Studies* 64 (1998).

9 Crerar, 134.

10 *RV*, ch. LIX.

11 "The Sacrament" denotes a Christian's reception, by faith, of their God by consuming the body and blood of Christ in the elements of bread and wine.

12 *RV*, ch. XC.

13 *RV*, ch. C.

14 *RV*, ch. LXXXI.

15 *RV*, ch. LXXIX.

16 *RV*, ch. XCVI.

17 *RV*, ch. XLIV.

18 *RV*, ch. XCVI.

19 *RV*, ch. XXXIII.

20 *RV*, ch. XXXV.

21 *RV*, ch. XXVII.

22 *RV*, ch. XXVII.

23 *RV*, ch. LXXIII.

24 *RV*, ch. XXIV.

25 *RV*, ch. LXXXII.

26 *RV*, ch. XCII.

27 *RV*, ch. XCII.

28 *RV*, ch. LXII.

29 *RV*, ch. LXIX.

30 *RV*, ch. LCII.

31 *RV*, ch. LXXV.

32 *RV*, ch. LXXXV.

33 "The Colours" refers to the country's flag, which in turn represents the nation.

34 Murdoch is careful throughout his work not to identify specific units and individuals who were guilty of such violations. He wanted to make his point but not have such minor incidents become the legacy of those who otherwise served so faithfully.

35 Typical of the times, Murdoch employs the term "Indian" to describe Canada's First Nations soldiers.

36 Irvin S. Cobb (1876–1944), well-known American journalist and syndicated columnist noted for the humour and irony of his writing.

37 Murdoch is quoting from "The Little Green Tents," a poem by Walt Mason (1862–1939), a Canadian-born American poet and syndicated journalist. His daily column was carried by more than two hundred American and Canadian newspapers. The poem, published in 1916, concerns American Civil War graves.

38 "Turpenide" appears to be Murdoch's spelling of "turpenite," a fictional war gas falsely attributed to French chemist Eugene Turpin. Tales of its usage abounded early in the conflict when the deadly effects of shell concussion were as yet unknown.

39 The "terrible disaster" was the Halifax Explosion of December 6, 1917.

40 LAC RG9 III vol. 4668 Reports on Operations. Individual Chaplains reports on Activities, France, 1918. R.C. Chaplains weekly reports; Murdoch: week ending February 3 and 17, 1918.

41 *PWT*, 28–64.

42 The building in question is named Notre-Dame-des-Ardents, not Ardennes.

43 Creamer, *Shepherd of the Woods*, 30.

44 N. Booth Tarkington (1869–1946), American novelist and dramatist. His 1916 novel *Seventeen* was a satirical treatment of a young American boy's first love.

45 The term "amenol" was used at the time to denote a high explosive substance similar to dynamite.

46 *The Katzenjammer Kids* was a syndicated American comic strip drawn by Harold Knerr from 1914 to 1949.

47 Tim Cook, *Lifesavers and Body Snatchers* (Allen Lane: Toronto, 2022), 373–5.

48 We might now use the term "human pride." Murdoch means to say that the devout had no undue concern for what others might think of them, no self-consciousness about how they might appear in the eyes of others.

49 From "The Burial of Sir John Moore after Corunna" (1817) by Irish poet Charles Wolfe (1791–1823).

50 Sir Gerald H. E. B. du Maurier (1873–1932), a famous stage actor and manager. Although he did not smoke them, he did assent to having the cigarette brand named after him—for a fee.

51 Murdoch has a slight error here; Rev. Coulthurst's first name was Percy.

52 The "Curé of Ars" was Jean Vianney (1786–1859), a French priest canonized in 1925. Noted for his devoted ministry, he is regarded as the patron saint of parish priests.

53 Murdoch is quoting from "Thanatopsis" by American poet William C. Bryant (1794–1878).

54 Lt. Col. Workman to Secretary of Chaplain Services, London, and to Assistant Director Medical Services, RG9 III C 15 vol. 4633, file CM9 Chaplain Services File for Padre Benedict Joseph Murdoch.

55 Benedict Joseph Murdoch, Personnel File, Library and Archives Canada, central.bac-lac.gc.ca/.item/?op=pdf&app=CEF&id=B6498-S010.

56 Lt. Col. Workman to the Right Reverend T. F. Barry, Bishop of Chatham, RG9 III C 15 vol. 4633, file CM9 Chaplain Services File for Padre Benedict Joseph Murdoch.

57 *PWT*, 209.

58 *PWT*, 222.

59 *Merriam-Webster's Collegiate Dictionary* dates the first use of "flashback" as an intransitive verb to the year 1944.

60 Barbara Rothbaum, "Understanding DSM-5 Criteria for PTSD: A Disorder of Extinction," Psychotherapy Academy, 2020, psychotherapyacademy.org/pe-trauma-training-ptsd/understanding-dsm-5-criteria-for-ptsd.

61 *PWT*, 227.

62 LAC Militia and Defence Headquarters Personnel Files, RG 24 C 1 a, Reel T-17603, file 203-M-54, image 3937.

63 Creamer, *Shepherd of the Woods*.

About the Author

ALTHOUGH ORIGINALLY FROM NOVA SCOTIA'S South Shore, Ross Hebb is now a long-term resident of his adopted province of New Brunswick. A graduate of King's College and Dalhousie University, Dr. Hebb received his PhD from the University of Wales, Lampeter in 2002. Along with volumes on Maritime Church history, he has also written about the golden age of shipbuilding at St. Martins on the Bay of Fundy. In 2014 he edited the collection *Letters Home: Maritimers and the Great War, 1914–1918*, and 2018, *In Their Own Words: Three Maritimers Experience the Great War*. In 2021, he edited *A Canadian Nurse in the Great War: The Diaries of Ruth Loggie, 1915–1916*. Dr. Hebb is married and lives in Fredericton, NB.